PORTRAIT OF WORCESTERSHIRE

Portrait of
WORCESTERSHIRE

PETER J. NEVILLE HAVINS

ROBERT HALE · LONDON

© Peter J. Neville Havins 1974
First published in Great Britain 1974

ISBN 0 7091 4587 X

ROBERT HALE & COMPANY
63 OLD BROMPTON ROAD
LONDON, S.W.7

PRINTED IN GREAT BRITAIN
BY EBENEZER BAYLIS AND SON LIMITED
THE TRINITY PRESS, WORCESTER, AND LONDON

CONTENTS

ILLUSTRATIONS

CREDITS

The illustrations numbered 9, 11, 20, 32, 33, 34 were
supplied by Geoffrey N. Hopcraft, and those numbered 12,
13, 14, 15, 25, 26, 28, 31 by Bill Meadows. All the other
photographs were supplied by Michael Bourne.

INTRODUCTION

In this book I have tried to give a comprehensive picture of Worcestershire, looking at both its past and present and occasionally attempting to see into its future. The picture, of course, is not a complete one for the county and its people are far too diversified to be covered in a single volume. Apart from this, the portrait drawn is very much that of the county as I see it and makes no pretence to be that of a purely dispassionate observer.

However, within the limitations of time and space, I have attempted to be fair to all parts of the county, from Bredon's cherry-blossomed villages to the industrialized towns of the north-west. Within the north-western area I have included Rowley Regis and Smethwick which, as part of the new Borough of Warley, were incorporated in the county in 1966 and also Dudley which, though no longer in Worcestershire, for so long formed a part of the county that it seemed to merit inclusion on this ground alone. Also included are parts of south-west Birmingham which, until 1911, were within Worcestershire and whose history and development has been closely associated with the northern region.

Rather than deal with questions of history, agriculture, communications, industry and so on separately I have chosen to divide the county into ten loosely defined areas and have attempted to trace the development of these and other factors as they affected each one. In some areas the general reader may complain that I have dwelt rather too long on matters of history, but this has been somewhat inevitable in a book dealing with a county that stands so close to the heart of England and has therefore found itself involved in so many of the major events of our past.

But, if this volume contains a plea it is not that we preserve Worcestershire's past—which can look after itself quite well without any help from us—but that we act responsibly as guardians of its future. This is not an argument against industrialism which, though necessary, need not be evil, but against mass urban expansion which threatens to engulf the countryside almost as if it were filling up the empty squares of a piece of graph-paper. Threatened by motorway proposals, New Town proposals and 'overspill dispersal' Worcestershire has become one of the most embattled of the Midlands' pastoral shires.

All, however, may not be lost and it is for those who know, love, remember and hope for the future of Worcestershire that this book is written.

I

THE LOWER AVON

In the months of high summer Evesham is beyond doubt the most pungent town in Worcestershire. The odour of fruit is everywhere, but nowhere is it more dominant than in the market at Merstow Green and along the Worcester Road where the town's canning factories are situated.

In these months the town seems literally to wallow in the products of the Vale of Evesham, the currants, asparagus, peas, runner-beans and other fruits and vegetables grown in the orchards and market gardens of the district. But the major crop is the plum—egg-plums, Victorias, Pershores—and it is these which provide the dominant odour as well as the hordes of wasps which no amount of pesticides seem able to eliminate. At this time of year the town is thronged with laden lorries bearing the harvest of the Vale to distant markets and factories, the railway station is piled high with crates and boxes of fruit and, in an effort to preserve their respectability, some of the town's many inns display 'No Pickers' notices on their doors.

It is largely the activity of these summer months that gives Evesham its reason for existence as the capital of the broad and fertile Vale in which it stands. Of all Worcestershire's major towns it is the one most closely wedded to the soil, a situation which shows no sign of altering even in the distant future.

From Saxon times until the Dissolution the development of the town was closely connected with the affairs of its Benedictine Abbey. Apart from the Bell Tower, a landmark for miles around and built during the abbacy of Clement Lichfield, little now remains of the former abbey for here Thomas Cromwell and his Commissioners were to do their work more thoroughly than at many other places.

According to local legend the abbey was founded as a result of

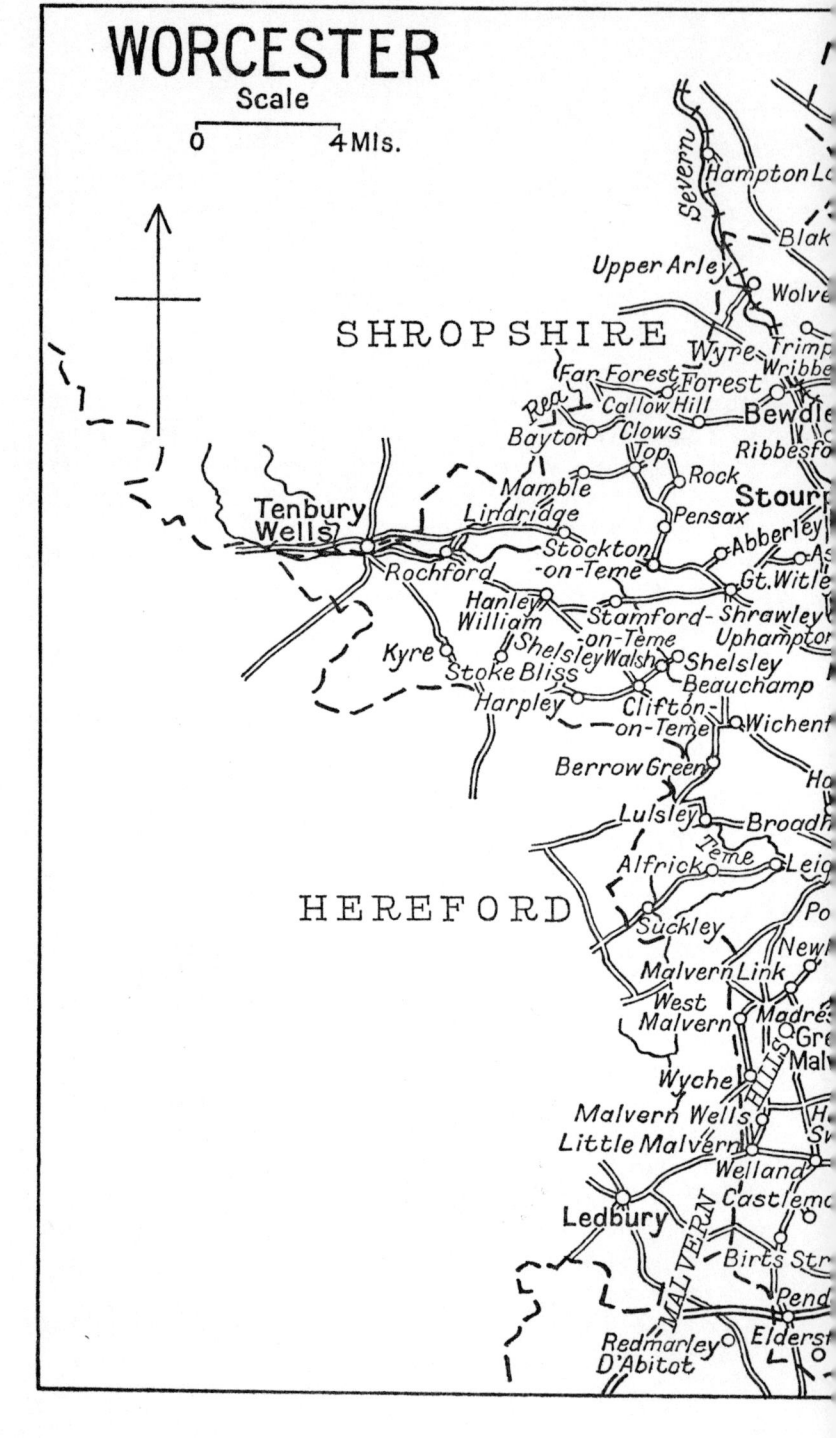

WORCESTER

Scale

0   4 Mls.

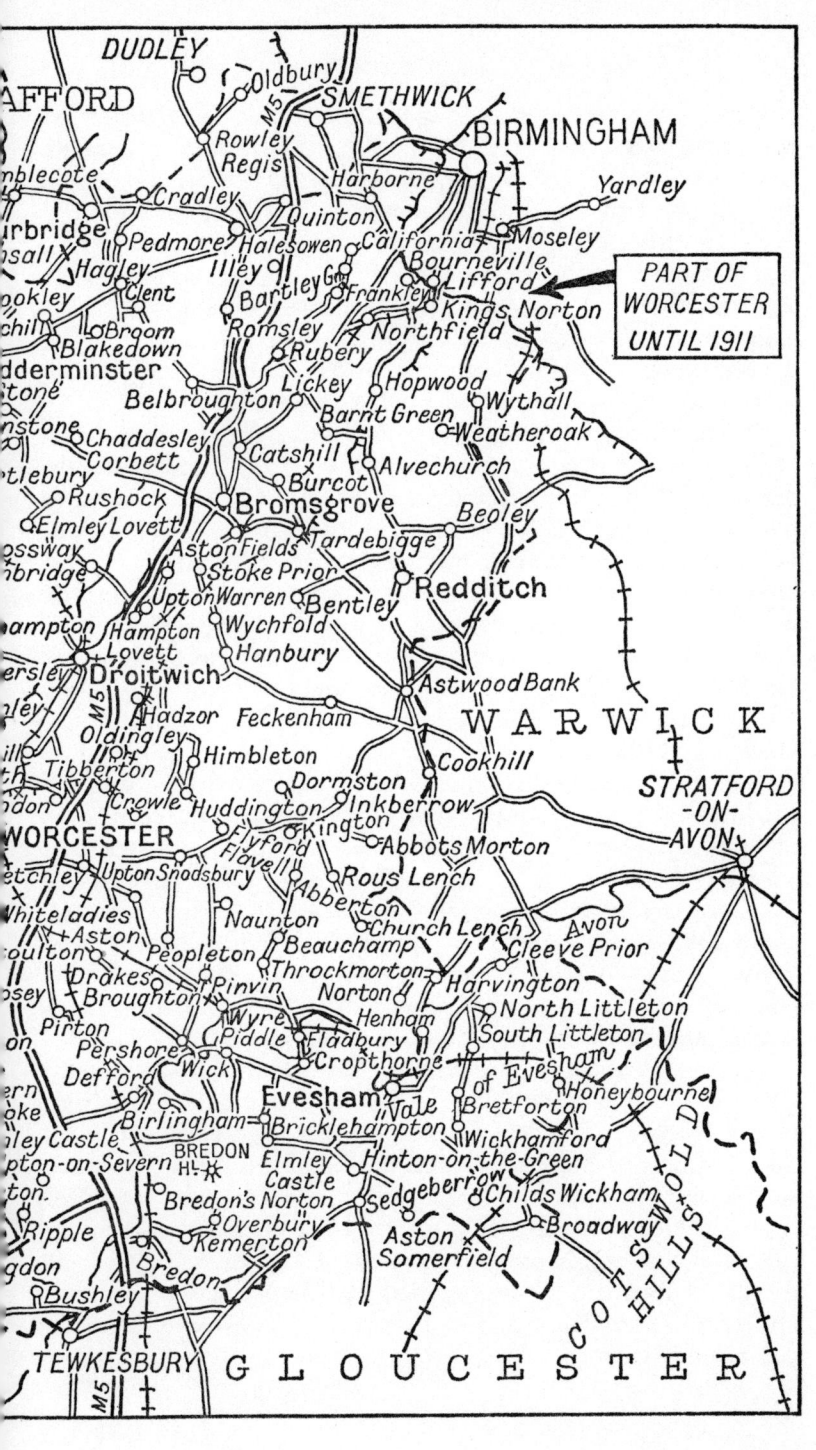

a vision first experienced by a swineherd named Eoves and from whom the town is said to have taken its name as Eovesham. Eoves was tending his herd in the Vale when he was confronted by a vision of the Madonna amongst the trees. He reported this to Egwin, Bishop of Worcester, who promptly journeyed to the spot and had a similar vision himself in which he was directed to build an abbey there. With special privileges granted by Pope Constantine and with grants of royal land he set about creating the beginnings of what was later to become one of the largest and most influential of all England's religious houses.

But, in the ninth century, a hundred years after work had first begun, the abbey was to be almost completely razed when the marauding Danes, penetrating into the Vale of Evesham, ravaged not only Evesham's abbey but that of Pershore as well. The building was later restored, but it must have been a rather jerry-built job for, at the end of the next century, a monastic chronicler was to record that the structure 'fell down'. Preparations were now made to provide an altogether larger and more impressive building which, though drawn up by the last Saxon abbot, was not erected until he had been replaced by a Norman in the aftermath of the Conquest.

The abbey now settled down to a life of peace during which it gradually extended its husbandry, which included the cultivation of vineyards, over a large area of the Vale. But its peace was to be abruptly shattered during the reign of King John. At the time John was acting as regent for his brother Richard I who was away having fun playing the unchivalric games that we now know as the Crusades. At home John never got on well with churchmen and was involved in something of a vendetta with the Archbishop of Canterbury, Stephen Langton.

When the abbacy of Evesham fell vacant John pointedly ignored Langton's candidate and instead appointed his own, Roger Norreys. This was something of a highspot even in the life of wayward John. As a dissolute monk Norreys' reputation was so bad that even John may later have come to regret his decision. Norreys had only just escaped from imprisonment for misbehaviour at his own monastery of Canterbury when the monks of Evesham were informed that he was to be their next abbot. They certainly had cause for apprehension. Gervase of Canterbury wrote that Norreys was, from youth, a monk proud of himself, puffed up, pompous in his speech, treacherous in his actions, covetous in his preferences, a despiser of religion, cringing to his superiors, contemptuous to his inferiors, gaudy in his clothing, negligent in the observance of order, a companion of females, a lover of horses, soon angry, eager at detracting, incorrigible in all things.

Far from mending his ways Norreys went his own merry way at Evesham and when rebuked by some of the monks retaliated by depriving them of food and clothing. He also squandered the revenues of the abbey to an alarming degree and, for 22 years, lived a life bordering on that of an Eastern potentate until, in 1213, he was finally deposed by the Papal Legate. Even then his career as a churchman was not over for he retired to Penwortham in Lincolnshire as prior, a post which he held until his death three years later.

But Roger Norreys' abbacy was also notable for the production of one cleric who was to exercise a far different influence on the abbey than Norreys had done. This was Thomas de Marleberge, who was destined to become one of Evesham's greatest abbots. He was at once a scholar, historian and craftsman and many of the later improvements to the abbey's buildings were due to his personal planning. He was also to be responsible for much other building on abbey land in the neighbourhood and personally supervised the painting of the Chapter House murals.

Later in the thirteenth century the abbey would have been at the height of its medieval glory when the sad battle that has forever placed the name of the town in English history books was enacted outside its walls in 1265. This was the battle in which Simon de Montfort, Earl of Leicester, and his son Henry were both to lose their lives fighting against a far superior force led by Edward Plantagenet, Prince of Wales.

De Montfort has often been called the "father of English liberty" and there is no doubt that the effect of his writ which "first summoned the merchant and trader to sit beside the knight of the shire, the baron and the bishop, in the Parliament of the realm" was to give representation to a class which had long been excluded from any direct participation in the affairs of government. But, while still being fair to de Montfort, it would be true to say that the Barons' War was fought largely over the question of whether England should be governed by feudal monarchy in the person of Henry III or by an oligarchy of the most powerful barons led by de Montfort himself and that the representation of merchants and traders in Parliament was very much an irrelevant side-issue. Eager to enlist all the support he could de Montfort's main aim in inviting the mercantile classes to participate in discussion was probably little more than one more manœuvre in his attempts to isolate the king. He would probably have viewed our modern versions of liberty as little more than anarchy and his meaning of the term was very much a restatement of the provisions of the Magna Charta of fifty years previously where liberty was largely interpreted as applying to the barons in relation to the powers of the Crown.

Even so, in his day, de Montfort was a popular hero. While the power of the king was impersonal that of individual barons was rather more localized and to a certain extent was more open to influence by the common man—and perhaps because of this, a large number of ordinary people actually favoured the barons' enjoying greater freedom. But it must not be forgotten that just as many ordinary men fought for the king as did for the barons and that, viewed from this standpoint, it was therefore the ordinary people who were ultimately responsible for his death. Loyalties to the king and his supporters, as to de Montfort and his, were of an almost tribal nature, based more upon locality and tradition than upon anything else. Ideas of liberty held their appeal, or lack of it, for the thinking man but, in the thirteenth century, his was a lonely face in a large crowd. For the common folk de Montfort was a hero as a warrior and as a dashing rebel, a 'saint' much after the style of Thomas à Becket who, fighting against a harsh and corrupt authority, automatically had good ranged on his side. It has been left to later centuries to make him, somewhat illegitimately, the father of the English Parliamentary system.

There is no doubt that the Battle of Evesham was enacted on a tragic stage. De Montfort and his army were resting in the town awaiting news of his son's earlier engagement with the loyalist forces. All expectations were of victory but, unknown to de Montfort, it was Prince Edward who had been the victor at Kenilworth. Now the Plantagenet prince was moving on Evesham at the head of a huge army.

The surprise was all the greater for de Montfort and his

The Bell Tower, Evesham

followers for, in order to deceive the rebels, the royalist army was marching behind the captured banners of the defeated baronial army. When the army appeared on the height of Greenhill over-looking the town de Montfort at first thought that it was his son Simon's victorious return.

But, when Edward replaced the rebel banners with his own, de Montfort realized that Kenilworth had been a disaster and that there could now be no hope of reinforcements reaching Evesham. Outnumbered by more than seven to one he is reported to have turned to his son Henry shortly before battle was joined with the words, "Let us commend our souls to God, for our bodies are already theirs."

The battle was fought in a lightning storm, searing flashes flaring across the Vale and thunder-claps reverberating from the hills. At Evesham the chronicler was later to say that much of the battle was fought in near-darkness as great clouds shrouded the sun and that inside the abbey the monks could not see to read their psalms.

Caught in the loop of the Avon there was no hope of escape for de Montfort's army. Everything was in Prince Edward's favour, for not only was his enemy hemmed in by the river, but he was attacking downhill. The battle lasted three hours during which de Montfort's supporters were systematically pushed back towards the Avon and at one point, King Henry, who was a prisoner in the rebel ranks, was almost killed by his own men and only saved himself by hurriedly pulling back his visor to reveal that he was indeed the king. At no time could Edward have had any fear of defeat for, when the battle was over, there remained more than a third of his men who had not been called upon and who had spent the whole duration of the battle as spectators on the slopes of Greenhill.

Both de Montfort and his son Henry were killed and amongst his supporters 18 barons, 160 knights and 4,000 soldiers also lost their lives. After de Montfort's death the battlefield became a place of chaos as his supporters tried to elude the pursuing loyalists. No doubt some did manage to escape, but more were butchered in the streets of the town or as they tried to plunge into the river. Some fled for sanctuary into the abbey but, despite the protests of the monks, were pursued and put to death in the cloisters.

Abbot Reginald's Gateway, Evesham

2

For ruthless savagery on the part of the victor the Battle of Evesham was not to be equalled until the barbaric struggles of the Wars of the Roses and it was partly Edward's ferocious treatment of de Montfort's supporters that was to endow him with the beginnings of the reputation he was later to enlarge in his campaigns against the Welsh and Scots. Even in death de Montfort was not allowed to rest, for Edward now ordered that the head, arms and legs be cut from his body for public display in London. The remains were later taken from the field by the monks of the abbey to be buried beneath their high altar.

Although de Montfort was never to be canonized his burial place soon became a shrine to which pilgrims flocked from all over England. The numbers became so great that the pilgrims' church of St Lawrence had to be enlarged. Evesham traders grew quite prosperous as a result of the pilgrim-trade, but it was something that could not last indefinitely and by the early sixteenth century the flow of pilgrims to Evesham had almost ceased.

But de Montfort is still commemorated in the town, undemonstratively in the names of Montfort Street and the more recent Simon de Montfort Drive and with rather more ostentation in the name of one of the town's many tea-rooms. But his most dramatic memorial is the stone which now stands in Abbey Park near to the site of the high altar of the vanished abbey. The memorial stone, which was brought from near de Montfort's birthplace in France, was unveiled in 1965 as the culmination of a festival to celebrate the 700th anniversary of the battle. Dedicated by the Archbishop of Canterbury, it was unveiled by Sir Harry Hylton-Foster, the then Speaker of the House of Commons. Sir Harry also opened a special Simon de Montfort room at the Almonry Museum. The plaque is inscribed:

Here were buried the remains of Simon de Montfort, Earl of Leicester, pioneer of representative government who was killed in the battle of Evesham August 4 1265.

This stone, brought from his birthplace, the castle of Montfort-L'Amaury in France, was erected to commemorate the seven hundredth anniversary of his death.

Unveiled by the Speaker of the House of Commons and dedicated by his Grace the Archbishop of Canterbury on the 18th day of July 1965.

The last Abbot of Evesham was one Phillip Hawford who was created abbot for the sole purpose of surrendering the abbey and its possessions to Cromwell's commissioners. Its last true abbot, from whom Hawford took over, was Clement Lichfield whose most eloquent memorial is the Bell Tower situated at the approach to the now vanished abbey. Abbot Clement was also responsible for the building of the town's ancient grammar school which stands on Merstow Green and which has recently been refaced and extended and acts now as the Evesham Working Men's Club. It is still just possible to read the Latin inscription above the doorway: "*Orate pro anima Clematis Abbatis*". A monastic school existed in the town as early as 1377 and the Old Grammar School was used until 1879. After this it was transferred to a building now housing Greenhill Private School from where it was removed to its present site in Victoria Road in 1910. The school has been known as Prince Henry's Grammar School since 1605 when it was re-established under a charter granted by James I and named in honour of his eldest son.

Apart from the Bell Tower various other fragments of the abbey survive, notably Abbot Reginald's Gateway approaching the abbey churchyard and which dates back as far as 1135. The Almonry also remains, now converted into a museum which is open during the summer months. It is a superb example of medieval domestic architecture and was originally the home of the abbey almoner whose duty was to dispense alms to wayfarers and the town's poor. On the lawn beside this old building are the town stocks, originally sited across Vine Street on Merstow Green and which are now preserved beneath a roof of Cotswold slate.

Some of the town's buildings still preserve a close association with the old abbey, notably the Crown Hotel in Bridge Street which is built around the site of the abbey well and probably developed from a tap-room and lodging house maintained by the monks for visiting traders.

That Evesham did not keep at least some part of its abbey, as did so many other towns, was due to its possessing in addition two other churches which adjoined the abbey churchyard. Prior to the Dissolution All Saints' functioned as the church of the townsfolk while its neighbour St Lawrence's was the church of the pilgrims who flocked to the shrine of Simon de Montfort.

Thomas Cromwell probably considered that Evesham was well enough provided with churches and would quite possibly have got rid of one of the remainder if he had been able.

After its dissolution the great abbey was let by the Crown for use as a quarry which effectively ensured that little of it remained by the end of the sixteenth century. Evesham must have felt the loss of its great religious house more keenly than many other towns placed in a similar situation. Many settlements which had originally grown up around religious houses had developed to such an extent that supplying the requirements of the religious community had come to assume no more than an incidental importance. But Evesham was not in their ranks and the loss of the abbey had the effect of plunging the local community into an economic depression from which it did not recover until the end of the century.

An attempt, largely successful, to set the town on its feet was made in 1605 when James I granted Evesham a Borough Charter with the right to send two members to Parliament, a situation which remained unchanged until 1867 when this was reduced to one. In 1948 the constituency was merged with that of South Worcestershire. The charter also incorporated the village of Bengeworth with the new borough.

With the charter making a real effort to re-establish Evesham's fortunes it was not long before plans were being made to make the town one of the leading commercial centres of the West Midlands. The initiative for this came from one man, William Sandys, who owned an extensive estate at nearby Fladbury, much of which was flanked by the Avon.

Although the Avon may have been navigable at some time long before William Sandys put in his appearance on its banks, it had become, by his day, a slow and sluggish channel of uneven depth and, in the words of Elizabeth Elstob, Evesham's eighteenth-century historian, "not capable of carrying a boat of any burthen". It was a situation which Sandys determined to alter. He declared his intention of making the river navigable from Tewkesbury to Warwick and, in 1635, was granted a licence for the undertaking from Charles I. The river, at this time, was navigable for only a short distance above Tewkesbury and most goods were brought into the Vale of Evesham via the Severn-port of Upton. But, with the Severn tidal at this point and often too shallow to be used and taking into account the pitiable state of the roads over which merchandise had to be brought from the Severnside port, there was no doubt that the existing means of transport left a lot to be desired.

Sandys was a businessman well aware that if he could convert the Avon into a through-waterway between the Midlands and Bristol he would divert a large amount of traffic from the Severn and make himself a fat profit. Although some landowners were opposed to the idea Sandys successfully formed a company and work began on the stretch of river between Evesham and Tewkesbury. Almost immediately he fell foul of the Avon mill-owners who feared that the new 'navigation' would curtail their water-supply. Their opposition was eventually withdrawn when Sandys undertook to construct weirs rather than locks. When not in use these could be left open so that the level of the affected reach remained unchanged. Today Pershore and Cropthorne weirs are their only survivors.

Work on the project was very slow, slower even than its promoter had anticipated. Almost all of it had to be done by hand and many men were needed. In fact Sandys seems to have been plagued by a continual shortage of labourers and those he could find refused to work on the project during the winter months. They could hardly be blamed for their reluctance for the work was arduous and unpleasant involving toil in almost continuous mud. In fact some of the silt proved so difficult to clear that, at a number of places, Sandys forsook the original course of the river in favour of the construction of mini-canals in the form of new parallel channels.

Time was an expensive commodity and by the time Sandys had carried his navigation to within sight of Evesham, the project was so behindhand that he was running dangerously short of capital. He attempted to raise more, but little was forthcoming. The dark clouds that were soon to burst in the thunderstorm of the Civil War were already massing and there were few people who found this the time to put their money into commercial ventures of any sort. In due course the war arrived—and William Sandys was not destined to see the completion of his project.

In the time of the Commonwealth work was restarted under the direction of William Say and it is to this man that we owe the completion of the navigation as far as Evesham and, more particularly, the delightful stretch of the river between Evesham and Nafford Lock.

The third and final engineer to work on the Avon Navigation and who extended it from Evesham to Stratford did not begin his work until after the Restoration. This was Andrew Yarranton, whose completion of Sandys' original project was backed almost solely by capital provided by Lord Windsor, who held land at Redditch and Bromsgrove. Yarranton had earlier, in 1665, been responsible for making the River Stour navigable from Stourbridge to Stourport and was one of the few people at this time who possessed any practical experience of this type of project.

By 1670 Yarranton had succeeded in extending the navigation as far as Stratford. He would have liked to have completed Sandys' original scheme and taken it on to Warwick, but Lord Windsor now decided he had spent quite enough on the Avon and declined to finance the project further.

For almost two hundred years the navigation successfully linked Evesham to the seaport of Bristol and carried a considerable volume of traffic. But, with the coming of railways in the nineteenth century, traffic, like that on almost all other waterways, steadily declined. In 1873 the river above Evesham was declared derelict and by the mid-1950s it was possible to use the Avon only as far as Pershore. A century of near neglect had put the Avon back to a condition almost as bad as William Sandys had found it in the early seventeenth century. Since then the Avon Navigation Trust has appeared on the scene and, using voluntary labour, the navigation has already been considerably restored and it will doubtless not be long before, once again, the river will be navigable from Stratford to the sea.

It was while work on the original navigation was in temporary suspension that Charles I held court in the town in 1644. Evesham was held for the Royalists until the following year when it was taken by the Parliamentarian Colonel Massey. In a Roundhead eulogy of the time one writer was to declare:

Who was he that went out from that command (as Governor of Gloucester) in such a blaze to adde glory unto conquest, and crown his actions with a never-dying honour: when he took the strong garrisoned Evesham, in a storme of fire and leaden haile, the loss whereof did make a king shed tears? Was it not Massey!

But though this later battle of 1645 has importance as one more Parliamentarian success on the road to the ultimate defeat of the Royalist cause it pales to insignificance when compared to that of 1265. It is very possible that, because of the dominance of the earlier conflict, Massey's Evesham victory has not been credited with the title of a battle at all.

Although architecture of most styles and periods are represented in the town, the seventeenth century is one that comes off rather badly. Perhaps the townsfolk feared a second visitation by Massey. In fact the only noteworthy building surviving from this century is the Friends' Meeting House with its gabled front which stands in Cowl Street and was built in 1676. Of earlier buildings there are many, including the Tudor 'Round House'—a half-timbered building now occupied by a bank and standing in black-and-white isolation on an island at the north side of the Market Place. In the early 1960s it was carefully restored and renovated. Parts of the Town Hall also contain Tudor work and the timber-framed Red Horse Inn, on the corner of Vine Street and Merstow Green, also dates from around this period; needless to say, its juke-box does not. Also dating from Tudor times is the Walker Hall, standing near the Post Office on the south side of the Market Place and which flanks the entrance to Abbot Reginald's Gateway.

Three of the town's Nonconformist chapels all date from the eighteenth century; the Unitarian chapel in Oat Street with its hipped roof and pedimented porch being the first to be built in 1737. Cowl Street Baptist chapel was built in 1788 and a year later the Plymouth Brethren Meeting House was erected in Mill Street with its austere but tasteful cream and chocolate colouring.

Bridge Street, High Street and Vine Street all contain examples of Georgian architecture although, especially in the case of Bridge Street, most of these are now occupied by ground-floor shops. One notable house, however, has not succumbed to the commercial pressures of modern times. This is Dresden House in High Street which dates from the reign of William and Mary and was once the home of Dr William Baylies. Baylies had a difficult time making a living in such a healthy place as Evesham and forsook the town for the less favourable climate of Germany where he eventually became personal physician to Emperor Frederick the Great of Prussia. He died at Dresden in 1787 and the name of his former house is thus, rather unusually, something in the nature of a posthumous memorial.

Evesham is well-endowed with inns and, apart from those I have already mentioned, my fancy is always taken by Bengeworth's 'Talbot', the Regency 'Falcoln' and High Street's 'Star' with its Classical entrance. It was to the 'Star' that I once repaired in the aftermath of a particularly ill-fated Literary Festival with which I was once associated in the town.

The main venue of the festival was the Walker Hall which, for its duration, was decorated by exhibits loaned by Coventry College of Art. Chief speakers were John Moore, the local novelist who is now perhaps best remembered for his *Portrait of Brensham Village* and *The White Sparrow*, and Vernon Watkins, the poet and early befriender of Dylan Thomas. Both are, unfortunately, no longer with us, but I never pass near the Walker Hall without recalling those July days, hot and languid and massed with creditors, when the success or failure of summer festivals did not seem to really matter at all.

Although the 'literary' side of this festival could hardly be said to have been an unqualified success the pure entertainment side, as is so often the case with these events, more than offset this. Its principal feature was a jazz group which packed out the town's Public Hall, a building which is as good a piece of nineteenth-century civic architecture as will be found in any part of the county and one that is perhaps long-overdue for a eulogy from Sir John Betjemen.

In the realms of music Evesham has more than an association with jazz-bands to its credit for Elgar was no stranger to the town and it was once home to the Italian composer Muzio Clementi. Just what brought Clementi to Evesham, or more correctly to Bengeworth, is not certain, though it is thought that he married a local girl. He is known, though perhaps only by musicologists, for having written sixty piano-sonatas and for the introduction of a new technique of pianoforte playing. He died in 1832 and is buried, not in Evesham, but at Westminster Abbey.

Another Italian also figured in Evesham's past, Count Francis Barnardi who is sometimes credited with the introduction of market-gardening into the district. In the mid-seventeenth century the Count was Genoese Ambassador to the Court of St James but, disagreeing with the policies of his native government, resigned his post and retired to Evesham where he lived the rest of his life as a country gentleman.

Count Francis, however, was a less than perfect husband and an even worse father. At the age of thirteen his son John decided, amongst other things, that he had had enough of market-gardening and ran away to be befriended for some years by the Pakingtons of Westwood Park. Eventually John became a 'soldier of fortune' fighting in the Continental wars that make European history such a laborious subject. Returning to England at a time of great political unrest he was arrested by officers of William III on an unsubstantiated charge of treason and lodged in the Fleet Prison to await trial. But events changed so rapidly that John Barnardi appears to have been forgotten and eventually he gave up hope of ever being brought to trial at all. In reality the prison now became his home. He married there and, his wife living with him, raised a family and finally died, still without having been brought to trial, when he was in his eighties. In all, John Barnardi had been an inhabitant of the Fleet for more than forty years.

Evesham grew steadily throughout the centuries following the granting of its charter but, in 1933, it was decided to enlarge the borough by the addition of the neighbouring parishes of Great and Little Hampton. The two parishes neighbour each other to the south of the town and are divided by the River Isborne, a tributary of the Avon. The Hamptons can be reached from Evesham via Boat Lane off Merstow Green where one of the few surviving chain ferries in Worcestershire still plies across the Avon at a one-way charge of 1½p for adults and ½p for children. Taking the ferry it is only a short walk to the summit of Clarkes Hill from where there is a view of Evesham nestling amid the orchards and market gardens of its Vale.

It is not long since the days when the spring blossom of the Vale brought annual traffic chaos to Evesham's streets and the lanes beyond as sightseers poured in from all over the Midlands. The sightseers still come to see the 'blowth' but, with the best routes now signposted by the RAC, they make a less dramatic impact.

But spring is still the best time for the stranger to visit Evesham and of spring's short months May is probably the best of all. Although May Day ceremonies have long since lapsed the town has replaced something of their spirit in its annual May Regatta.

Here crews compete from all over the country and, on a fair and sunny day, there are few better sights than that of a well-disciplined eight straining downstream towards the finishing post on the banks of Abbey Park. Both the May Regatta and the annual Head of the River Race are organized by Evesham Rowing Club which was established over a century ago and has its Boat House in Abbey Park.

All this is not to say that Evesham has remained unchanged within the present century for it is now something much more than a reminder of a vanishing bucolic England. Light industry has been established in the town for some time with Smedleys' canning factory standing alongside the Worcester Road and other food processing factories on the north side of the town. Light metalwork is also carried on and a small industrial estate has recently been developed off the Worcester Road while another is planned for the south side of the town. Since the late 1940s the town has been considerably enlarged by the creation of private and council housing estates especially to the south and south-west.

In recent years there has been some attempt to develop Evesham as a 'tourist trap', but the attempt now appears to have been largely abandoned. With Stratford and the Shakespeare country lying to the north and with the Cotswolds to the south-east Evesham must be content, from the tourist point of view, to function mainly as an overflow town. This is probably all for the good for large-scale tourism has already blighted two of Evesham's near-neighbours. At Broadway the village is fossilized, pleasantly fossilized certainly, but no one could say that, even taking into account the 'Lygon Arms', it was a place that throbbed with vitality. But perhaps fossilization is a better fate than that which has overtaken Stratford-on-Avon where commercial exploitation, from postcards to garages with literary names, has turned Shakespeare's birthplace into a cultural fun-fair.

Casting a glance in the direction of these two neighbours I feel sure that the people of Evesham are content with their fruit, Bell Tower and busy pavements. The summer crowds and small-boat enthusiasts who throng the river's banks at Abbey Park and Crown Meadow are enough for them. They have few ambitions for Evesham to become yet another chintzed-up tourist town and are happy to inhabit one of the least spoilt of Worcestershire's towns. Though the stranger may visit it and find himself welcomed, he should not forget that, despite all its historical associations, it is very much a working town, its face firmly turned towards a future which will entail no less toil than that required to shape its past.

Beyond Evesham the meandering Avon becomes a sunlit silver band lazily looping its way about the Vale, and to take a small boat downstream in spring is an experience which few people could forget. Then the whole Vale is brushed with blossom and riverside orchards bear their white and pink cascades to be mirrored at the water's edge. In summer the river is often the only real cool place to be found, the orchards hot and languid and coloured by the heaviness of ripening fruit.

In these summer months children from such Vale villages as Fladbury and Cropthorne would appear to spend most of their days at the river-bank. Undoubtedly the river can be dangerous, but at this time of year some stretches are relatively shallow and the currents are generally less powerful than at most other periods. The last time I took a boat along this stretch of the river the weather had become so hot that a group of children had abandoned their nets, fishing rods and clothing and while some were splashing in the water at the river's edge others lay sprawled upon the deep grassed bank drying themselves in the burning late-July sun to form a scene that was reminiscent of a Renaissance fresco. Perhaps there are those who would claim that even the Avon is no place for bathing these days. But, with only the minimal amount of industry on its banks, it is one of the least polluted of England's rivers and I doubt if any of those particular young bathers came to any harm.

Fladbury village was the site of a monastery as early as 691 and though no trace of this Saxon foundation now remains, a Saxon cross preserved at nearby Cropthorne church may have originally come from it. Fladbury was the medieval home of the Throckmorton family, who were later to take up residence across the Warwickshire border at Coughton Court, near Alcester. In later days the family, in common with other Catholics, was to be persecuted for its religious beliefs and Coughton Court has tragic associations with the ill-fated gunpowder-plotters. While at Fladbury, however, the family enjoyed happier fortunes.

The Throckmortons first rose to power and influence as followers of the Earls of Warwick and in Fladbury church, which

dates from Norman times, Sir John Throckmorton has lain for
over five hundred years with his wife Alianora and their son
Thomas. Sir John died in 1445 after a career as a soldier and an
adviser to Richard Beauchamp, Earl of Warwick, in which he
rose to occupy the position of Under-Treasurer of England. It
was Sir John's grandson, George, who was to marry an aunt of
Katherine Parr and to become a man much favoured by Henry
VIII. But, by then, the family was firmly established at Coughton
Court and its influence and entanglements in Tudor politics lie
outside the scope of this book.

Lying some distance from the village is Craycombe Hill whose
lower slopes are studded with the orchards of Chadbury Lodge, a
farm in the ownership of one of Evesham's largest fruit-growing
companies, and whose upper slopes are crowned with woodland
of a wilder sort. The hill rises three hundred feet above the Vale
and, for those wishing to make the climb, gives a superb vista
across the Avon to the height of Bredon and the more distant
Malverns. At the foot of the hill Craycombe Manor was once the
home of the Worcestershire novelist, Francis Brett Young. His
works, at the moment, are rather out of favour, but no doubt are
only waiting to be rediscovered by some enterprising television
producer. This figure of the future may even have received some
aspects of his early training on the slopes of Craycombe Hill
itself, for here, tucked away below the main hill, is Woodnorton,
which is now used as a BBC training school. Before the BBC's
trainee engineers arrived here Woodnorton was used as a private
school and earlier still had associations with French royalty. For
many years it was the home of the Duc d'Orleans and his Duchess
whom the French Legitimists regarded as rightful king of
France. It was also, for a short time, the home in exile of King
Manuel of Portugal after he had been deposed in 1910. The
estate of which Woodnorton was then the centre has since been
broken up and memories of foreign royalty have almost faded
from this hill above the Avon.

Another 'foreigner' to the Vale, this time a Welshman, is
however, still remembered at Fladbury church. This was William
Lloyd, one of the 'Seven Bishops' who were tried on a charge of
seditious libel against James II for protesting at the enactment of
the Second Declaration of Indulgence. Regarded as near-heroes
at the time, these same men might find themselves labelled

bigots today, for the gist of their protest was that Catholics should be debarred from holding high office in government. But it must also be remembered that, at the time, many Englishmen feared that the Catholic James II was paving the way for a Catholic take-over of the country which would have brought England into alliance with the France of the despotic Louis XIV and against the Protestant countries of Holland and Northern Europe. There was great popular rejoicing when it was declared that the Seven Bishops were not guilty.

In later life Bishop Lloyd came to believe that he was a prophet and, in 1712, Queen Anne, who doubtlessly fully appreciated Lloyd's entertainment value, invited him to give his prophecies an airing at a special performance for the Court and herself. Earlier Lloyd had held long conversations with the diarists Pepys and Evelyn, though only Evelyn wrote-up the conversation in any detail. Lloyd died at the episcopal palace of Hartlebury in 1717 aged 91, expressing a wish to be buried at Fladbury where his son was then rector.

At Fladbury stands an islanded mill-house now converted to use as a private house which can be reached only by boat. The chain-ferry which once linked the mill to the 'mainland' is still occasionally used. No doubt William Sandys and his successors had trouble with the mill-owners here when constructing the original Avon Navigation. There was a mill at Fladbury at the time of the Domesday Survey and the present one was in continuous use until the early 1930s. Nearby is the eighteenth-century rectory with its terraced garden falling in waves to the river-bank and which must have made a delightful home for the son of William Lloyd.

In distant days there was considerable rivalry between the inhabitants of Fladbury and Cropthorne, a rivalry which often led to violence. In those times many villages existed almost as a family unit, everyone knowing everyone else and without the influx of weekend outsiders to break up the continuity of village life. Radio, television and the modern transport revolution has dealt a body-blow to this type of existence, but between the men of Fladbury and Cropthorne a friendly rivalry has outlasted even these and, darts and cricket matches apart, a man from either village will still try to score a point off someone from the other if he can.

Cropthorne church, which dates from the early twelfth century, has many monuments to the Dingley family who were lords of the manor of neighbouring Charlton from the fourteenth to the end of the eighteenth century. The line came to an end in an extraordinary fusion of mayhem and eccentricity.

Sir John Dingley-Goodere succeeded to the family estate in the early eighteenth century. He was the elder of two brothers, the other Samuel, as was often the case with younger sons of no fortune of their own, entering the navy. All this was relatively normal practice. But here it was complicated by an intense personal rivalry which, it would be no exaggeration to say, verged on hatred.

In 1733 both brothers were elected Mayor of Evesham by exactly the same number of votes. As neither would stand the impasse was finally solved by Samuel forcibly throwing his elder brother out of All Saints' church where the swearing-in ceremony was taking place. As head of the family Sir John resented this slight to such an extent that he now announced that, as he was childless, he intended the Charlton estate to pass to relatives of his mother who held land near the Herefordshire village of Burhope.

Samuel was duly fearful that Sir John would keep his word and deprive him of his expected inheritance. He had now attained the rank of captain and his ship was moored for refitting in Bristol dockyard. On the pretext that he wished to discuss the affairs of the estate Samuel now lured Sir John to Bristol where the discussion took place over supper in a quayside inn and in the presence of a lawyer. The lawyer was later to relate that the brothers parted on the best of terms.

But all was not quite as it seemed. Sir John left the inn before the others and as he was making his way along the quayside was surrounded by a gang of sailors from his brother's ship. When they began to bundle him into a boat to take him out to Samuel's frigate Sir John began to fear the worst and called out to passers-by that he was being taken to be murdered. But the sailors countered this by maintaining that Sir John was drunk and no-one interfered.

Once on board the ship, Sir John was locked in a cabin where he was later to be strangled by two sailors whom Samuel had hired. Unfortunately for Samuel the lawyer who had earlier been with the brothers at the quayside inn grew suspicious when he heard of the dockside brawl and set out to investigate. The murder had also been witnessed by two of the ship's crew who had watched through a crack in the cabin wall.

Samuel and the two sailors were brought to trial and all were hanged. Samuel's eldest son, Edward, now succeeded to the Charlton estate at the age of 12. Edward seems to have been as unstable as his father and uncle and died insane twenty years later.

The last of the Dingleys was Edward's younger brother Sir John, who was as deranged as the rest of his family, but hardly dangerously. Within a few years he had galloped through his fortunes and the estate at Charlton had to be sold, friends obtaining for him the pension and residence of a poor knight of Windsor. Sir John's ruling passion in life was to find himself a wife, but his eccentric behaviour and dress did not really appeal to the ladies. He had the habit of approaching any likely female he happened to see and, after the preliminary courtesies, would present her with a document he had written himself in which were set out the terms of his marriage offer, topped off by the declaration that a trifling lawsuit would put him in possession of an enormous fortune. He even advertised his offer in the newspapers, but, despite all efforts, he remained unmarried and died, the last of the Charlton Dingleys, in 1809, at the age of 82.

Downstream from Cropthorne lies Wyre Piddle which, with many of its cottages stretched out along the Worcester Road, has always seemed to me to be a rather dusty village. But perhaps this is only because I have mostly happened to come to it in those months when local growers are loudly bewailing the lack of rain whilst almost everyone else seems to be doing little else but laze around soaking up sun and alcohol.

The village has the remains of a wayside cross standing beside the Worcester Road at the junction with Church Street. The top part of the cross is missing, and probably has been since the image-breaking days of the Reformation, though steps, base and much of the shaft remain. The church stands on the site of a prehistoric burial ground and dates from the twelfth century. It was, however, much restored in 1888 and can hardly be said to have emerged from the experience as an aesthete's dream. Church Street has a good group of black and white cottages neighboured by a private housing development. Some of these houses are of the more expansive type and make a bid to be instant historic houses of the bits-stuck-anywhere brigade with bow windows, bottle-glass porches, Georgian entrances and wrought iron gateways and are perhaps inhabited by twentieth-century high-waymen. In the main road inn, 'The Anchor', Wyre Piddle possesses as good a rural inn as will be found anywhere in the county.

To the north-east of Wyre Piddle, set upon the high ground beyond the Avon's northern bank and in a countryside which contrasts sharply with the lushness of the Vale, is Throckmorton. In distant days Throckmorton must have been a desolate place and even today it still possesses a certain air of isolation. It is from this village that Fladbury's Throckmortons took their name and the remains of their original moated manor house lie near the church. Nearby Court Farm still has the remains of two separate moats. Not far away one of the Evesham produce firms has established what it calls its pulping station where plums are pulped to provide the basic filling for jams and cakes. Although it is away from the road and screened by trees it makes its presence known in summer by the pungent odour imparted by the pulping process.

Below Wyre Piddle the Avon runs on to Pershore whose fourteenth-century packhorse bridge is nowadays used only by anglers and pedestrians for there is a newer one beside it. The old bridge has been lucky to survive at all for, after their defeat at the Battle of Worcester, it was partly destroyed by the retreating Royalists in an effort to slow down the Roundhead pursuit.

The town had its origin in the seventh-century reign of Ethelred I of Mercia and, although it is not certain, it would seem that the abbey was originally founded by Ethelred's nephew Oswald. As was the case with neighbouring Evesham, Pershore's fortunes were to be closely connected to those of its abbey. Both town and abbey were twice pillaged by the Danes and the abbey was twice severely damaged by fire, in 1223 and 1330. But, from the monks' point of view, the greatest disaster to befall the abbey, apart from the Dissolution, was the appropriation of a large part of its lands by Edward the Confessor to endow his newly created Westminster Abbey. Part of the town itself was granted to Westminster and, smarting under such treatment, the monks now built the nearby parish church of St Andrew so that they would not have to share that of Holy Cross with the Westminster tenants.

Packhorse Bridge, Pershore

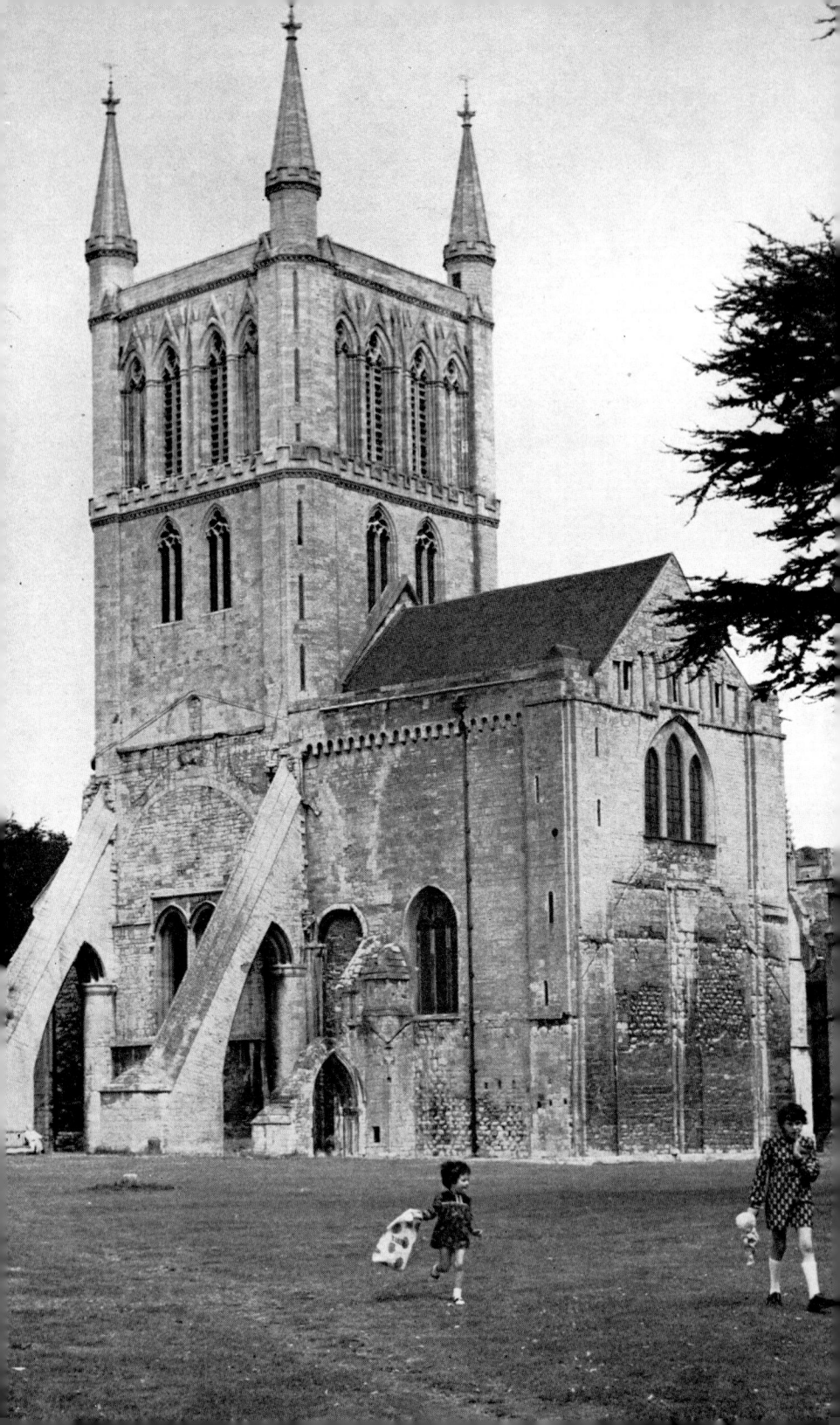

The church of Holy Cross is remarkable in possessing a stained glass window depicting the Dissolution of the abbey. In this one of the monks, Richard Beesley, is shown kissing the feet of Thomas Cromwell's commissioners. It was Richard Beesley who was most eager to give the commissioners a helping hand with the destruction of the abbey, though whether this was through true piety, as Beesley maintained it was, or in an attempt to curry favour with the representatives of the new order, we now cannot be certain. But a letter written by Beesley to the commissioners and now preserved in the British Museum is one of the most curious documents to survive from the years of the 'visitations'. After addressing Cromwell in elaborate style Beesley states that:

> Now y wyll ynstrux your grace sumwatt of relygus men. Moncks drynk an bowll after collacyon till ten or xii of the clock, and cum to mattens as dronk as myss and sume at cardes, sume at dyss and at tabulles, sum cum to mattens begenynge at the mydes and sume when yt ys allmost done, and wold not cum ther so, only for boddly punnysment, nothyng for Godes sayck.

Of course, Beesley's letter cannot be said to have influenced the course of events at Pershore for, like all other religious houses, it was already doomed. But it does demonstrate, if nothing else, that under the threat of imminent destruction, some of the religious houses must have become divided amongst themselves.

At the Dissolution the abbey site was granted to the Sheldon family, who also took over Bordesley Abbey, near Redditch. The nave of the abbey church was granted to the townspeople who afterwards exchanged it for the choir.

After the Dissolution time and neglect reduced even the small part of the abbey that had survived. In the sixteenth century the chapel of St Eadbury was considered to be unsafe and was dismantled. The Lady Chapel was also pulled down and in the seventeenth century the north transept collapsed.

Until the nineteenth century the town's annual fair was held in the abbey churchyard. Victorian Puritanism then being in full swing it was considered that this was a practice that amounted to sacrilege and the fair was consigned to the Market Place, where it still takes place.

Apart from the abbey, the church of St Andrew and the packhorse bridge little medieval work remains in the town, although

Pershore Abbey

3

some of the remains of the former monastic buildings survive in
the grounds of Abbey House and a house in the High Street
possesses a medieval undercroft which may have formed part of
the chapel of St Michael.

The architecture of Pershore is basically Georgian and, as at
Bewdley, its dominant tone is of red brick. Georgian houses
predominate in both High Street and the town square and a
number of them have retained their canopied balconies.

Not long ago the town seemed to be a rather neglected place
and hotels such as 'The Three Tuns' and 'The Angel' were
visited mainly by travellers staying overnight on their way to
somewhere else. Pershore then seemed thoroughly absorbed in
itself as a centre of the produce industry. But change has come
to the town, at least in the summer, for Pershore has since become
one of the growing band of 'festival' towns. Unlike so many
other places Pershore provides a perfect setting for a small,
intimate festival and there can be no doubt that the town's trades-
people welcome its existence. There can be few more pleasant
experiences than to attend a festival week concert in the ancient
abbey and then to stroll, first along the town's High Street and
then along the bank of the Avon that runs behind it with, all
the time the Abbey Tower just visible above the rooftops. Such
an evening can be perfectly rounded off over drinks in one of the
many inns.

There has been considerable housing development around the
town in recent years but in most cases this has been well planned
and laid out and does not jar with the town's older building.
Buildings of a larger nature include the Catholic primary school
and new swimming baths whose multi-coloured roofing appears
rather garish, especially when viewed against the backdrop of the
older buildings that line the High Street beyond. This is perhaps
the worst angle from which to view the town and it would be
something of an improvement if Pershore's Smithfield could be
tidied up a little.

As if to emphasize the fruit-growing associations of the town
there is a horticultural training college on its southern outskirts.
From here students go on to farms and market-gardens all over
the country, in many ways carrying on a tradition first established
by the monastic cultivators of the Vale. The town also has a
working mill which stands on the west bank of the river just

above the old bridge. The banks of the Avon were once dotted with water-mills, in medieval times the majority being not flour, but fulling-mills. These were the days when Worcestershire was a considerable sheep-rearing region and the fulling-mills, where local cloth was prepared, was the basis of a thriving local industry. Like the mill at Fladbury that at Pershore is of ancient origin, though the visitor must not expect Fladbury's picturesqueness to be repeated here for a working mill must keep abreast of the times if it is to remain working at all.

A mile beyond Pershore, lying just off the Worcester–Evesham road, is the village of Wick with many fine half-timbered cottages and a manor house that is a splendid example of Tudor domestic architecture. Wick has largely resisted the pressures to become another commuter village and those new houses that have been built here are not discordant with their surroundings. The village has remained a dominantly agricultural community and its surrounding fields grow some of the best peas in the county.

The small churchyard must be one of the best maintained in the region though the church itself has been largely rebuilt and contains little of interest. That at neighbouring Pinvin, however, escaped with only the more general 'restoration'. These restorations, more often than not, altered not only the fabric of the church but its life as well. The provision of tiled floors in most of our rural churches dates from these times, a provision which did away with the need for rush floor covering and consequently with the 'rush-bearing' ceremonies of earlier days. The restoration also often did away with the old galleries which had formerly housed the church orchestra and, with the disappearance of the orchestra, came the organ which has remained as the major musical instrument in our churches.

But Pinvin's nineteenth-century restoration did produce one unexpectedly good result for during the work a series of wall-paintings were discovered and fortunately it was decided not to obliterate them in the name of Victorian progress. The series are painted over each other, the most recent being in the form of now-illegible texts dating from the Commonwealth, while beneath them are prayers from the time of Elizabeth I. Beneath a part of these is a painting of the Virgin and Child and a figure of St Roche dating from the fifteenth century whilst to the east of these is a set of fourteenth-century paintings. Taken together this series presents a remarkable example of some of the changes which have taken place in the religious lives of the English people over the past centuries.

Not far away at Besford is another ecclesiastical rarity, this time the church itself which is now the last of the once-common wooden forest churches to remain in the county. Today the major legacy of what could be called the county's well-wooded past are its many half-timbered houses. But, with the exception of Besford, all the county's fully-timbered churches have been rebuilt, in part at least, in other materials. Even Besford's church contains some stone work, in this case its chancel, but this does not really affect the older structure as it is a late nineteenth-century addition. Its survival is all the more remarkable when it is discovered that the church was refurbished in 1880 when the restoration movement was at its height. Within, the small aisleless nave is framed and roofed in oak while two ancient bells hang in the timber bell-cote.

But the most remarkable feature of its interior must surely be the sixteenth-century rood loft which is a rare and fortunate survival for the Tudor reformers were successful in destroying most of them in the iconoclastic years of Edward VI. The church also possesses an Elizabethan triptych to the memory of the 15-year-old heir of the manor who died in 1576. The Harewells, of whom this unfortunate boy was one, became lords of Besford manor in the early fifteenth century, selling it to William Sebright, Town Clerk of London, at the end of the sixteenth; the church contains a number of memorials to members of both families.

It should be said that Besford church is rather small, which may account for it being largely overlooked by succeeding waves of reformers and restorers. Being of timber construction it can be something of a hot and oppressive place to linger on a sunny summer's day. But it is undeniably worth a visit, not only for its own sake, but as an illustration of how so many of our churches appeared in the times when England was largely an afforested country. It was because of the plentiful supply of timber that our Saxon ancestors built almost entirely in wood and that, in consequence their architectural legacy has simply rotted away over the centuries. Besford church cannot be claimed as a Saxon survival, but as an example of timbered construction with its roots reaching

back into Saxon times, it is a rarity for any part of our countryside.
The black and white Tudor home of the Harewells remains the
centre-piece of the present Besford Court which now houses a
Roman Catholic institution. In the early years of the present
century the Court was bought by a North Country industrialist
who was responsible for most of the additions to the original
building. In an episode which recalls a similar incident in
Galsworthy's *Forsyte Saga* his wife ran off with the architect and
in disgust he sold it to its present owners. Thomas Harewell of
Besford Court is commemorated by a seventeenth-century
monument at Birlingham church.

The stretch of Avon between Besford and Birlingham lies on
that reach terminated by Nafford Lock. It is one of the most
beautiful parts of the river with Housman's immortal Bredon
Hill dominating the western skyline. Birlingham is enclosed on
three sides by a loop of the river to create a situation which recalls
the position of Evesham.

The bridge at nearby Eckington is one of the oldest to bestride
the river. Across this once came the heavily laden packhorse-
trains and now it is a perfect place from which to watch the
river's summer pleasure traffic though perhaps Sir Arthur
Quiller-Couch, who was to compose a memorable poem here,
would not appreciate the abundance of fibre-glass and gleaming
metalwork that has changed the near-deserted river of his day
into one of the main arteries of the waterway leisure boom.

Strensham is the last village reached before the Avon becomes
part of the county boundary with Gloucestershire. The village
was once home to the Russells who had a castle here, though this
has long since mouldered back into the land from which it came.
The last lineal descendant of the family was Frances, the widow of
Sir Charles Trubshaw, who died in 1774. In 1826 William
Cobbett, on his rural ride into Worcestershire, wrote that
"Strensham has been bought by a Birmingham banker of the
name of Taylor for, it is said, seventy thousand pounds." It was
Taylor who was responsible for the erection of the present
Strensham Court, though his descendants, like those of the
Russells, no longer live at Strensham.

The church, standing somewhat apart from the village on high
ground overlooking the river, contains a virtual gallery of
memorials to various members of the Russell family as well as a

diminutive one to Samuel Butler, whose fame as a seventeenth-century satirist was destined to long outlive the memory of his wealthy patrons.

According to some accounts Samuel was not born at Strensham at all but at Bartonbridge, then a village near Worcester. But this seems to be a case of the county-town wanting to grab all the local literary 'goodies' for itself and it is difficult to see how such an assertion could ever have been made. Samuel's father wrote the entry of his son's christening in the parish register himself and was probably one of the leading yeoman farmers of the district. He rented land, valued at £300 per year, from the lord of the manor, Sir Thomas Russell, and owned a house and land of his own which, up until the middle years of the last century, was still locally referred to as Butler's Tenements. He was apparently well-enough off to be able to send Samuel to receive his education at Worcester School. Little is known of Samuel's youth and early manhood but during his twenties and thirties, which were the time of the Civil War and Commonwealth, he found employment as a private secretary to various powerful Puritan families. Much of his time was spent at nearby Croome Court, where he took up painting under Samuel Cooper and is said to have painted a portrait of Oliver Cromwell from life. Unfortunately no-one seems to have placed much value on his paintings and later they were used to stop up broken windows at Croome Court.

Yet his fame was not to come from the brush, but from the pen. During the dying year of the Commonwealth, with Oliver dead, his self-effacing son Richard installed as a makeshift Lord Protector and General Monck rapidly coming to the opinion that the Army must be used as the instrument to secure the restoration of Charles II, Samuel began to write his satiric poem 'Hudibras'. This, piteously lampooning the Puritans, was guaranteed to appeal to anyone who had but the faintest of Royalist sympathies.

The Restoration was effected whilst Samuel was still writing his lengthy poem and momentarily he benefited from the changed circumstances becoming one of the secretaries attached to the reconstituted Council for Wales and the Marches which was established at Ludlow. But, like many other poets, Samuel was hardly the most economical of people and was soon running up impossible debts. Working almost to the sound of creditors he finished off his poem and, aiming high, sent it off to Charles II.

Charles certainly liked it but, apart from saying so, did nothing to help the now struggling poet. 'Hudibras' went into print in 1663 and brought Samuel in a fair sum which, however, only temporarily relieved his distress.

The King himself liked the poem so much that he was continually giving away copies to his friends, but perhaps he felt he could not help Samuel for political reasons. Charles was deliberately treading the middle way between the Puritans and the Royalist extremists and had made no secret that he did not intend to resume his 'travels'. Open praise for 'Hudibras' might have been construed as too anti-Puritan a move for the new king, who was determined that nothing was going to rock the throne he had so recently gained. As a result Samuel's pleas for support or for a position at Court went unanswered and Charles apparently determined that he could offer the poet no more than his good wishes.

Samuel, meanwhile, at first brought out additions to his poem, whose success did not prevent him from ultimately slipping into actual penury. When he died, in 1680, his circumstances were so bad that it is quite possible that he died of malnutrition. It was a sad ending for a man who was undoubtedly one of the literary geniuses of his age.

II

THE SOUTHERN BORDERLANDS

NORTH-WEST from Evesham and lying close to the border with Warwickshire the group of villages known as the Lenches are scattered on the flank of the rising ground above the Vale. These six black-and-white villages, all nestling at the foot of the low-rising Lench Hills, have long been labelled as some of the most picturesque in the county and, at this moment in time, I can see no reason why anyone should attempt to remove the label for it remains a true one.

Of the six, three—Aitch Lench, Sheriff's Lench and Abbot's Lench—are more correctly described as hamlets. Over the correct name of Abbot's Lench there exists some confusion. In its oldest form this would appear to have been Hob's Lench which, for devotees of the occult, would perhaps endow it with far more than its more obvious rural character. Just when it was dubbed Abbot's Lench is now uncertain but, in a spirit of compromise between old and new, popular mutation now more generally renders it as Ab Lench.

Rous Lench is the largest of the group, existing almost as a parent surrounded by its offspring. It was originally named Lench Randolph, the present name being substituted in the sixteenth century when the Rous family became lords of the manor. Within the church are various memorials to the family including one to Edward Rous who died in 1645. He was a Royalist who had the misfortune to be captured by the Round-heads in his own garden. Taken to Warwick Castle he became ill and died there, but was brought back to his village for burial. The village has other Civil War associations for Cromwell spent some time at Lench Court after the Battle of Worcester.

It was the Rous family which built the half-timbered Court which was well-known to Richard Baxter, the Puritan divine and a friend of Sir Thomas Rous who is commemorated by a striking mural tablet in the nearby church. But what is surely the most memorable sight here is the intricate topiary work, clipped yews surrounding falling terrace-steps of lawn and garden. It is a wonderful sight and one can only wonder at the work involved in its maintenance. Though a garden on the grand scale Lench Court never seems to lose its feeling of intimacy.

Nearby Church Lench has a Norman church though it was much restored in the last century and what medieval work survives is largely of the fourteenth century.

Norton-with-Lenchwick, as its name denotes is really two villages, Norton bestraddling the Evesham–Stratford road and Lenchwick lying a mile or so to the north-west. In Tudor times Norton manor was owned by the Biggs family, later being sold to Sir William Craven and members of both families are commemorated in the fifteenth-century church. Like most villages in the Vale region Norton lies in orchard country, with the fruit trees growing profusely in the village itself. Within its towered, red-sandstone church is a twelfth-century marble lectern dug up near the site of Evesham Abbey in 1813 and subsequently transferred here. The main road at this point can become extremely congested and Norton is in some danger of being strangled by the motor-car. The situation has brought about the inevitable cry for a by-pass, but if all the county's main-road villages are ultimately to be by-passed it will involve a tremendous loss of agricultural land. The time must surely be drawing near when we must call a halt to the endless tarmacking of our countryside. Worcestershire is a county particularly menaced by the process with plans to construct a new motorway from Strensham to Solihull to 'syphon off' M5 traffic travelling north-east and a motorway-link, the projected M42 which would complete the triangle with a motorway from Lydiate Ash to Solihull. Protesters against the M42 maintain that the correct solution to the congestion of the two-lane M5 is to widen it to a three- or four-lane motorway. Should these arguments succeed Worcestershire may yet be spared from another carve-up in the name of the motor-car.

Cleeve Prior is another village in this corner of the county much praised for its beauty, though this is not so much in the familiar black-and-white tradition but in that of the Cotswolds of which it forms a low-lying part. Its gardens, with their massed arrays of flowers, give as much, and probably more, pleasure to visitors as they do to their green-fingered owners.

The manor was once the possession of the Bushell family one of whom, Thomas, was to experience in full the vicissitudes of the Civil War. Thomas was born at Cleeve Prior in 1595, later becoming friend and pupil of the philosopher-statesman Sir Francis Bacon. When the philosopher died Thomas spent three years living in seclusion on the bleak and desolate Calf of Man writing later that he had undertaken this lonely sojourn "in obedience to my dead lord's philosophical advice".

On his return to the mainland Thomas did not immediately return to Cleeve Prior but bought an estate in Oxfordshire in the grounds of which he discovered a natural spring and an unusually formed rock. These fired Thomas Bushell's imagination and led him to improve upon nature in a way that would have been fully appreciated by those later eighteenth-century lovers of the Gothic and the picturesque. He laid out gardens with artificial springs, fountains and grottoes in such profusion that he created a virtual waterscape whose fame was sufficient for it to draw Charles I and his Court on a visit. The entertainment Bushell laid on certainly appears to have been appreciated by the king and, not long afterwards, he mounted a second display for Queen Henrietta Maria who had been unable to accompany her husband to the first of 'the waterworks'. The upshot of this double bout of royal patronage was that Thomas was awarded the monopoly of the royal mines in Wales and he must have been quite satisfied with the outcome of a rather esoteric entertainment which had included "artificial thunders and lightening, rain, hail-showers, drums beating, organs playing, birds singing, and waters murmering all sorts of tunes".

But the grant of the monopoly of the royal Welsh mines was really as beneficial to Charles as to Thomas Bushell. For many years they had scarcely been worked at all and were in a serious state of dereliction. By putting much of his own money into the undertaking Bushell revitalized them and a mint was established at Aberystwyth issuing various denominations of silver coins.

During the Civil War Thomas Bushell acted on the Royalist side and was appointed Governor of Lundy Island, a position of great importance as Lundy commanded the seaward approaches to the Royalists' port of Bristol. Later, following the fall of the port and most of the south-west towns Thomas was sanctioned by the king to surrender the island. It was one of the last Royalist strongholds to fall into Parliamentarian hands and its former governor now found himself a hunted man with a price on his head. After playing the desperate part of a fugitive over most of south-western England Thomas at last went to earth at his manor at Cleeve Prior. Here he was successfully hidden while friends negotiated with Cromwell on his behalf.

For once Cromwell seems to have been moved more by business sense than bigotry. Thomas was granted both his freedom and a licence to operate not only the Welsh mines but also those in Somerset. Undoubtedly Cromwell did not wish to remove a man who had made the mines so profitable for the king and who could now run them just as profitably for the Commonwealth. But Thomas Bushell was to remain a confirmed Royalist and was later, after the Restoration, to secure favours from Charles II. He died in 1674 and was buried amongst the great in Westminster Abbey.

Locally nearby Harvington is primarily known as the head-quarters of a large tour-operating coach company. Many of the village's black-and-white cottages are thatched, in some cases the work being relatively recent. Indeed, locally the ancient craft of the thatcher is one rural trade that is enjoying something of a revival, for the new owners of many old cottages are having later tiled roofs replaced with the more traditional thatch and, in their own way, are proving more zealous in at least preserving the appearance of these villages than the true countryman who has lived in them all his life. This is not to say that some cottage restorations are not grossly overdone, for where it may be perfectly in character to restore a thatched roof to one that only later became tiled it is clearly an absurdity to clutter up the exteriors of these old cottages with farm-cart wheels, Edwardian lamp-posts and sufficient plaster gnomes and attendant animals to turn it into something resembling a Disney grotto.

Harvington's church occupies a hilltop overlooking the village and is neighboured by a half-timbered house with a large stone dovecote. Although dovecotes such as this are now almost solely ornamental they serve to recall days when the winter months were once meatless for most of Worcestershire's inhabitants. Together with fishponds, dovecotes were kept well stocked to provide an additional meat supply, when normal meat was scarce and what did exist almost inedible due to the vast amount of salt needed for its preserving. It was this paucity of fresh winter meat that led to the enactment of the stringent Game Laws whereby it was illegal, at one time, for the poor even to hunt woodcock. In rural areas dovecotes did not become ornamental buildings until the general introduction of the refrigerator.

In name the Littletons are three villages, but in reality are only two, for North and Middle Littleton have merged over the centuries to become one large village generally referred to as North Littleton. It is however at Middle Littleton that the major buildings of this double village stand, the thirteenth-century church, the sixteenth-century manor-house and the buttressed tithe-barn built at the direction of Abbot Ombersley of Evesham in 1376. The tithe barn is an enormous building indicating just how productive was the land of this region even as long as six centuries ago and eloquently illustrating the power of the Church in medieval agriculture.

At South Littleton a business-like vicar once agreed to provide new service books for his parishioners if in return they would allow him to keep doves in the tower; presumably he had no dovecote of his own and had decided that a little cooing from birds ultimately destined for the clerical pot would not unduly affect the quality of his sermon. The church was a medieval foundation but most of the restored building dates from Victorian times. The tower, however, minus pigeons, is of the fifteenth century and there are a number of earlier remains in the church, including a Norman tub font and, above the priest's entrance, a carving with the head of a medieval bishop on one side and, perhaps as an appropriate comment on the part of the sculptor, with an ass upon the other. As at Middle Littleton, the church has a collection of truly horrific gargoyles. The churchyard cross was one of those which attracted the destructive zeal of the Puritans at the time of the Reformation though its base and steps still remain.

Close to the Gloucestershire border and closer still to the ancient trackway of Buckle Street is Pebworth. Buckle Street is not a Roman road, though the Romans probably made use of it, but an ancient Celtic highway which later became one of the major routes taken by the Droitwich salt traffic. Pebworth's

Elizabethan manor-house stands on the site of an earlier moated building and traces of the former moat may still be seen.

Still keeping close to the Gloucestershire border is Church Honeybourne, a village which, in late medieval times, was a prosperous place on the edge of the Cotswold wool region and with a church that dates from those times.

Honeybourne railway station, or rather the site of it, was once the scene of a curious conflict. It was here that a tunnel piercing the Cotswold escarpment was constructed for the Oxford, Worcester and Wolverhampton Railway Company. Unfortunately, while the tunnel was being built, the OWW Railway went bankrupt, and the local contractor for the tunnel workings refused to leave the tunnel until he had been paid enough to pay off his men. While the local men were staging their sit-in at the tunnel, control of the railway effectively passed to the Great Western Railway Company who placed the famous civil engineer, Isambard Kingdom Brunel in charge of those works based on Evesham of which the Honeybourne Tunnel was part.

Brunel sent a request that the local men leave the tunnel so that his own work force could complete the job. He was met with a blank refusal. Further delays in construction were just what Brunel was trying to avoid and, in an effort to speed up work, he now transformed himself into a temporary general. He gathered an army of workers from the Evesham site and, marching at their head, reached the tunnel determined to occupy it by force if necessary. But the local magistrates had heard what was happening and, with a party of special constables at hand, read the Riot Act and succeeded in preventing a clash.

A few days later, however, Brunel and his workers were on the march again for in this, as in all his other undertakings, he was to prove himself nothing if not persistent. This time there were no magistrates present and a day-long battle resulted in Brunel ultimately expelling the local men. By some miracle no-one was killed, but a large number were injured. I have always found the little-known incident a fascinating insight into the ruthless character of the man who was probably the foremost engineering genius of the mid-Victorian age.

Offenham is said to have derived its name from Offa, King of Mercia in the ninth century, who had a palace here. Seven hundred years later Clement Lichfield, Evesham's last abbot, spent his last days here after the Dissolution, although nothing now remains of the manor-house where he stayed, the present Court dating from somewhat later times. The village once lay on the main road to London, the road being carried over the Avon by a ford, with a narrow bridge for the use of pedestrians and pack-horses.

This is the heart of the Vale's market-gardening industry though, in these drought-ridden summers, the waters of the Avon are no longer being used as freely as once they were. Although new housing development has occurred in almost all the villages they are still basically linked to the soil and Bretforton's Fleece Inn exists to quench the thirsts of today's rural workers just as it did those of sixteenth-century predecessors. Bretforton was once a grange in the ownership of Evesham Abbey with monastic administration centred on Sexton's Farm. This dates from the seventeenth century, but in the original rebuilding a medieval undercroft dating from the fourteenth century was retained. At nearby Badsey another fourteenth-century monastic building in the ownership of Evesham's abbey was later to be replaced, this time in the sixteenth century by Badsey's timber-framed manor-house. The original building had been built by Abbot Cheriton as the medieval equivalent of a convalescent home for sick monks. The manor-house was to be the home of the Hoby family and within the church is an effigy to Sir Richard Hoby who died in 1617. Locally the name of the village is now commonly linked with that of the neighbouring Littleton's in the name of an enterprising growers' co-operative.

It would be stretching a point to say that Wickhamford, with its American associations, stands in Shakespeare Country, but it has certainly come to enjoy a place on what could be termed the Shakespeare business circuit. This has been a little inevitable for, of the three places in England most closely associated with the Washington family—the other two being Northamptonshire's Sulgrave and Washington in County Durham—Wickhamford is by far the most attractive and easily the most accessible. In blossom time the village is a delightful piece of rural England with the Badsey brook taking a sparkling course through wayside orchards and gardens.

At Wickhamford lies Penelope Washington whose mother married Sir Samuel Sandys, lord of Wickhamford manor, as her second husband. On Penelope's simple tomb are the Washington coat of arms, the stars and stripes, which were subsequently to become the basis of the national flag of the United States. George Washington was a collateral descendant from Penelope's family and for many generations Wickhamford has been one of the major centres of American pilgrimage in England.

Penelope died in 1697 and the Latin inscription on her tomb has been translated to read:

Sacred to the memory of Penelope, daughter of that most distinguished and renowned soldier Colonel Henry Washington. He was descended from Sir William Washington, Kt, of the county of Northampton, who was high in favour of those illustrious princes and best of kings, Charles the First and Second, on account of his gallant and successful military achievements in both England and Ireland; he married Elizabeth, of the ancient and noble stock of the Pakingtons of Westwood, a family of unstained loyalty and patriotism. Sprung from such famous ancestry, Penelope was a diligent and devout Worshipper of God: she was the great consolation of her mother (her only surviving parent); to the sick and needy she was an especially ready and generous benefactress. Humble and chaste, and wedded to Christ alone, from this transitory life she departed to her Spouse. February 27. *Anno Domini* 1697.

The Sandys family also had other connections with the New World, for Sir Edwin Sandys was head and treasurer of the Virginia Company. The manor-house in which Penelope lived was formerly the possession of the Throckmortons from whom Sir Samuel Sandys, father of Penelope's husband, bought it in 1594. This Sir Samuel was the second son of the Cumbrian Edwin Sandys, one-time Bishop of Worcester and later Archbishop of York who laid the basis of the fortune of this important local family.

The timbered manor-house stands on the site of a grange once belonging to Evesham Abbey to which it was given as early as the eighth century. Within the medieval church are numerous memorials to members of the Sandys family whose glory is now, however, rather eclipsed by the reverence accorded to the far more simple memorial to the daughter of the Washingtons.

Not far from Wickhamford lies Worcestershire's Cotswold village of Broadway, now the only true Cotswold village to be included in the county though, in earlier days, even such a

'High Cotswold' town as Northwich came within its boundaries. Broadway has been praised and damned by so many writers that people's views of it have almost come to mean as much as what it actually possesses.

Its long main street has some affinities with that of Oxfordshire's Burford, though perhaps the Oxfordshire town is the more homely of the two for, while Broadway retains the appearance of a village it has long ago ceased to be one. The 'clean-up' campaign here which has resulted in the removal of most advertising posters, vending machines and so on, has made Broadway somewhat reminiscent of West Wycombe where the village now seems to lie under invisible wrappers, air-tight and removed from life. This preservation obviously has its good points though at the cost of creating a museum rather than preserving a village.

Yet, in this age of the commuter and the retired resident perhaps the term village is in need of redefinition. If this is so then Broadway can claim to have been something of a pioneer of the type of dislocated village which is now becoming so widespread in our countryside. A century ago its population was essentially an agricultural one; today many of its inhabitants are people who have retired from city lives or, as is increasingly the fashion, live here while still conducting business lives in the cities.

As a fashionable village Broadway dates roughly from the late Victorian period. It was here that Madame de Navarro, more commonly known as Mary Anderson, a popular American actress, retired to live at Court Farm, though it was a retirement, which like that of Madame Patti's, was destined to fill her adopted home with many of the great artists and writers of the day. To the fourteenth-century Abbot's Grange, now a tastefully-designed hotel, came the painters Sargent and Frank Millet. Mary Cannon, the former wife of James Barrie, lived here and Thomas Hardy is said to have visited the architect Sir Reginald Blomfield at Broadway after he had retired to the village.

Of Broadway's buildings the triple-gabled Tudor House and the Prior's House are amongst the best examples. The fourteenth-century Prior's Manse is reputed to be haunted by the ghost of a monk strumming a lute. But the building best known to Broadway visitors is almost beyond doubt the 'Lygon Arms' which, in part, is said to date from the fifteenth century. Its most recent addition, on the grand scale at least, is the Great Hall which was

The Avon at Fladbury Mill
Wick Manor House

built in 1909, though with its minstrel gallery this is at first a little difficult to believe.

Broadway has two churches, the older one standing more than a mile from the village and having been founded as long ago as the seventh century. The parish register dates from 1539, the year of the Dissolution of the greater monasteries, and contains a solemn denunciation of Henry VIII for sanctioning their closure—something which, even in those hectic days, could only have been written by a particularly forthright cleric.

In the churchyard is buried Sir Thomas Phillips, the nineteenth-century bibliophile who succeeded to his family's property near Broadway in 1818. Sir Thomas set up a printing press at Broadway to produce copies of ancient manuscripts so that they could be readily available to students. Later, however, the press was removed from the village to Cheltenham.

Broadway Hill, which rises to the south-west of the village, is more than a thousand feet above sea-level. The tower by which it is crowned was built in 1800 by the then Earl of Coventry so, it is said, that his wife could enjoy the view. In later days it was to be the temporary home of William Morris, the artist and social reformer.

Nearby are a group of villages which once formed part of Gloucestershire and, as with much of this south-western area of the county, still in spirit seem to belong to its West Country neighbour. Childs Wickham has a medieval wayside cross which is topped by a Renaissance head and a group of thatched cottages grouped alongside a small stream. Neighbouring Ashton Somerville has an ancient medieval church while at Hinton-on-the-Green the gateway of the Tudor manor-house was destroyed by a marauding band of soldiers during the Civil War.

Sedgeberrow is perhaps just near enough to Bredon Hill to rank as a Bredon village. The manor was granted to the Church of Worcester as long ago as 777. Since those far-off times the manor-house has been divided into cottages standing on the site of an older building which was once the farmhouse of the grange belonging to the prior of Worcester's Benedictine monastery.

To the west Bredon Hill rises to over nine hundred feet to give wide views across the Vale and westward towards the more distant peaks of Wales. It was the site of an important Celtic settlement in days long before the Roman Occupation and when

Hampton Ferry, Vale of Evesham

4

most of the low-lying ground below its slopes was covered largely by forest. Not far away the Bredon Camp is neighboured by the remains of another ancient settlement, generally referred to as Condderton Camp. Within Bredon's Iron Age fortifications is the Banbury Stone, a great slab of oolitic rock upon which it has been suggested that the Druid priests once made human sacrifices. Modern research, however, has tended to establish that human sacrifice was something that the Druids did not practice and if sacrifices ever did take place here they would probably have been of domesticated animals.

The size of Bredon's Camp appears an obvious indication that primarily it was a settlement rather than a fortress, though in time of need, it doubtless served as both. There are double ramparts to the south and east and I would hazard the opinion that these were constructed during the early years of the Roman Occupation before the all-conquering legions had penetrated into the region. The Romans almost certainly took and made use of the camp, for a large number of Roman coins have been found here.

Near the summit are two rocks known as the 'King' and 'Queen' and, in medieval times, this was the place selected for the meeting of the local manorial court. Before the court met the two stones would be whitewashed and it has been argued that this may have been an unconscious survival of old fertility rites once thought to have been conducted here.

At the summit of the hill is a square stone tower known as Parson's Folly. This was built towards the end of the eighteenth century by the then-owner of Kemerton Court and once had two rooms looking out over the Vale. The upper floor has long fallen in and the Folly is in some danger of degenerating from a building to a hilltop cairn.

The hill has provided inspiration for many writers though, thank Heaven, there are no seats with inscriptions to declare that Shakespeare—or Byron or Browning for that matter—'sat here'. In Housman's 'Summertime on Bredon' the hill has its own hymn when:

> Here of a Sunday morning
> My love and I would lie
> And see the coloured counties
> And hear the larks so high
> About us in the sky.

In this famous poem, as in others such as 'The Chestnut casts its Flambeaux', Housman catches, for me at least, the essential spirit of Worcestershire. But it is this poem, more than any other, which sways me to think that so many of the Shropshire places he mentions were really Worcestershire ones in disguise and that for Ludlow and Wenlock Edge we should perhaps read Evesham or Wyre Forest. Certain it is that Housman came to Bredon and that this most famous of Worcestershire hills led him to write the most well-known of all his poems.

Bredon Hill also inspired William Cobbett, who passed this way on his *Rural Rides* and who was, temperamentally, a man as different from Housman as it was possible to be. The iconoclastic radical wrote of the area he viewed from the hill as "one of the very richest spots of England, and I am fully convinced a richer spot that is to be seen in any country in the world".

Even earlier Henry Fielding had passed this way and it is probable that Mazard Hill, which Tom Jones climbed in the famous novel of that name, was really none other than Bredon.

But, though many people visit the Bredon villages, which as a group are probably the best representation of English domestic architecture in the county, there must be few who tackle the hill. Climbing the hill myself not long ago on one of those May mornings in which Housman took such delight, I encountered no one though in the villages clustered beneath its slopes there were visitors in plenty.

As long ago as the eighth century the manor of Bredon was church property and, in the time of King Offa, a monastery was established here. Not surprisingly, as the Saxons built largely in timber, little of their work survives and the church, which stands on the probable site of the Saxon monastery, dates from Norman times. Unlike the majority of Worcestershire churches that at Bredon has a spire rather than the more usual tower.

Within the church are some magnificent memorials to the Reed family. Giles Reed founded the almshouses still to be seen in the village and both he and his wife Katherine died in 1611, their monument being the most outstanding in the church. Katherine was the daughter of Sir Fulke Greville, the friend and boyhood companion of Sir Phillip Sidney.

In the chancel is the tomb of Bishop Prideaux, Royalist Bishop of Worcester at the time of the Civil War. Prideaux had earlier been Master of Exeter College, Oxford and was appointed to the bishopric of Worcester in 1641. He achieved a deserved reputation for fairness and impartiality in religious matters but, when Worcester was taken by the Parliamentarians in 1646, his reputation was hardly enough to prevent the confiscation of the episcopal estates and revenues. Prideaux, who had been in the city when it fell to the Roundheads, was forced to seek the hospitality of Dr Henry Sutton, his son-in-law and rector of Bredon. Sutton himself was hardly well off in the changed circumstances of Puritan rule and the Bishop was to find himself living in rather straitened circumstances. Things were not helped by the Bishop being temperamentally adverse to frugality. In his later days he was forced to sell his library and most of his personal possessions to provide for his needs and those of his family. His sojourn at Bredon, however, was relatively brief, for he died in 1650.

The rectory in which Bishop Prideaux spent his last years dates from the fifteenth century, though it contains some additions made in the sixteenth. It is a noble building of a scale more grand than most rural ecclesiastical buildings, but it is completely eclipsed by the magnificence of Bredon's fourteenth-century tithe-barn. Tithe-barns had a habit of being large, but that at Bredon is truly in the jumbo category and it comes as little surprise to be told that it is the second-largest such building in England. It has two great cart porches and above one is a room, reached by an external flight of steps, which was once used by the bailiff in charge of the barn. Within, the roof is supported by great wooden pillars which give it something of the air of a church.

About a mile northward is Bredon's Norton with its manor-house lying amid orchards. The house was once home to Thomas Copley who was an associate of Sir Walter Raleigh in the Virginia Company. Copley accompanied Raleigh to America where he was partly instrumental in laying the foundations of what later became first the colony and later the State of Virginia. He died in 1593 and was buried here. His coat of arms is still to be seen emblazoned on the doorway of the manor-house.

The manor-house also has more recent associations with the United States for it was here, in the latter years of the last century, that Mrs Victoria Woodhull Martin chose to go into respectable retirement. Born Victoria Claflin at Homer, Ohio in 1838 she first arrived in England in 1877 and later married John Biddulph Martin, chairman of Martin's Bank. Her life at Bredon's Norton, where she died in 1927, was one of utter respectability, dented only a little by a passion for fast cars and an interest in progressive education for girls. But her earlier life in America had been one of scandal and controversy and at one time she had stood as the first woman candidate for the Presidency on a campaign platform which had as its main planks female suffrage and equal rights for women. Prior to this Victoria and her sister Tenessee had been New York's first female stockbrokers—highly successful ones— and had also founded a newspaper. All this could have had appeal to the mid-nineteenth-century American voter; but Victoria was damned on two other counts in that she publicly advocated and privately practised free-love and also made claims, later discovered to be bogus, that she was a medium. Victoria Woodhull Martin was probably a woman of genius, but her genius also had its lunatic fringe. She seems to have left America under a cloud which emanated largely from the will of Cornelius Vandebilt which she was alleged to have influenced even though she did not herself profit from it.

In old age Victoria turned away from many of the policies she had once advocated so vehemently and even spoke out against the women's suffrage movement which she came to believe had gone too far. At her death *The Times* published a subdued and sedate obituary which only served to show that both its establishment and Victoria had been passing through a mellowed old age.

Unlike neighbouring Warwickshire, Worcestershire is hardly to be classed as a well-crenellated county, though if names are anything to go by, the visitor to Elmley Castle might reasonably expect to find a few surviving battlements. But today there is no more than a mound of old stones to mark the site of the castle which was once the home of the d'Abitots and which witnessed the beginnings of the rise to power of the Beauchamps. The castle was one of the many which fell into neglect after the blood-letting of the Wars of the Roses. When Leland passed this way he noted that only the tower remained and that he "saw carts caringe stone thens to amend Pershore Bridge". Much of the original stonework must have also been incorporated into many more local buildings.

In 1544 Henry VIII granted the manor to Christopher Savage and he and his successors were responsible for the building of the Tudor manor-house, additions to which were made at the beginning of the eighteenth century. The Savages are well-remembered by their memorials in the village church which dates in part from the distant days of the d'Abitot war-lords.

There are a large number of half-timbered houses in the village and a small stream runs the length of the high street. Here the village inn, 'The Queen's Head', is also half-timbered. Its signboard, which showed 'Good Queen Bess' on one side and on the other a representation of her reception when she visited the local Savage family, has recently been removed.

In the sixteenth century the Savages also held the neighbouring manor of Little Comberton. In distant times it would seem that Little Comberton was known to the Romans for Roman coins and fragments of Roman pottery have been discovered here and it is possible that a Roman villa, the home perhaps of a retired officer or administrator was once sited here. Little Comberton has a Norman church as does its twin Great Comberton which also possesses the largest dovecote in England with walls more than three feet thick.

Close to the Evesham–Cheltenham road is Beckford standing on the lower slopes of Bredon Hill. Beckford's church, Norman like those of so many of its neighbours, stands on the site of an earlier Saxon monastery. A monastery has been re-established here of recent years based upon Beckford Hall which was formerly the home of the Wakemans. The Hall is in the Cotswold style and is approached by a 100-yard avenue of box trees. There was a priory here in the twelfth century, its possession, at the time of its suppression in the fifteenth century, being assigned to the newly-created Eton College.

Beckford is a village of the Cotswold type as to a lesser extent is Kemerton and to a far greater that of Overbury. Indeed, as I have said before, many of these villages seem more truly to belong to Gloucestershire, which in fact they once did, than to Worcestershire, for their lime-stone buildings are more generally associated with the western county than with our own.

Yet, not far away, on the slopes of Bredon is a building which brings the half-timbering of traditional Worcestershire to this southern boundary. This is Woolas Hall, built by John Hanford and a fine essay in Tudor architecture. A stream from the hill was once channelled to turn the kitchen-spit. On the hillside above there once stood a chapel dedicated to St Catherine and which was built upon the site of a well which was reputed to be able to cure diseases of the eyes. The chapel has long ago disappeared and the site of the well is no longer known.

From here it is not far to the summit of the hill with its views of the huddled Bredon villages below its slopes and beyond, to the north-west, the rich panorama of the pastoral Vale. There can be no better place to end this journey into the county's southern borderland.

III

THE UPPER SEVERN VALLEY

B E W D L E Y is separated from the suburban sprawl of neighbouring Kidderminster by a tattered and steadily contracting green-belt in which is rather incongruously set one of those modern phenomena, a safari park. Lions and giraffes now live out an exiled existence here while bored baboons make sallies at tourist cars to acquire various fittings for their vehicle accessory collections. Since its opening the park has proved very popular and the concept of such open-areas has many advantages over the more traditional zoo.

However, I feel that it is rather illogical for England to now have so many safari parks housing the animals of Asia and Africa when it does not have a park of this nature containing animals from our own continent. Asia and Africa still retain many of their wild animals in their natural state, but in Britain and Europe generally, we have almost destroyed the indigenous wildlife. Perhaps it would be more appropriate for a British wildlife park to contain, not lions and tigers but the European lynx, bison and red deer. Europe once teemed with wildlife, with beaver, elk, grey seal, bear, wolf and wild boar as well as the fox, pine marten, badger, fallow deer, squirrels and otters that have survived into our own day. Some of these animals have not been seen in England for centuries, yet they were once part of our heritage, unlike, for example, the giraffe. Wolves were hunted in England in the Middle Ages and the last wild boar was not killed in this country until the seventeenth century. Of those animals that do survive in England not all that many are seen by the casual observer and there is much to be said for the creation of an environment in which they can live and yet still be seen by the visitor.

Most of the animals now extinct in Britain still exist in isolated parts of Europe, wolves being found in Northern Finland and a few scattered bison surviving in the forests of Poland. In Europe one National Park dedicated to the ideal of preserving the animals of our own continent already exists in West Germany's Bayerischen Wald in Bavaria and perhaps it is about time that Britain, whose national parks seem to lack a unified wildlife policy, followed its example before there are only the animals of other continents left to preserve.

However unpalatable the thought may be Bewdley and Kidderminster seem destined to ultimately coalesce. But, at the moment, it would be difficult to find two such contrasting towns in so close a juxtaposition. Kidderminster is a bustling, industrialized town sitting firmly upon foundations largely laid in the early years of the Industrial Revolution. Bewdley, on the other hand, appears positively decorous and, scorning the new industrialism as long ago as the 1780s, has for almost two centuries become a place where time has apparently hung still.

I say apparently for even Bewdley has been unable to resist change completely. In the present century it has welcomed and bade farewell to the Garden Cinema which once stood beside the Telford Bridge. In the late 1940s, before we were all so preservation-conscious, the town lost its Angel Assembly Rooms for redevelopment with scarcely more than a murmur of protest and, at about the same time, came the beginnings of the caravan settlement that lies to the north-west of the town. More recently it gained an impressive new secondary school on the east bank of the Severn—balanced, perhaps, by the loss of some of its eighteenth-century quayside warehouses on the west bank.

But though change has taken place here over the past hundred and fifty years it has been of the gradual sort and not of the wholesale bulldozer-and-grab variety that has ravished so many English towns. Just how many local authorities, I wonder, trying to keep abreast of the times, would be content merely to replace the footpath notices directing pedestrians to the old tow-path arches benaeth the Telford Bridge, with ones which now update it as a pedestrian underpass.

Much of Bewdley's past is inseparable from the Severn, though little commercial use has been made of the upper waters of the river since before the Second World War and the remaining quayside warehouses are either derelict or used for other purposes.

Summer pleasure traffic is, however, continually increasing and may yet provide the impetus for some revitalization of the old waterfront.

It was in the Middle Ages that the town first rose to importance and that it did so was almost solely due to its position on the Severn and to the fact that its bridge made it one of the major gateways into Wales and the Marcher baronies. Even in Saxon times Wribbenhall, as Bewdley was then called, had been in existence as a port. Growing from small beginnings it was destined to become one of the leading Severnside towns.

In medieval England most of the nation's merchandise was transported by river. Most of the old Roman road system had crumbled to dust after a thousand years of misuse and poor maintenance and, though many might bemoan the state of the old roads, there were few who would even contemplate the construction of new ones. In the winter months the mile-wide dirt-tracks that passed as main-roads were often turned to swamps of impassable mud while conditions during the summer were little better when the slightest breeze could raise a dust-storm that made movement almost impossible.

Transporting goods by road was a slow, laborious and risky enterprise and so, wherever possible, the merchant saw to it that they went by water. In fact, so much was this the general rule, that the rivers became the highroads of medieval England carrying more than half the nation's commercial traffic, while the roads were used as little as possible and then chiefly as links between one navigable river and another.

From early medieval times down until the beginning of the nineteenth century the Severn was to carry more traffic than any other river in England. Its major port was Bristol, after London the nation's largest sea-port. Downstream from Bewdley and other Severnside towns such as Bridgnorth, Worcester and Upton, went the cloth, wool, timber and metalware of the Midlands while upstream came French wine, lace and spice. Later, in the hey-day of Bewdley's prosperity, the town's now forsaken quays would have seen tea, rice, cotton, sugar and even slaves who had been trans-shipped to England from the Caribbean. One Bewdley inn, the 'Black Boy', still serves to recall the town's distant connection with the slave trade.

Special flat-bottomed boats, known as trowes, were built at

Bewdley and other riverside towns to cater for the Severn trade. These boats were fitted with sails but most of their motive power was provided by teams of men known as bow-hauliers who heaved the great craft along the river by ropes. The masts of the trowes were especially designed to that they could be lowered to enable them to negotiate the river bridges.

The Severn trowes may have been a more efficient means of transport than the packhorse teams that used the roads, but they were still very slow, providing ideal targets for river-pirates. In the fifteenth century Bewdley earned itself an unfavourable reputation as the base of pirates who attacked the laden trowes, usually at night, bearing off as much of their cargo as they could carry. The overhanging trees of the forest wildernesses of Malvern Chase and Wyre Forest gave ample cover for their nocturnal operations.

Scarcely less illegal were the attempts of the Bewdley trowe-masters to corner all the traffic passing Bewdley for themselves. Early in the sixteenth century a petition from the citizens of Gloucester and Bristol was sent to Parliament complaining that:

> Certain persons of Bewdley, having great boats called Trowes, had confederated themselves together for their singular profit, and would let no one pass through the said port with their goods and chattels, except they hire the said boats for the carriage of the said goods: and that on the Eve of St Michael last past, they had seized upon a great dray or flote going to Gloucester, such as com-plainants had used to carry their timber and fuel, and made the masters of it cut it in pieces, the said flote upon the said water, or otherwise they would cut off their heads.

By the time that accusations such as this were being made Bewdley had become important not only geographically but also politically. As long ago as the time of the Norman Conquest the manor had been given to Ralph de Mortimer. Although it was subsequently to be granted to the Prior of Worcester the Mortimers continued to lease it and by the mid-fourteenth century it would seem that they were once more in full possession.

The Mortimers were one of the most powerful and influential of England's Norman families and during the Wars of the Roses Bewdley's fortunes rose and fell in relation to the alternate risings and settings of the Mortimers' 'Sun of York'. Bewdley people

were no doubt grateful when Richard Duke of York, who inherited the manor in 1425 and who was the main instigator of the
York–Lancaster power-struggle, obtained a licence for a weekly
market to be held in the town and for an annual fair, the Fair of
St Agatha the Virgin, to be held on 5th February. They were
probably even more grateful when Richard was instrumental in
providing the town's first bridge in 1447. Richard actually lived
in the town for some time, rebuilding Tickenhill manor-house
as far as possible in the style to which he had become accustomed
at the family fortresses of Ludlow and Wigmore.

But neither Richard nor his bridge were to last long. In 1459
the first Yorkist rebellion was nipped in the bud at Ludlow and
Richard, his son Edward, Earl of March, and Richard Neville,
Earl of Warwick were amongst those who made a hasty getaway
to France. As part of a Lancastrian reprisal Bewdley's new bridge
was demolished. The following year Richard staged a come-back,
but his army was defeated at the Battle of Wakefield and the
Mortimer Duke was killed.

But the Yorkist sun was not to be banished from Bewdley
skies for, within a mere three months, the tide of fortune had
swung heavily against the Lancastrians and Richard's son, the Earl
of March, was crowned king as Edward IV. Although the Lancastrians were far from being a spent force it was the Mortimer
House of York which was to effectively rule England for the
next quarter of a century.

It was Edward who was to create Bewdley a borough, its
charter of incorporation being granted in 1472. Six years later he
further increased the importance of the town by making it the
headquarters of the Council for Wales and the Marches, the
royal manor at Tickenhill being made the seat of the Council
which was responsible for royal administration in Wales and
the Marcher lordships. The Council, as befitted a bureaucratic
machine, was staffed by a vast army of officials and Bewdley's
merchants must have been well pleased that the king had decided
to provide them with such an affluent market for their wares.

Bewdley was now substantially the town which so delighted
Leland when he visited it at the beginning of the sixteenth century,
and although a certain amount of new building has extended the
town in recent years, especially in the area around Wyre Hill,
Leland's description is still basically accurate:

The towne of Bewdeley is set on the syd of an hill, so coningly that a man cannot wishe to set a towne better. It riseth from Severne banke by este upon the hill by west, so that a man standinge on the hill trans pontem may descrive almost every howse in the towne.

As I have just pointed out, the latter part of the description is not as accurate as it was—but that is hardly Leland's fault. He went on to describe how "at the rising of the sun frome the este the hole towne glittereth, being all of nuy buyldings, as it were of gold". Given that Leland may have been exaggerating a little, many of Bewdley's buildings certainly were new at this time, for the town was expanding not only as an administrative centre but as an industrial centre as well.

Here again the existence of the Severn was of tremendous importance. Then, as now, industry needed a reliable means of transportation for its products and this was just what the river provided. Bewdley's main industry in Tudor times was cap-making which gave employment to about a thousand people. Whole families were employed in the trade in which it was forbidden by law for any machinery to be used. Almost as important to the town's economy was the tanning industry, with no less than a dozen tanneries existing in the town in the reign of Elizabeth I. Given the somewhat primitive conditions of the time Bewdley must have welcomed the traveller with a rather pungent odour.

These were heady days, not only for Bewdley tanners, but for the whole of England. Freed from the restraints imposed by the medieval Church, England was embarking on a free-enterprise bonanza. The rise of Bewdley's cap-making and tanning industries, as well as that of the local craft of hornware, was only part of a greater whole. Everywhere trade and industry was entering a boom-period, and, looked at in one light, the activities of Drake and Hawkins were only taking this spirit of Elizabethan free enterprise to its logical conclusion.

But there were clouds looming to darken this prospect and the fear of invasion by Philip of Spain was felt even here. As every schoolboy knows—or used to know—the Armada was launched in 1588 and was defeated by a combination of bad weather and nippy little English ships. But, though the Spanish fleet was broken up in the North Sea following the initial skirmishes in the

English Channel and the fire in Calais Roads, it was some time before most of England knew that the danger had in fact passed. As late as the spring of 1589 the bells were rung in Bewdley "when the Spanniardes' shipes were taken in Irelande".

Bewdley was now well-established as one of 'the pearls of the Severn' and in the early years of the next century James I renewed its charter, granting it at the same time the right to send a member to Parliament. This was later to give rise to a rather complicated situation. In 1685 James II forced a new charter on the town which gave the Crown wider powers than it had enjoyed under the old. Later, in the reign of Queen Anne, an irregularity in the second charter led to the first one being restored, though without the newer one being rescinded. Bewdley was now to find itself with a member of Parliament, a bailiff and a corporation all in duplicate. A Whig majority in Parliament declared that Henry Herbert was the town's legal representative but, when the Tories gained a majority, they opted for his rival, Salwey Winnington of Stanford Court. Perhaps this was all for the best, for it at least insured that Bewdley always had its member on the ruling side.

Both James I and later his son, Charles I, stayed at Tickenhill House and the royal manor-house once knew many other royal visitors. The most ill-fated of those to visit the house was undoubtedly the young Prince Arthur, eldest son of Henry VII, who when only 7 years old, was appointed by his father to be Justice in Shropshire, Hereford, Gloucester and the Marches of Wales. The first Tudor king made as much as he could of his Welsh ancestry, largely in the hope of staving off a possible rebellion on the lines of that which had earlier been taken by Owain Glyn Dŵr. His eldest son had been christened Arthur in something of a concession to Welsh national spirit and in an attempt by his father to bring to a practical reality the Welsh belief that a Welsh king bearing the name of the great warrior Arthur of legend would one day rule the lands of his ancestors. But, tragically, Henry was destined to discover that even kings cannot tamper with legends.

The young prince was installed at Tickenhill where, assisted by his council, he carried out the duties of governing the lands under his authority. It must have been a rather dismal childhood for the affairs of the council were conducted within a round of almost unrelieved formality. Yet it should not be forgotten that people of the Tudor era saw little strange in this, for it was an age when children tended to be regarded and treated as miniature adults and Arthur, more importantly, was being schooled for the serious task of kingship.

It was at Tickenhill that, in 1499, Arthur now 13, was married by proxy to Catherine of Aragon. Later the Prince and his bride visited the house several times, but his final visit was the most sombre of occasions. At the end of March 1502 the Prince journeyed to Ludlow and almost immediately after his arrival complained of feeling ill. He had never been strong and the journey through the bad weather had brought on a bout of pneumonia from which he was never to recover. On 25th April the body of the Prince rested overnight at Tickenhill on its way to its final resting place at Worcester Cathedral. This last journey was made in the most appalling weather, it being recorded that the road was so bad that "in some places they were fayne to take oxen to drawe the chase so ill was the way" and that it "was the foulist could windy and rayney day".

Some years later Prince Arthur's brother Henry VIII, sent his 8-year-old daughter Mary to Tickenhill while he was involved in the complicated negotiations that finally led to his divorce from Catherine of Aragon.

In the Civil War Charles I stayed here and Prince Rupert also stayed at Tickenhill in September 1643 when, on his arrival at the town, he was greeted by a peal of bells and presented with a hogshead of claret. At the time Rupert visited the town he was still the darling of the Royalists and the performance of his Cavaliers at Edge Hill was regarded as the finest action of the war. Under its Governor Thomas Littleton, Bewdley was firmly for the Royalist cause and in 1643 Royalist hopes of victory were still high. But when less than a year later, Charles stayed at Tickenhill, the Royalists were already on the defensive. It was from here that the harassed king despatched a troop of horse which was temporarily successful in raising the Parliamentarian siege of Dudley Castle. This was a minor victory. Far more important were to be Charles's orders which now sent Rupert northward to the crushing defeat of Marston Moor.

Although this disaster was a severe blow to the Royalist cause Charles was still capable of fielding an army. But this was at the cost of drawing men from garrison towns such as Bewdley itself and, over the country as a whole, the forces of Parliament were now in the ascendancy. In the autumn of 1644 a force of Roundhead 'shock-troops', based on Edgbaston Hall near Birmingham and led by Colonel 'Tinker' Fox, surprised the weakened Bewdley garrison in a night attack. They were unable to hold the town, but carried off Thomas Littleton from his bed at Tickenhill.

When, on 17th June 1645, Charles returned to Bewdley for the last time after his army's decisive defeat at Naseby, he found that the Roundheads had done so much damage to Tickenhill that he was compelled to spend the night at the Angel Inn.

The town's trade suffered badly during the war, commercial traffic on the Severn being severely hit, especially after Bristol fell into Parliamentarian hands. But prosperity was due to return, though it was not until the more settled years of the eighteenth century that Bewdley entered upon its years of greatest activity and began to assume the appearance it has so largely retained.

With the development of the colonies in North America, the Caribbean and later India—and of industry at home—traffic on the Severn flowed at boom proportions. Bristol merchants began to build the first of Bewdley's Georgian warehouses to hold their goods while local merchants and trowe-masters were responsible for the building of many of the Georgian houses that now delight both visitor and townspeople alike. The town was thriving, and, from those who took their pleasure in the rarefied atmosphere of the Angel Assembly Rooms to those who preferred that provided by such quayside inns as the 'Mug House' and 'The Cock and Pie' it was a prosperity in which almost everyone shared.

That Bewdley was now so connected with the sea is borne out by the fact that it became one of the principal Severnside haunts of press-gangs operating from Bristol, and there must have been many an unwilling Bewdley sailor who fought in English naval actions in the French Wars.

Since Tudor times the domestic cap-making industry had declined but still enjoyed a fitful existence while, in addition to its tanneries, the town now possessed a foundry established in 1697. But the bulk of Bewdley's prosperity came, as it had always done, from the river. Although few people in the eighteenth century would have thought it possible, it was not destined to last forever.

One effect of the Industrial Revolution was to create a need for

Rous Lench Court

transportation greater even than the existing navigable rivers could provide. As most commercial traffic was conveyed by river it seemed logical to extend the existing natural river-network by the creation of a supplementary artificial one. Within the space of thirty years—1760–90—'canal fever' produced inland waterways in many parts of England, some successful and some not. But, though Bewdley was not to have a canal, its fortunes were to be decisively influenced by one.

When proposals were made in the mid-1760s to build a canal linking the Severn at Bewdley with the Trent and Mersey Canal at Great Heywood in Staffordshire the town's corporation declined to have anything to do with "the stinking ditch". This was to prove a fatal error for, undeterred by Bewdley's rejection, James Brindley, the engineer in charge of the construction of the Staffordshire and Worcestershire Canal, now decided to construct his canal so that it entered the river at what was then the small Severnside hamlet of Lower Mytton.

When the canal eventually reached Lower Mytton, Brindley built not only those buildings essential for its operation but also warehouses and those houses that were to form the basis of the 'New Town' of Stourport. Goods which had previously been trans-shipped at Bewdley from the trowes to the waggons and packhorse trains serving the West Midland area now went on to Stourport where they were trans-shipped to the canal boats. Although Bewdley still handled a certain amount of traffic, mostly for Wales and the immediate locality, almost all long-distance freight now by-passed the port in favour of its newer rival. Conditions for the town were to become even worse as the canal system was extended and the opening of the Birmingham and Worcester Canal in 1815 dealt Bewdley a further hammer-blow.

Local merchants began to feel the pinch, those who could moving out to re-establish their businesses at the canal centres while their Bewdley warehouses emptied and in time fell into disuse. The port's bow-hauliers were also to be affected. The opening of the new canal actually put more traffic on the river and, for a time, it seemed as if prospects of steady employment were better than ever before. But manual haulage had not found favour with most canal-boat owners who early turned to the use of horses. It was logical that horse-haulage should now spread to

Harvington Hall
5

the river, though not without a battle on the part of the bow-hauliers.

In 1774 work was begun on the construction of a Severnside tow-path, but was brought to an abrupt halt by riots. There were more riots the following year when the work was resumed, but, despite the efforts of the threatened bow-hauliers, the tow-path was finally completed. The bow-hauliers, in fact, remained on the river, though in diminishing numbers, until the early decades of the nineteenth century when they were finally defeated by the introduction of steam-tugs. By then river-traffic had slowed to a trickle, most goods now being carried by the new and faster railways and 'the King's High Road of Severne' had, from a commercial viewpoint, become little more than a watery byway. It was a situation which could scarcely have been foreseen at the close of the eighteenth century when Bewdley's citizens had commissioned Thomas Telford to construct the graceful three-arched bridge that now spans the river. The earlier five-arched bridge, which it replaced, had been severely damaged by floodwater in 1795.

The bridge, apart from the Town Hall built in 1808, was the last major building work to be undertaken in the old port until relatively recent times. Bewdley was now in decline and, after 1815, also in the grips of depression.

Cap-making, which, in the words of local poet John Tibbett "once was called the staple trade" had now virtually ceased to exist, the local tanneries had shrunk from twelve to three, boat-building was in decline and was soon to almost cease while even Bewdley Foundry was going through hard times. Many of the townsfolk were unemployed and trekked to neighbouring Kidderminster where work in the carpet manufactories was already scarce and, if found, involved long hours, unhealthy conditions and a meagre wage.

Conditions were to improve, but the town was never again to know such prosperity as it had experienced in the eighteenth century. In 1769 it had been, for its size, one of the most prosperous and important towns in Worcestershire. Within a hundred years it had assumed the character of a small market-town, with only its Georgian houses, deserted quays and empty warehouses to tell anyone that it had ever been anything more.

It was in this garb that Bewdley entered the present century and, with the development of the motor-car and, more importantly, the motor-bus, soon found itself linked firmly to Kidderminster. This is a position which has been maintained and which now seems unlikely to change. With an industrialized town almost literally on its doorstep there has been very little incentive for Bewdley to encourage new industry of its own. Indeed, the impact of anything large-scale on the intricate structure of the present town could scarcely be anything less than disastrous. This is borne out by the existence of the present Kidderminster–Leominster road which, even today, still crosses Telford's bridge to climb out of the town by a roadway originally designed for packhorse teams. If any town could be said to cry out for a by-pass it is Bewdley, but just where it would be sited must remain a planner's headache and fortunately not mine.

The shortsightedness of the town's eighteenth-century civic leaders has left Bewdley with an architectural inheritance which it would be equally shortsighted for its present leaders to ignore. This is not to say that the town's future lies in it being 'prettied up' as part of a scenic showcase, but then neither is it to say that it should be thoughtlessly despoiled. New building there has to be, such as the secondary school which, in its position on the willow-edged east bank, can offend no-one. But it is almost certain that the majority of its pupils are destined to earn their livelihoods in the offices and factories of Kidderminster and not in Bewdley itself. It seems a small price to pay for allowing their town to remain as the least tarnished of all the ancient Severn ports.

In the realm of personalities Bewdley, like all other towns, has produced its crop of native worthies. It is more than probable that the future Royalist commander, Sir Charles Compton was born at Tickenhill in 1624. In the Civil War Compton was to distinguish himself as a man of almost foolhardy courage, his most famous exploit being the 'commando' raid on Cheshire's Beeston Castle where he surprised the sleeping garrison and took the fortress for Charles with only six men who were disguised as butchers and bakers. Just why he neglected to include candlestick makers I am at a loss to say.

The town was the birthplace of an impressive list of eminent churchmen among whom was John Inett whose *History of the English Church* was published at the beginning of the eighteenth century. Richard Willis, son of a local tanner, gained a reputation as an off-the-cuff preacher at St Clement Danes and, on the strength of this, was appointed Chaplain-General to the army of William III.

In the world of literature Bewdley has produced two minor poets in George Griffith and John Tibbett, the latter having his rather unoriginally titled volume *Poems* published in 1811.

In the present century Bewdley was the early home of Stanley Baldwin, Prime Minister from 1924 to 1929 and again from 1931 to 1938. In some circles Baldwin's career is still a matter of controversy and, as the years spanned by his political life were ones of great conflict and bitterness in British politics, it would be fatuous to say that all the people of Bewdley held him in the same regard. Suffice it to say that he had a great affection for the town which, no doubt, was something he shared with many others, supporters and opponents alike.

Lord Baldwin's birthplace still stands at the corner of High Street and Lax Lane—the name of the latter being of Viking origin and meaning 'salmon'. The lane leads to the site of the old ford which was used before the river was bridged. Salmon are not so plentiful as once they were and the Severn cannot pretend to match the Wye as a salmon-river. But the river still attracts its anglers who on a good day, or a bad one for that matter, will patiently line the banks hopefully waiting for something to take their bait. It is not so long ago that local fishermen used coracles on this section of the river and fished, not by line, but by net. Netting is now illegal and coracle-making a dead craft, revived only by those societies who exist to preserve rural industries but who have only succeeded in fossilizing them. But, while the coracles are no longer with us, it is certainly possible to hire a canoe or motor-boat to explore the river.

Downstream and lying beyond the west bank of the river stands Ribbesford surrounded by its cherry orchards and with a history quite as long as that of its larger neighbour. In Saxon times the manor was in the ownership of the Cathedral-monastery of Worcester but, after the Conquest, passed through the hands of various Norman lords finally coming into the possession of the Mortimers. In the seventeenth century it was purchased by Sir Henry Herbert and became something of a cultural hot-spot, a local story asserting that at one service in the parish church George Herbert preached the sermon, Henry Vaughan read the lesson while Milton played the organ. In more recent years Ribbesford House became, for a brief time during the Second World War, the headquarters of General Charles de Gaulle and the Free French Army.

Above Ribbesford, as above Bewdley also, hangs what is left of the once great Forest of Wyre. It is still the largest of Worcestershire woodlands, though much of its area spills over into neighbouring Shropshire. It was timber from Wyre that once supplied one of Bewdley's major trades, that of shipbuilding, which was carried on extensively at the river-port from medieval times until the end of the eighteenth century. In days before the extensive mining of coal and before the process of smelting iron-ore with coal was discovered the Forest was also a centre of the charcoal-burning industry which survived, on a considerable scale, until quite recent years. Today evidence of these former industries has largely disappeared and the woodcutter and charcoal-burner have all but become figures of the past.

Wyre Forest and its scattered villages are now quiet places, though the old cottages are finding new tenants from those who wish to escape the rat-race and clamour of the nearby industrial towns and the new houses for those commuters willing to brave the choked roads are beginning to make an impact on the local scene. So far the forest has been able to absorb these new developments without great loss of character. But the day may not be too far distant when it becomes as embattled a region as the Clent and Lickey Hills and a rigorous policy of conservation will have to be applied if Wyre is to be consciously retained as an amenity. 'Amenity' seems a horrible word to use in this connection yet, if we are realistic, this is what Wyre has become for so many who live in the industrialized areas to the east and who are often no more than a short drive from its wildness. It is something the planners must bear in mind before they allow too many small housing developments to be inserted piecemeal into the woodlands.

As an example of all that should not be done in Wyre I would cite the delightful-sounding, but less delightfully-created, village of Far Forest. This collection of bungalows and small houses straggles the Bewdley–Cleobury Mortimer road for some distance at the approach to the Shropshire border. Far Forest is not so much a village as a latter-day encampment and as an encampment

I am only sorry that it is of bricks and mortar and cannot be moved on.

In this upland region lie a cluster of small villages with a past that belies their very rural situation. Most of the inhabitants of Rock, Bayton, Clows Top and Pensax once drew their livelihood from the small local pits, none of which are now working and whose spoil heaps have been gradually obliterated by spreading vegetation. Yet, as long ago as the reign of Elizabeth I, the Pensax pits were in production and some were apparently in the ownership of Worcester Corporation.

Coal also made the fortune of the Brock family of Pensax Court, a house whose gardens are still famous for their beauty and whose outstanding feature is the Japanese rock-garden. At the end of the eighteenth century the gardens were sufficiently renowned to merit a visit by the Whig leader, Charles James Fox who, apart from being a radical and a thorn in the side of William Pitt, was also something of a botanist.

But the local collieries were to bring sadness to the family on one occasion for, during the eighteenth century, the young heir to Pensax Court lost his way one night and rode unsuspecting into the mouth of an abandoned shaft. Search parties were sent out, but when they finally discovered him at dawn next day he was dead. With his death the estate passed to another branch of the family which, in our own time, has given us the Clutton-Brock whose multi-racial and humanitarian activities at Cold Comfort Farm have recently been discontinued at the insistence of the Rhodesian authorities.

Pensax church was rebuilt in 1832 on the site of an earlier building and, in common with a number of churches in the area, occupies an imposing hilltop position above the Teme Valley. The name of the village is a fusion of Welsh and Anglo-Saxon meaning Hill of the Saxons.

Like Clows Top, Bayton stands on high ground looking north-westward towards the Clee Hills. It once possessed what could have been classed as a 'half-forest church', but much of the old timbering and all of the bell-turret were swept away at the time of its Victorian restoration.

Rock is no exception to the general rule of hilltop churches, though the buildings, parts of which date from Norman times, would be impressive even without its elevated position. Rock was once the home of the Coningsby family and it was Sir Humphrey Coningsby who was responsible for the building of the church's south chapel. Sir Humphrey was England's Lord Chief Justice who, turning aside from legal affairs, also rebuilt the church tower and provided for the parish priest to assume the additional duties of schoolmaster.

At Heightington the church is unusual for the region in that it is set on low ground amid orchards. It is a chapel rather than a church and I feel tempted to describe it as more of a cottage than either. It has a low gallery, which is something of a hazard for anyone above medium height, and an organ illuminated by a skylight. The building dates back to at least the fourteenth century and for those who seek the unusual in the countryside it is well worth a visit.

Areley Kings has been almost entirely engulfed by neighbouring Stourport and no doubt the day is not too far distant when it will have been completely absorbed. Long before Stourport first appeared on Severnside this was the home of Layamon, the twelfth-century poet, who was priest here. It was Layamon who led the vanguard of the revival of English letters with his poem 'Brut', which was an attempt to provide a narrative verse history of Britain, though, historically, it is almost completely a work of fiction. Yet the importance of his poem does not lie in its accuracy, for Layamon was helping to keep alive many legends which had their origins in the dim depths of Celtic antiquity and which were to provide the inspiration for the work of many later writers. Unlike most medieval authors Layamon was not content to shroud his work under the conventional cloak of anonymity, boldly declaring his name and where he lives in the first lines of the poem. In all he seems to have been something of an egocentric and, although he was not canonized, the inscription on the base of the font in Areley church declares that he was a saint. Layamon probably thought he ought to have been and may have put it there himself. All of which rather bears out the theory that he was originally banished from the monastery at Worcester so that, in seclusion, he should learn self-discipline and abandon his vainglorious ways. For once the old remedy obviously failed to work.

Some two miles downstream from Areley is Redstone Rock where it was once believed Layamon had lived as a hermit. This theory is now generally discounted but the rock-chambers probably began life as some form of hermit's cell later being enlarged to form a retreat for monks from Worcester. Nashe records that, in the late eighteenth century, the chambers had recently been used for the manufacture of cider.

Within Areley church is an inscription to one Walter Walsh declaring that he was "ruinated by three Quakers, two lawyers and a fanatick to help them". Just what fate overtook poor Walter at the hands of this strange alliance is now a matter of mystery. The church is also the burial place of Sir Harry Coningsby of Rock who, as a young man living at Hampton Court, had the tragic misfortune to drop his infant son into the palace moat where he was drowned. The incident so affected him that he retired to Areley where he lived the life of a recluse until his death in 1701. But Sir Harry was not soured completely for he planted walnut trees in the churchyard and in his will directed that local schoolboys should be allowed to crack the nuts on his tomb on a particular day in the year.

Bewdley's successful eighteenth-century challenger Stourport owes its existence almost solely to the building of James Brindley's Staffordshire and Worcestershire Canal. Before the advent of the canal the hamlet of Lower Mytton was no more than a scattering of cottages with a riverside inn. Brindley transformed this into a throughgoing eighteenth-century inland port and in so doing quite literally 'sold Bewdley's fortunes down the river'. Of course Bewdley's fortunes did not exactly wane overnight, yet the transformation was almost as dramatic. No sooner had the canal been cut than Brindley set about the creation of a new town complete with streets, wharves, warehouses and loading basins. In fact Brindley's Stourport was something of a commercial counterpart to the planned spa centres of the same period.

Stourport was destined to become a major inland port, served not only by its canal but by the river as well. It replaced Bewdley as the main centre of distribution for goods from Bristol and seemed set to enjoy many decades of increasing prosperity, its commerce augmented by those industries attracted to the town where they were assured of rapid transportation for their products.

But Stourport's prosperity was shortlived and the town was certainly not to experience anything like the century-long 'golden age' of rival Bewdley. Its rapid growth as a river and canal port was largely brought to an end by the development of the railways, but even before this it suffered by the opening of the Birmingham and Worcester Canal in 1815. This was to syphon off a considerable volume of Birmingham and Black Country traffic which, up till then, had passed through the Severnside port. This was bad enough but, when the railways began to spread their iron tentacles across the countryside, Stourport as an inland port was doomed. Over the years its wharves and warehouses fell derelict and its boat-yards became disused. A purely local trade did linger on, but only tenuously and, if it had not been for the creation of the new leisure traffic of present times there is little doubt that the waterways of what was once almost solely a 'canal town' would have ceased to exist. Today it is leisure traffic which keeps Brindley's inland port alive and puts this most westerly of the county's industrialized towns in touch with memories of river-borne commerce and the open sea.

The presence of the canal was a major factor in bringing to Stourport its first iron-foundries which were later to become centralized in the Baldwin ironworks at Wilden on the outskirts of the town. The works were founded by Stanley Baldwin's father, Alfred Baldwin who, unlike his son, preferred to live almost on the doorstep of his company so that he could be in daily touch with the running of its affairs. Stanley Baldwin, sprung from a man of iron as he was, was also something of an aesthete being, on his mother's side, the nephew of Burne-Jones, the pre-Raphaelite artist and cousin to Rudyard Kipling. As soon as he was able he seems to have forsaken Wilden House and the blighted land of smelters for the more pastoral surroundings of Astley House.

To the south-east of industrial Stourport, Hartlebury lies in a landscape as different from that of Wilden as it could be possible to imagine. The castle, standing on high ground above Hartlebury Common and surrounded by a reed-tinged moat, has been the episcopal palace of the Bishops of Worcester for close on four centuries and has been in their possession since the thirteenth century. At the time of the Reformation Hugh Latimer lived here in grinding poverty. Henry VIII at one time decided to have him executed but Latimer was saved by the unexpected intervention of Thomas Cromwell, who had scarcely carved out a reputation for himself by defending the clergy. Unnerved by this unusual behaviour Henry relented and the poor bishop was saved only to be burnt by Henry's daughter a few years later.

The manor-house suffered in the time of Elizabeth I when Bishop Sandys was in occupation. It has been alleged that the Cumbrian bishop sold many of the manor's furnishings, even down to tables and benches, in the process of building up a personal fortune from church lands and property. Sandys was an unpopular bishop at Worcester and was later to become first Bishop of London and later Archbishop of York. But when he arrived at York the Dean refused to let him enter the cathedral on the grounds that he was tainted with the sin of simony—the selling of church offices to the highest bidder. Sandys ultimately gained access to his cathedral, but was soon behaving in such a high-handed manner that the clergy determined to be rid of him. A plot was hatched which resulted in the bribing of an innkeeper to introduce his wife into Sandys' room while the archbishop was asleep. This was duly done and Sandys was 'caught out' by the innkeeper and a number of his clerical opponents. The clergy at Worcester, who had suffered greatly at his hands, must have been well pleased when they heard that their former bishop had laid down his high office and had retired in disgrace.

Leland described the manor-house which Latimer and Sandys knew as "well-builded" and with "fair ponds, a park for deer, and a warren for conies". During the Civil War it, at one time, functioned as a prison for captured Royalists, but it was later gutted and much of the present building is a mixture of Stuart and Georgian styles, although part of the original thirteenth-century structure is incorporated in the building. The north wing of the castle is now a County Museum, much of it built up from the collection of the late Mr J. F. Parker and which was formerly housed at Bewdley's Tickenhill House.

One good thing that Bishop Sandys did while he was here was to persuade Queen Elizabeth to refound Hartlebury Grammar School. Under Elizabeth's Statutes the schoolmaster and usher were given the right to "the profits of all such cock-fights and potations as may be commonly used in the schooles". The school is now housed in new buildings on the hillside and, to my knowledge, produces no more gamblers or drunkards than any other in Worcestershire.

A little to the south, at Crossways Green, is the site of the oak, so it is claimed, under which St Augustine sat when trying to reach agreement with the dignitaries of the Celtic Church. Rock, amongst the Abberley Hills, is only one of the other places in Worcestershire which also claims to have been the site of this meeting place. Indeed, there are so many places in the West Midlands and Border Counties claiming Gospel Oaks and Mitre Oaks that, if St Augustine sat under all of them, he must have had little time for anything else. No-one can now say with any certainty just where this far-off meeting place was but, not meaning to be disloyal to Worcestershire, I plump for Shropshire's Cressage, where the village name is a corruption of Christ's Ac—or Christ's Oak—as the most probable spot. Not that the meeting did any good, for it was not until almost four hundred years later, at the Synod of Whitby, that the native British Church finally agreed to follow the doctrinal practice of Rome. By some logic all of their own some of the zealots of the sixteenth-century Reformation managed to claim that, in England, the Reformation was in fact re-establishing the native church which had surrendered its independence at Whitby. It was a somewhat dubious claim and no-one went around sitting under Worcestershire oak trees to prove it.

From Crossways Green it is only a short distance to the group of villages which border the Severn immediately above the county town. Shrawley does not actually lie upon the river but Shrawley Woods spill to its edge from a hillside crowned by a Norman church. The Normans also built a castle here which ultimately came into the hands of Richard Neville, 'Warwick the Kingmaker'. Since then it has crumbled to become yet one more of the county's vanished medieval fortresses.

Within the church are commemorated members of the local Severne family, though local tradition once asserted that they were not the members of one family at all. According to this, in medieval times, a group of hermits living in caves in the sandstone rocks near Astley discovered a new vocation in the rescuing of infants who, Moses style, had been launched upon the river in sealed coracles. A large number of the water-born children so collected are said to have been taken to Shrawley for baptism, something which, in view of their recent experiences, they could hardly be expected to appreciate. Locally it was alleged that most of the children came from Bewdley, which was a nice piece of calculated malice directed at a town which, at the time, was attempting to dominate the Severn river-trade. Bewdley probably regarded the allegations as no more than typical of the bad press it would get on other parts of the river, but local members of the Severne family must have had their work cut out trying to combat the belief.

Like Shrawley, Holt has its church positioned on a hilltop overlooking the river. It is also more fortunate than its sister village in that it has retained its castle and, though much of the structure has been rebuilt and extended over the centuries, the fourteenth-century tower still remains as Sir John Beauchamp, the last of the Beauchamps of Holt, would have known it. The castle later came into the hands of the Bromleys and within the church is a tablet to Sir Henry Bromley who tracked down four of the Gunpowder Plotters at Hindlip Hall.

Holt is really three villages, the old village centred around the church and castle, most of the modern village grouped at the junction of the Stourport–Worcester road and the Tenbury–Droitwich road, while on the riverside Holt Fleet has an existence all of its own. It used to be said that this was one of the most beautiful stretches of the river, and, in many ways, it still is. But its very attractiveness has been Holt Fleet's downfall—caravans and ramshackle huts catering for the weekend trade have sprung up and have completely altered the character of the area. Caravan sites must present the county's planners with an awesome head-ache for they must be well aware that no-one wants them apart from those who actually use them, those who own them and those local traders who profit by their presence. In their efforts to become places where people can momentarily get away from it all caravan sites almost invariably create places which everyone seeks to get away from too. There seems to be no solution to the problem, other than that of banning caravans altogether, which would seem rather a harsh measure. Perhaps, however, some attention should be directed to the scale of places where caravans are allowed to be sited. Bewdley and Bridgnorth, for instance, seem examples of other Severnside resorts which are able to cope with the caravan's existence, but places as small as Holt Fleet find it impossible to absorb such sites without being drastically affected.

Just above the northern outskirts of Worcester lies Grimley

with a Norman church which was much rebuilt in the last century. The village was once famous as the rather unlikely home of Napoleon's brother, Prince Lucien Bonaparte. Lucien had married the widow of a stock-broker and refused to give her up even though his brother offered him the crowns of Naples and Spain if he would. Napoleon was quite put out about this and Lucien took ship for France to avoid the imperial wrath. But the ship was intercepted by a British frigate employed in the blockade of the French ports and Britain now found itself with an anti-Napoleon Bonaparte.

Lucien requested that he and his wife be allowed to stay in England and, after the authorities had convinced themselves that it was not all part of a fiendish Bonaparte plot, he was allowed to do so. He purchased Thorngrove House where his son, Prince Louis Lucien was born in 1813. Prince Louis was later to go to France when his cousin ruled the country first as President and later as the Emperor Napoleon III. But when the Second Empire fell in defeat in the Franco-Prussian War of 1870 he again returned to England, though not to Thorngrove, and lived here until his death.

On the eastern bank of the river is the parish of Ombersley, one of the largest in the county and including, besides Ombersley itself, the hamlets of Hadley, Northampton, Dunhampton and Uphampton. Apart from being one of the county's largest parishes Ombersley is also one of its largest villages. In medieval times the manor belonged to Evesham Abbey, being often used by the abbots as a retreat. With the Tudors it came into the possession of the Sandys family who were later to take up residence at Ombersley Court. After the Battle of Worcester Charles II is said to have made a stop at the 'Kings' Arms' undeterred by the fact that two of the local Sandys family had been fighting against him in the Parliamentarian ranks. But, judging from the famous Bromsgrove incident, this type of situation held few fears for Charles and the visit seems perfectly in character.

Ombersley's long main street contains many black-and-white cottages whose grime may be a little lessened when the new by-pass is constructed. The church, the interior of which is dominated by memorials to the Sandys family, dates from the thirteenth century, though much of it was rebuilt by restoring Victorians.

To the north-east lies Westwood Park, the Elizabethan home of the Pakingtons, though the house was much extended in the late seventeenth century by work modelled upon that of a French *château*. The house occupies the site of a Benedictine nunnery founded by Eustacia de Say in the thirteenth century which survived until the Dissolution when Henry VIII granted it to Sir John Pakington, whose legal skills had come in rather useful to the king in those rather tangled times.

At the time of the Commonwealth Westwood was to become a refuge for members of the Old High Church party, who had supported the policies of Archbishop Laud and was later to be associated with Worcestershire clerics who were opposed to the religious policies of William of Orange.

In what may have been an attempt to frustrate the efforts of historians all the heads of the Pakington family were named Sir John. But historians had little to fear as few of the Pakingtons were to leave noticeable marks on the pages of English history, being content with the rural rather than the political life. Probably the best known of this long line of Sir Johns was an eighteenth-century version who is often alleged to have been the original of Addison's 'Sir Roger de Coverley'. This Sir John sat as a member of Parliament for Worcester from the age of 19, but unfortunately his life was not one that exactly paralleled that of Sir Roger.

One might, perhaps, expect to find the Pakingtons commemorated in Doverdale's restored Norman church, but this is not the case for most of them rest at Hampton Lovett. About them lies the countryside which they husbanded so carefully through the centuries and which, like that of so many of the county's great landowning families, is their most enduring legacy to Worcestershire.

IV

THE STOUR VALLEY

KIDDERMINSTER and Stourbridge, the two major towns of the Stour Valley, could in many ways be considered a natural part of that area of the county which I have termed the Industrial North-west. That they have not been so included is partly because the Stour Valley has an industrial history which considerably pre-dates that of the towns to the north and partly because their inclusion would leave this book with eight fingers and one very over-sized thumb.

The Severn and its tributary the Stour have been decisive factors in the development of the region and for this reason I have included Bewdley's twin-town of Wribbenhall in this chapter. The quays of Wribbenhall and Bewdley once functioned as the major trans-shipment point for products of the Stour Valley destined for the sea-port of Bristol. When the Stour was first made navigable in the latter part of the seventeenth century some of this traffic by-passed Wribbenhall, but much of it continued to use the port until Wribbenhall's fortunes, together with those of Bewdley, declined upon the completion of the Worcestershire and Staffordshire Canal and the creation of the canal-port of Stourport.

Wribbenhall was once the name given not only to the river-port on the east bank of the Severn but also to Bewdley and the surrounding area. Originally Crown property, the manor was granted to Manser de Biset by Henry II. Later it passed into the hands of the Burnells and in the nineteenth century was purchased by the Earl of Dudley.

Wribbenhall's main period of prosperity was in the late seventeenth and eighteenth centuries when its quays handled a large proportion of the traffic using the river. But like Bewdley it was also engaged in industry itself, producing caps, sail-cloth and the famous Bewdley hornware, which despite the name was produced in more or less equal proportions at Wribbenhall as well.

Wribbenhall was once the home of the man who was to become Bewdley's leading eighteenth-century industrialist. This was Samuel Skey, a Bewdley grocer's apprentice, who prospered so well that he was able to fulfil his youthful ambition to erect a large house on Jackystone Hill, the sandy common lying behind Wribbenhall. It is the sort of dream that still has its attractions for poor boys, though nowadays they are likely only to inhabit a jerrybuilt structure of brick-faced breeze-blocks and to find themselves saddled with a mortgage whose interest rates will serve to make them poorer still.

But Samuel Skey, like the fabled Dick Whittington, was poor in only a relative way, for on the completion of his apprenticeship he was lucky enough to be left £1,000—no chicken-feed in the eighteenth century—and promptly set up as a drysalter and dye manufacturer on his own account. His industrial speciality was later to become the manufacture of sulphuric acid, which he was to do on such a scale as to rank as its second largest producer in England. He had wide interests beyond his business concerns and was a member of the philosophical and scientific body known as the Lunar Society which, meeting in Birmingham, numbered amongst its members Joseph Priestly, Matthew Boulton and James Watt.

As already mentioned, along with Bewdley, Wribbenhall was to suffer a reversal of its fortunes with the opening of the Worcestershire and Staffordshire Canal. The appearance of the railways was to even further depress the town, though Bewdley's own station, on the GWR Severn Valley line was to be located here. This line was one that, not so long ago, was lopped by a particularly shortsighted swing of the Beeching axe. It is, however, now enjoying a fitful existence as a privately operated passenger-carrying railway running between Bridgnorth and Hampton Lode and there are plans to eventually reopen the track to carry steam-hauled trains to Upper Arley and Bewdley Station. I am given to understand that, having overcome some administrative difficulties, work is now progressing well on the undertaking although, as it depends on voluntary labour, no firm date can be given for the reopening of the whole Bewdley–Bridgnorth line.

Not far upstream from Wribbenhall and also on the east bank

Bredon Tythe Barn, showing the Bailiff's room

of the river is Upper Arley, lying close to the South Staffordshire border. The village remains essentially rural though the new reservoir below it has not been without its effect. Within the ancient church is the figure of a cross-legged knight of the fourteenth century which is believed to represent Sir Walter de Bohun. While waiting at Southampton to embark on a crusade for the Holy Land, Sir Walter, as so many soldiers on embarkation before and since, decided to be married. To celebrate the wedding-day a tournament was arranged in which the newly-wed Sir Walter was a leading participant. Perhaps, in trying to impress his bride, he was less than cautious in the lists. But, at all events, Walter rode his last that day, for he was accidentally killed and the sorrowing bride accompanied his body here to find its resting place on the bank of the Severn.

A century before Sir Walter, Arley was the home of Hubert de Burgh who in the reign of King John unsuccessfully defended the castle of Chinon for this maligned king and later successfully defended Dover against the army of the French dauphin.

Arley's manor-house was demolished in the last century to make way for the battlemented Arley Court. More recently the Court was used as a college but it, too, has since been demolished. The village remains one of the most peaceful on the river with its flower-decked gardens terracing the steeply rising bank.

On high ground above the eastern slopes of the wooded Habberley Valley is Trimperley, a scattered hamlet lying on a lane off the Kidderminster–Bridgnorth road which has become well-used as a short route to Bewdley. It is an unremarkable place but the ridge road upon which it stands offers some of the most superb views in the county. From here it is possible to look across the Habberley Valley to the tangled Forest of Wyre, with Cleobury Mortimer in the middle distance and the hills of Clee and Wales beyond. It is this north-western edge of the county that has influenced so many Midland writers, Housman, Brett Young and Mary Webb amongst them. It is a mysterious, romantic landscape which must stir the imagination of all but the most phlegmatic.

Wolverley is a large village a mile or so to the north of Kidderminster which has so far managed to avoid total absorption by its large neighbour. But there has been very considerable development here of recent years and it cannot be all that long

Worcestershire's Cotswold vernacular: Broadway
Stourport Canal Basin, Stourport on Severn

before it completely surrenders its separate identity. The village lies in the Stour Valley and its old centre of church, school and a number of aged red-brick houses is situated on a red sandstone escarpment high above the valley. A steep road cut through the rock leads from the main village to the church and within the cliffs are caves and one of the most unusual cattle pounds in the country. The village still possesses the school founded by William Sebright in the seventeenth century, though the present school is housed in buildings to the north of the village.

Wolverley is famous as the birthplace of John Baskerville, one of the greatest innovators in the art of printing. Baskerville was born at Sion Hill, Wolverley in 1706, later moving to Birmingham where he tried his hand at a number of trades before turning to printing. It is often said that at the time he took up the occupation which was to make his name and fortune he was employed as a footman. There seems little evidence for this, but it is a nice story and perhaps not all that improbable.

Baskerville was little short of a graphical genius and had earlier practised as a teacher of handwriting, the fine, flowing copperplate and secretary hands, mastery of which was then sought by those who wished to be considered intelligent and cultivated. Later he had moved to engraving and from here it was but a short step to the making of types for mechanical printing.

Baskerville entered the printing field with a bang, for his first effort was a magnificent edition of Virgil. As Macaulay was later to write, this edition was "to astonish all the librarians of Europe". Later he printed Milton's poems and was appointed printer to the University of Cambridge. He printed many editions of the Bible and the Book of Common Prayer and his Bible of 1763 was hailed as "one of the most beautifully printed books in the world". Baskerville's volumes are amongst those books most highly prized by bibliophiles.

Despite the fact that he printed so many Bibles and prayer books John Baskerville was a confirmed atheist. In accordance with his wishes he was buried in a tomb in his own garden with the inscription:

> Stranger
> beneath this cone, in UNCONSECRATED ground
> a friend to the liberties of mankind directed his body
> to be inurr'd.

May the example contribute to emancipate thy mind
from the idle fears of Superstition
and the wicked arts of the Priesthood.

But the tomb was not to remain undisturbed for long. The
house was gutted by fire in 1791 and later the Birmingham
Canal was cut through its grounds. The coffin was recovered
some years later and finally, in 1827, it found its ultimate resting
place in the churchyard of Cradley chapel. Today the great
printer is remembered in the name of Baskerville House, formerly
known as Birmingham Civic Centre, and of Baskerville Place
which runs through ground which once formed part of his home.
In the 1890s Sir Arthur Conan Doyle lived near here when
practising as a doctor and was so drawn by the name of the street
that he incorporated it into one of the most famous of his Sherlock
Holmes stories, *The Hound of the Baskervilles*.

Another Wolverley family was to have associations with
Birmingham, though of a more tenuous nature. Within Wolverley
church is the broken effigy of Sir John Attwood who was born
at the long-demolished manor-house and who fought under the
Black Prince in the Holy Land. It is probable that Thomas
Attwood, who was born at Hawn House, Halesowen and who
was Birmingham's first MP was a descendant of the fourteenth-
century Sir John.

A strange story attaches to this knight for it is said that he was
so long upon the Crusades that his wife, receiving no word from
him, gave her husband up for dead. After a time she agreed to
marry another, but near to the wedding day, her husband was
discovered lying fettered in a nearby field. Sir John had been
absent so long that his wife was unable to recognize him but he
proved his identity by showing her his part of their wedding ring
which they had cut in two before he had joined the Crusade.
Sir John was to tell how he had been taken prisoner by the
Saracens and how he had prayed that he might be released to
return to his wife. One night a light had appeared in his dungeon
and an angel stood before him to announce that his prayers were
to be answered and that he was to be restored to his family. Sir
John said that he knew nothing more until he found himself in
his own meadows. The fetters in which he was found used to
hang above his tomb but they have long since disappeared.
This is a good story but it seems far too good to be true and I

suspect that some chicanery was going on here. Perhaps a rather unchivalric knight had somehow got hold of the real Sir John's half of the wedding ring and knowing that he was dead or captive of the Turks had decided to pass himself off as its owner. Or, on a more chivalric note, perhaps a dying Sir John had given the ring to a close companion who had agreed to impersonate him for the sake of the lady he had left behind. The truth will never be known and maybe it is better to accept the story of Sir John mysteriously turning up in his meadow.

Wolverley church is an eighteenth-century building in the Italian style, rather an unusual possession for the county and rendered even more imposing by its cliff-top position. From the former church on the same site survive a six-sided font, an old carved pulpit canopy and Sir John's effigy. There is also an unusual relic in a chained copy of Bishop Jewell's *Apology* recalling the days when books were rare treasures and even the Bible was chained to the pulpit in most churches. Nearby, via a road cut through the sandstone rock, is Blakeshall, its hilltop church almost twinning that of Wolverley.

These villages are now firmly in the orbit of Kidderminster with most of their population working there and local life truly dominated by the nearby town. If Worcestershire can boast of a one-trade town then Kidderminster is it, for if the streets of London are paved with mythical gold then those of Kidderminster are, or should be, fitted with rather less mythical carpets. If Worcestershire were some brash American state and not an English county I am sure that some sales promotion stunt would long ago have brought this to pass. Kidderminster does, even in the county, have its one-trade challenger in the form of Redditch which still declares itself to be "the expanding needle centre of the Midlands". But, although the needle industry still occupies an important place there, other industries have appeared which have attacked its former dominance in the town's economy. Other industries also exist at Kidderminster, but none has so far made a bid to eclipse the town's traditional carpet manufacture and it seems rather unlikely that any such bid will ever be made.

Although I have said that carpet manufacture is traditional to Kidderminster it has not been associated with the town for all that long and is first recorded as being carried out here in 1736. What were then called Kidderminster or Scotch carpets were then woven on hand-looms, their weaving being primarily a small-scale domestic industry carried out in the weavers' own homes. But, before the coming of the carpet industry, the town had been a weaving centre for many centuries, cloth weaving beginning here at least as early as the thirteenth century. As such it prospered by the expansion of England's wool and cloth trade in the fifteenth and sixteenth centuries when it became one of the major 'cloth' towns of the Midlands. This prosperity continued into the seventeenth century but, a hundred years later, the Midlands and West Country textile manufacture was to find itself being eclipsed by the growing factory industry in the North.

As Kidderminster's cloth industry waned the carpet manufacture sprang up first to supplement it and finally to supplant it completely. This process was greatly accelerated when, in 1745, carpet-weavers from Tournai settled in Kidderminster and began the manufacture of Brussels and Wilton carpets. For the next two or three decades cloth and carpet weaving were carried on in roughly equal proportions. After the close of the Napoleonic Wars a post-war trade depression hit the whole country and the ancient cloth industry virtually ceased to exist. When economic conditions improved the carpet manufacture re-established itself and began to expand—but the manufacture of Kidderminster cloth was at an end.

The reason for the demise of Kidderminster's cloth industry was, strangely enough, largely because it had been so long established. When textile manufacture in the North changed from domestic production on the hand-loom to factory production on the power-loom Kidderminster had been slow in responding to the new challenge. Power production in the North turned out vast quantities of textiles at rates so cheap that the Kidderminster hand-loom weavers could not hope to compete and make a living from their ancient craft. A possible answer may have been found in the creation of textile mills in the town itself; but there was fierce opposition from the local weavers to the creation of factories and the consequent introduction of machines which, they considered, would throw many of them out of what little work they had. Kidderminster was spared the terrible working conditions of the North's 'Satanic mills', but ultimately only at the complete loss of her centuries-old industry.

On the other hand, the new carpet industry was not fettered

by centuries of traditional working and organization and even though it was a related weaving trade it was possible for it to start with a clean slate. Its creation as a factory-based industry offered no threat to the hand-loom cloth-weavers and, in fact, was later to prove their salvation for, as the cloth industry declined in the face of mass-produced competition, many of them were to find employment at the looms of the carpet factories.

Yet, even though the carpet factories were to enable Kidderminster's weavers to make a livelihood in their native town rather than joining in the general county migration to the Black Country, this is not to say that they were entirely unaccompanied by the evils of the Industrial Revolution. The conditions in the Kidderminster factories do seem to have been better than those existing in the northern mills—but only marginally. Up until the 1830s there existed virtually no enforceable regulations on factory conditions and matters of hours, pay and the use of children were entirely at the often dubious judgement of the employers. As an industrial town Kidderminster probably had, on average, employment conditions that were slightly better than those found in most other places at the time. But this is not to say that, judged by modern standards, they were not brutal and callous in the extreme.

A report prepared for a Parliamentary enquiry in the 1840s, gives some impression of life in the carpet factories at this period—and earlier conditions had probably been even worse:

In Kidderminster, the workshops are generally well-built, and, if kept clean, may be considered not unhealthy: but, owing to the dirt, the size used in the carpets, and above all, the want of common care in sweeping on the part of the workmen, and lime washing on the part of the masters, they are noisesome holes . . .

The weaver, in most instances, employs a drawer, which is usually either a young boy or girl. This drawer has to perform the most laborious part of the work, and not only is he obliged regularly to work, but when either idleness, dissipation, or any other cause, prevents the weaver attending to his work at the beginning of the week, the drawer, whether boy or girl, is obliged to wait his time, and frequently to work fifteen or eighteen hours incessantly, to get the piece finished . . .

Nor is this all; for, from the constant opportunity in the workshops, great immorality takes place, even at a very early age, between the drawers, and frequent instances of seduction on the part of married men and fathers of families takes place, from the facilities offered by the solitary night-working, with their drawer girls.

This early slavery . . . must have and does have a baneful effect upon them in after-life. Consumption, diseases of the joints, and ruptures, are of frequent occurrence; and . . . the mortality among children at an early age is alarmingly great.

Not until the latter decades of the last century were safety regulations properly enforced, hours regulated and young children finally removed from those factories which had not already effected more enlightened working conditions for themselves.

Carpet manufacture in present-day Kidderminster is a booming business and one of the most striking things here is the number of new glass and concrete office blocks of the various companies that have sprung up over the past two decades. The tendency since the Second World War—and for some years before—has been for the old family-owned businesses to coalesce into larger groupings and now most of the carpet manufacture here is carried on by less than half a dozen major concerns. Yet the old manufacturers are still well represented and Kidderminster's present MP, Sir Tatton Brinton, is himself a member of one of the best known carpet-manufacturing families in the town.

It is rather strange to realize that Kidderminster produces no carpet which it can truly call its own for even the traditional Kidderminster carpet is more usually known as the Scotch, whilst it also produces the Wilton, the Brussels which in origin dates back to those eighteenth-century Flemish weavers, the Axminster, which it has produced since the Devonshire town discontinued its own manufacture, and the Venetian. Kidderminster College of Further Education greatly assists the local industry with courses in carpet design and the local museum houses a display of the many different types of carpet made in the town.

Kidderminster's parish church is that of St Mary's standing on a hilltop site above the Stour. Much of the fourteenth-century building was restored during the last century but a church must have stood on this site long before for in the twelfth century the lord of the manor, Manser de Biset, founded a convent upon his marriage and gave it the rectory of Kidderminster as an endowment.

Until recent years St Mary's was rather removed from the bustle of this busy town, but road development has now brought the town-centre by-pass almost to its main entrance, something which gives more people an opportunity to glimpse its beauty and which seems to link it more strongly with the vigorous life of the town. Its nave and arcade date from the fifteenth century and the fourteenth-century chancel has a roof copied in this century from the medieval roof that once adorned the Guesten Hall at Worcester Cathedral.

The chantry chapel was built at the direction of a London merchant only a few years before Henry VIII ordered the suppression of chantries. The local authorities, however, decided that the building was far too good to be pulled down and for more than three hundred years it served as the town grammar school. The present King Charles I Grammar School (boys only) is housed in buildings on the Bewdley Road while the girls' equivalent, Kidderminster High School, stands on the Chester Road.

The Whittal Chapel was built in 1922 to the design of Sir Giles Scott and was given by a native of the town who established a prosperous carpet business at Worcester, Massachusetts. Its panelled roof is spanned by three arches and the oak reredos has finely carved borders with figures of Christ and the Disciples. The glass in the window depicts the Virgin Mary, Joan d'Arc and Florence Nightingale and was presented by his widow in her husband's memory.

Within the church is the chair often used by Richard Baxter, the Puritan divine whose statue stands in the Bull Ring near the town centre. A pillar in the church is known as Baxter's Pillar, for it was here that the pulpit from which he preached was once fixed. Baxter is not only remembered at St Mary's for in the Baxter Congregational Chapel is his communion table, in the Unitarian Chapel is a canopied and lavishly carved pulpit from which he also preached and his house still stands in the town bearing the date 1641. Kidderminster's Reference Library houses a large collection of his published work, the most famous of which is *Saints' Everlasting Rest* which was to prove the forerunner of a spate of popular Christian literature.

Baxter suffered much for his religious beliefs and once fell foul of the 'Bloody' Judge Jeffreys, who wished to have him whipped through London "at the cart's tail". Baxter was appointed curate of St Mary's in 1641 and later became its vicar retaining the living until 1660. In that year the newly-restored Charles II offered him the bishopric of Hereford, for although Baxter had been sympathetic to some of the aims of the Parliamentarians he had never abused the Royalists and had always remained true to the monarchy. Matters of conscience, however, prevented him from accepting the bishopric and soon afterwards he felt compelled to leave St Mary's and establish his own chapel.

Preserved in the church is a fifteenth-century triple brass to Sir John Phillip, his wife Matilda and her first husband Sir Walter Cokesey. Sir Walter was a friend of Henry V and accompanied the king to the Siege of Harfleur where he died in October 1415. The English army suffered few casualties in the campaign, most deaths being from dysentery, from which Henry V himself was to die on a second expedition a few years later. Walter's October death robbed him by only a few days of a place in the battleline of that most famous of all English victories—Agincourt.

Besides its monuments the church also possesses an Elizabethan cup, almost two feet high, which once saw service at mayoral banquets, and a sixteenth-century Processional Cross of copper, silver and enamel brought from Florence.

Kidderminster is a town which has undergone—and is still undergoing—a process of vigorous change and is undergoing it largely not for the benefit of its people, but for that of their and others' motor-cars. Like most of our towns it has found that its old streets just cannot accommodate the hordes of vehicles wishing to use them. So, in the name of the new god of fuel consumption, many of the old streets and buildings have had to go and Kidderminster is now emerging from the trauma with wide streets, a host of characterless office blocks and a market centre that looks indistinguishable from all the other new market-centres that have sprung up in so many of our towns. Perhaps, in years to come, we or our successors will appreciate the lines of these new blocks and chatter enthusiastically about moulded concrete and the qualities of mid-twentieth century safety-glass. It is not impossible if only for the reason that future historians will have to talk about something. Amid all this the town still has its idiosyncratic railway station, a large black-and-white building that rumour has it was intended for Stratford which presumably refused it on the ground that even that town could not stomach the chintz and pseudo on such a scale. Kidderminster accepted it willingly enough and curiously it does not appear out of place.

The town has a second statue, other than that of Richard Baxter. It is of Rowland Hill, the pioneer of penny postage, who was born here in 1795. Hill was what the Victorians used to call "a man of many parts" and took a hand in many things before turning his attention to the reform of the nineteenth-century postal system. His father was something of a reformer and founded a school in Kidderminster at which his six sons and two daughters were educated. Rowland seems to have learnt all the school had to offer by the age of twelve for it was then that he turned teacher himself and over the next few years not only taught at his father's school but generally took over its administration, pulling it out of the debt into which his father had placed it.

It was while running the school that Hill established a form of education later to be known as 'The Hazelewood System' and which was one of the first excursions into what is now termed progressive education. A school constitution was drawn up with the consent of both staff and pupils and offenders were tried by a jury of pupils. The constitution could not be amended without the agreement of a majority of both pupils and staff.

After initial experiments with the system at Kidderminster, Hill transplanted it to a school which he founded in Birmingham and, in 1822, an account of its organization, published by his brother Mathew, created a considerable stir. Jeremy Bentham, the economist and political philosopher, declared that Hill's school had caused him to cast aside all that he had previously written on the subject of educational reform. For a while Hill's school became very popular, almost fashionable and children from some of the nation's leading families were sent there rather than to the public schools, many of which had gained an unenviable reputation for brutality and corruption. Hill's work had an influence even beyond England for a school following his principles as set down in his brother's book was founded at Stockholm, where it ran until 1846. By then, however, Rowland Hill had turned to other things.

He was to invent a waterwheel and a printing press, and to interest himself in the colonization of Australia, becoming secretary to the South Australian Commission. Later he was to be

Chairman of the Brighton Railway Company and it was during this time that he also turned his attention to the reform of the postal system. This was a monumental task for any man to undertake, for, despite the reforms of the previous fifty years, the operation of the service was still a bureaucratic nightmare and hidebound by traditional methods of working. Hill was to encounter strenuous opposition to his new proposals, but this was overcome and the Penny Post finally came into being. It is sad to reflect that its recreation, in the light of present postal charges, seems a complete impossibility.

As is the case with so many English towns most of Kidderminster's ancient customs have long since perished. Yet one custom, which Rowland Hill and Richard Baxter both doubtless knew, still survives, for every Midsummer's Eve the inhabitants of Church Street celebrate a 'Feast of Peace and Good Neighbourliness'. Church Street, with its neat little houses, has lost some of its upper portion to the new by-pass, but otherwise it has escaped the fist of the developers.

The feast seems to date back to at least the fourteenth century when a Kidderminster spinster bequeathed forty shillings to the inhabitants of the street to be put in trust and the interest used to provide farthing-loaves for children born in and living in the street. She also proposed that all the men in the street should gather on one day each year to compose any differences that had arisen amongst them.

This situation seems to have carried on until, in 1778, John Brecknell, a bachelor living in the street, left a bequest which enlarged upon that of his fourteenth-century predecessor. John Brecknell, in his will, placed £150 out at interest

> to provide and pay for and give to every child or unmarried person that is born in or an inhabitant of that Church Street aforesaid one two-penny plum cake upon the Eve of every Midsummer's Day—and further to provide and pay for, pipes and tobacco and ale, etc, for the entertainment of the male inhabitants which shall then assemble—and the remaining part of the interest on the £150 to be given to such poor persons as the company then assembled on the majority of them shall think the fittest objects.

As a result of these two bequests Church Street has a tradition which goes back more than five centuries and which is still continued in our own day.

South-west from Kidderminster and lying close to the borough boundary is the small village of Stone with its nineteenth-century church, standing on the Bromsgrove–Kidderminster road, partnered by the former village school. Nearby is Shenstone, whose Court is now an Adult College of Education.

The road through Shenstone leads on to Rushock where the church was restored in 1758 but incorporates part of a building which dates from the thirteenth century. Rushock Court has been rebuilt since Father John Wall was arrested here in 1679 for ministering to the Roman Catholics of the region. John Wall was priest-in-charge of Lady Yate's Harvington Hall chapel and, attending to the religious needs of a large group of Worcester-shire's Catholics had, for many years, lived a cat-and-mouse existence with his Protestant pursuers. He was tried at Worcester and his execution took place on the same day as that of John Kemble at Hereford, these two men becoming the last Roman Catholics to die for their faith in England.

At Elmley Lovett the Department of the Environment has been the uneasy inheritor of the former Air Ministry store-sheds which stand near the church. There seems little reason for them to be housed here and it is about time that the conservation-minded Government department had them dismantled. Behind the sheds is Elmley Lovett church, much restored in the last century, but with its fourteenth-century tower and spire remaining intact.

Nearby Elmbridge is a small village which, in the past, was dominated by Purshall Court lying a little way to the north of the village. From the end of the fourteenth century the Court was in the ownership of the family from which it takes its name and many of their memorials are to be found in Elmbridge's Norman church. The Court has links with the Gunpowder Plot for the conspirators held a number of their meetings here. An upper room was used as a chapel which John Wall probably knew in the days of the Catholic persecution.

This area of small villages to the south-west of Kidderminster is one into which the developer has only gingerly pushed his speculative fingers. The same hardly applies to the area to the north-east of the town for here Kidderminster has crept out along the main road to Birmingham and a deluge of development has swelled both Cookley and Caunsall to the point where they have almost completely coalesced. Indeed, the road from Caunsall to Kidderminster is now largely built-up and both villages have become fine examples of unplanned, centre-less suburbia.

Cookley is a good illustration of what I prefer to term a submerged village. These are the villages which lie about our large towns and industrial centres and which have been either absorbed into the towns themselves or else drowned in overspill or ribbon development. Evesham has already done this with Great Hampton, Worcester with Whittington and a number of other villages, while Birmingham has swallowed up a whole slice of the north-east of the county. At Cookley the nineteenth-century church stands with a few older houses in a sea of new development. It is a forlorn Canute almost alone with its memories of fertile pastures and pleasant views whose attractions have brought so many people here that they have long ago been obliterated.

Blakedown, on the Kidderminster–Birmingham road is in something of a similar situation though it has not been 'got at' quite so rampantly as in the case of Cookley, while Churchill some miles further on, has been fortunate enough to escape with only minor additions. It is this question of scale that is all-important. Our villages have evolved gradually over many centuries and are quite capable of absorbing a certain amount of new housing without losing their character. It is when a village is suddenly deluged with piecemeal development that doubles or trebles its size within a matter of months that it is robbed of identity.

To distinguish Churchill from its namesake on the outskirts of Worcester it was once generally referred to as Churchill-in-Halfshire, the suffix being the name of the ancient Hundred in which it was situated. From 1429 to 1606 the Dickens family of Bobbington in Staffordshire were lords of the manor and it has been claimed that Charles Dickens was one of their descendants. The main village lies off the busy road and its main street contains an interesting group of cottages and barns, some in red-brick, others faced with sandstone and many decked with flowers in the summer months. In the last century the thirteenth-century church was dismantled, but the great yew in the churchyard was probably here more than a thousand years ago.

Rejoining the Birmingham–Kidderminster road and travelling north-eastward true commuter territory is reached at the first of the Hagley villages, Lower Hagley which leads imperceptibly into Hagley itself. For the majority of people Hagley's main claims to fame are as a crossroads for the Birmingham–Kidderminster road and that from Bromsgrove to Stourbridge—this has been reinforced in recent years by the opening of the Hagley–Lydiate Ash link-road to the M5—and for the seat of the Lyttleton family, Hagley Hall.

Immediately to the north-west of the village rise the Clent Hills, which because of the abruptness of their slopes, seem to be far higher than they really are. Hagley Hall lies in a hollow beneath the hills with its parkland bounded on the west by the new link-road. Much has been written about this house, which was built in the mid-eighteenth century, but externally at least, I have always found it rather unprepossessing, perhaps because the nearby hills dwarf so much of its reputed grandeur. At the present time the Hall is being steadily encroached upon by new houses, reasonable if unexciting examples of their type, which are being built almost on its doorstep in Park Road.

Hagley has been the main seat of the Lyttletons since 1564 when the family bought the estate and moved here from the manor-house at Frankley. At one time it looked as if both properties would pass out of the hands of the family for John Lyttleton was involved in the Earl of Essex's abortive plot to seize the throne and when it was discovered his estates were forfeited to the Crown. His widow, however, succeeded in having the estate restored to their son Thomas who became the first baronet. Thomas Lyttleton was a firm supporter of the Royalist cause in the Civil War and was taken prisoner by the Round-heads. His house at Frankley was burnt down by the Royalists to prevent it falling into Parliamentarian hands.

In the mid-eighteenth century the eighteenth baronet was created the first Baron Lyttleton. George, Lord Lyttleton, was to be known as 'the Good Lord Lyttleton' and as the friend of Pope and other poets. In political life he rose to become Chancellor of the Exchequer while, on the domestic scene, it was he who was responsible for the rebuilding of the Hall. He was both generous and intelligent, but absent-minded to a marked degree and Lord Chesterfield, in his letters, remarked on his "distinguished inattention and awkwardness" as a warning to his son.

The first lord died in 1773 and was succeeded by his son who over the next six riotous years was to be generally known as 'The Bad Lord Lyttleton'. An endless round of fashionable vice was all but ended when he had a dream that a bird had flown into his room, changed into a young woman and told him that he had only three more days to live. The 'bad lord' evidently believed in dreams for he lived the next three days in fear and dread and, his agonies of mind playing havoc with a weak heart, appropriately followed the ghostly woman's suggestion on the appointed night. This event was to become one of the classic ghost stories of the period.

With the 'bad lord's' death in 1779 the title lapsed, but was recreated some years later in favour of a kinsman who had been Governor of South Carolina and, after that colony had seceded from the Crown in the American 'War of the Revolution', Governor of Jamaica. William Lyttleton, the third baron of the recreation, was a strong advocate of Parliamentary reform. But his reforming activities were not so well remembered as his account of his being smuggled aboard HMS *Northumberland* when she received the fallen Napoleon from the frigate *Bellerophon* and of the conversation he had with the defeated Emperor.

The fourth baron, George Lyttleton and W. E. Gladstone both married sisters on the same day and remained firm friends for the rest of their lives. This Lord Lyttleton took a part in promoting popular education, taught in the local Sunday School and gave assistance with the restoration of Worcester Cathedral. He also played cricket and produced eight sons who, with their father and two kinsmen, were later as the Lyttleton Eleven, to take on Bromsgrove School and give it a sound thrashing. A port in New Zealand was named after him to commemorate his work in promoting settlement there.

One of his sons was Alfred Lyttleton who became an outstanding wicket-keeper and tennis champion. Alfred Lyttleton was to succeed Joseph Chamberlain as Colonial Secretary and helped to sort out the mess we had got ourselves into with the Boer War.

Lying beneath the slopes of Wychbury Hill is Pedmore, a village which has been all but incorporated into Stourbridge which merges to the north-west. Like neighbouring Kidderminster, Stourbridge can claim a past that goes back well before the Industrial Revolution established the basis of its present fortunes. Like Kidderminster, too, it has, until the recent past, been a one-trade town, Stourbridge glass being justly famed for its high quality. The industry was founded in Elizabethan times by Continental immigrants fleeing from religious persecution, the Tyzack family, who were responsible for so much of the industry's development, originally coming from Lorraine. The centre of the industry is now, however, largely located over the Staffordshire border at Amblecote.

The town was anciently known as Bedcote and did not adopt the name Stourbridge until 1454. It was originally centred south of the present town-centre where, at Old Swinford, the tower and spire of the church date back to the thirteenth century. The church, most of which dates from its Victorian restoration, is shaded by beech trees and stands in what is now a quiet corner of the town. Within are memorials to various members of the Foley family who built one of England's first industrial empires in the region and one of whom, Thomas Foley, founded the Bluecoat School which stands nearby on the main road.

It was at Stourbridge that Dr Johnson went to school, though he did not attend Foley's foundation, but the older King Edward's School in the High Street. The school was founded in 1552 but was largely demolished in 1864 to be replaced by the present building. Johnson came to stay here as a result of his uncle, Dr Ford, living in the town and his cousin, Cornelius Ford being 'a parson of Pedmore', and was later to declare that he learnt nothing from the town's grammar school. Perhaps this was a somewhat prejudiced judgement for, before he had set out for London and fame as the Don of English Letters, he had been seriously smitten by the charms of Olivia Lloyd, the daughter of the founder of Lloyds' Bank and had hoped to secure an ushership at his old school so that he could remain in the town. The school, however, had evidently had quite enough of Johnson and turned him down flat and in so doing probably did both Olivia and Stourbridge a good turn.

Stourbridge industries include, amongst many other things, tanning and the manufacture of anvils and garden implements. But, although it is now largely carried on across the county boundary, its true industry remains glass-making which employs a large proportion of its working population. Although modernization has moved into the trade many traditional methods are

South Quay, Bewdley

still used and it is difficult to see how methods of working in such a highly individualized type of industry can be improved.

That the glass-making industry came to be established at Stourbridge was due, in the first instance, to the presence of local fire-clay deposits. This clay is not quarried, but is mined and whilst most of it is used for the fire-bricks which will line the glass-makers' furnaces the finest, called pot-clay, is used to make the pots in which the mixture of dried sand, red lead, arsenic, potash, borax and saltpetre is fused into molten glass.

The glass-making mixture is subjected to a temperature of 1400 degrees Centigrade in large furnaces. Nowadays the used gases are used to preheat the incoming air, passing beneath the floor of the glasshouse to a detached chimney. In former times, however, the spent gases were allowed to escape from the top of the furnace and because of this method of working the old glasshouses were shaped like great bottles.

After some hours the molten glass is ready for working and it is fascinating to watch the skill of the 'footman', more commonly known as the blower, as he creates the beginnings of a piece of fine glassware. The glass may be blown into a mould or may be regulated in size by the 'footman' himself, whose cheeks, acting as bellows, seem capable of feats of inflation beyond the range of more ordinary mortals. Once blown a base may be added by either flattening the glass or by the addition and shaping of new molten glass. It is then passed to the 'gaffer' for final finishing, which includes trimming and possibly the deft operation of adding a handle.

The finished glass must be cooled very slowly to prevent cracking and when this has been done it is ready to receive its design, which is done by either cutting or engraving. After cutting the glass so rendered will have acquired an opaque surface and the final operation is to dip the cut glass into a chemical bath which removes this outer layer, leaving a glass of perfect clarity.

Stourbridge glass has a world-wide reputation for quality and is exported to all parts of the world. It is the product of many generations of craftsmanship and it is this which sets it apart from so many of the newer industries to be found in the towns to the north.

The Parish Church of St Mary, Kidderminster
Hagley Hall

V

THE INDUSTRIAL NORTH-WEST

STOURBRIDGE lies at the threshold of the Worcestershire Black
Country, though I should add that, of recent years, the term has
become something of a misnomer for much of the region has
undergone an intensive scouring process.

Apart from both its density of industrialization and population
when compared to the rest of the county the region's most obvious
difference is one of accent, which towards the Staffordshire
border, broadens to the complexities of a full-blown dialect.
Black Country speech, along with that of parts of East Anglia and
Lancashire, has been claimed as the nearest survival of the speech
of our Anglo-Saxon forebears. There could be some truth in the
assertion, though its origins are more probably to be found in the
region's settlement by a group of invaders who, although associated with the main body of Saxon migrants, were of a somewhat
different stock. At all events, the Black Country accent is not the
product of industrialism as is so often supposed for it was spoken
here long before the exploitation of coal and other mineral
resources led to the area taking over from Shropshire's Coalbrook-
dale as the centre of the Industrial Revolution.

On the outskirts of Stourbridge, Lye owes its growth almost
entirely to industrial development in the late eighteenth and
early nineteenth centuries and one of its former major industries
was the manufacture of frost-cogs. Frost-cogs are small triangular
spikes which are fitted to horseshoes to prevent slipping on icy
roads. They are still made here but obviously, in this age of the
motor-car, on a far smaller scale than formerly.

Cradley and Cradley Heath have remained the centres of the
chain-making industry which, like frost-cogging, was once
carried on by master-men at their own forges. Of recent years the
industry has tended to move into factories and most of the old

domestic forges have been either demolished or remain empty and derelict. But centuries of largely independent manual labour have contributed much to the sturdy and ebullient character of the typical Black Countryman which has managed to outlive the inevitable ending of his old methods of domestic working. He is still to be found with his whippets and pigeons and often with his fishing tackle ready to spend a weekend by the river if he has the chance; for the true Black Countryman, despite his surroundings and two centuries of industrialism, remains at heart a countryman who, in his mind's eye, has never lost sight of the green pastures that now lie buried beneath interminable acres of housing, spoilt and throbbing factory sheds. Apart from chain-making other industries are carried on around Cradley, including the manufacture of fine enamel-ware and, more prosaically, the heavy toil of making manhole-covers.

In the seventeenth and eighteenth centuries Cradley was renowned for the work of its local gunsmiths and one of her most famous sons was originally apprenticed to the trade. William Caslon was born at Cradley in 1692 and was destined to become one of the greatest of English type-founders. It is a strange coincidence that John Baskerville, who assumed Caslon's mantle later in the following century, should have ultimately come to rest at Cradley. Forsaking the craft of gunsmith Caslon eventually went to London to turn out tools for the bookbinding trade. In his association with this he made his first tentative attempts at type-founding with results that so pleased a leading printer that he urged Caslon to take up the trade full-time. Assured of a market for his work Caslon readily adopted the suggestion and launched himself on a career that was to end with him heading the largest type-founding business in the world.

His type was sought by leading printers not only in England but also on the Continent, where printers had previously taken a dim view of English type. He was chosen to design the type for 'English Arabic' when copies of the New Testament were first sent to help Christian missionary work in North Africa and the Middle East.

To the north-east of Cradley, Halesowen stands on the edge of the Black Country proper and, unlike some of the industrial towns to the north, has a past which goes back well before the turmoil of the Industrial Revolution. The sandstone church which dominates the centre of the town dates from Norman times and it is thought that it may have been partly modelled upon an earlier Saxon church which stood upon the site.

Not far away, between the 'Black Horse' public house and the Manor Abbey sports stadium, on the left of the by-pass leading to Birmingham, is all that remains of the once great abbey of Hales which in the past exerted its influence throughout the whole region. The remains of the abbey are now incorporated in farm-buildings and are only just visible from the main road. The abbey was founded in 1215 by King John, who obviously had his good points, and was occupied by a body of monks variously known as the White Canons, the Austin Canons or the Premonstratensians. The order had been founded in 1120 by St Norbert at Premonstratem in Picardy and was one of the smallest in Europe. Halesowen was to become their largest house in England. This did not mean that it was highly populated, for the number of monks at no time rose above twenty-one. But the abbey was important locally because of the large area of land it controlled, including Romsley, Warley, Oldbury, Lutley, Cradley, Lappal, Illey, Cakemore and Ridgeacre. Tithes were also due to the abbot from the manors of Clent, Walsall and Wednesbury and it controlled the chapels at Kenelmstowe (Clent) and Frankley.

As lord of all these manors the abbot enjoyed a number of important feudal rights. He could claim half the horse-colts, bees, hogs and goats at a yearly count of his tenant's possessions. He claimed payment from an heir gaining possession of his lands, a fee on the marriage of a tenant's daughter, service of tenants on his lands, part of all corn that was ground at his mill (and corn from the manor lands could not be ground anywhere else), and in general prospered most when times were good and suffered least when they were bad.

Whether the abbots were on the selfish side and refused to give the brethren a fair share of all these 'goodies' no one can say, but the monks seem to have become a little tired of the sight of all this going to the abbot and, presumably, very little of it coming their way. In 1272 the Assize Rolls record that various monks from Hales armed themselves and set out on a systematic pillage of the neighbourhood. The actions of the brothers were high-handed enough for at least one of them to be outlawed for robbery.

In the last century of its existence the abbey began to acquire a rather dubious reputation. Various disorders occurred and the abbot was at one time accused of ploughing up the king's highway to plant barley. In 1478 two of the monks were accused of incontinence and immorality and in 1491 one Margery Coke and an assorted band of women were ordered to cease their frequent visits to the abbey grounds.

Six years later some of the monks staged a mutiny and Roger Walsall was sent for ten years imprisonment to Croxton Abbey while Roger Wednesbury, Richard Bowen, Thomas Dudley and Richard Hampton all received lesser sentences for their part in the rising.

The abbey table was one of the most lavish in the district. In 1489, with less than twenty monks in residence, twenty bushels of rye and wheat were used weekly for bread while the annual consumption of food included 60 beef-cattle, 40 sheep, 24 calves and 30 swine. Beer was plentiful with over a thousand bushels of barley being used. Of course, not all this was used by the monks themselves, and much of it was dispensed by way of general hospitality.

Besides the income from his feudal dues the abbot kept the money rolling in by the possession of relics which attracted many pilgrims. Chief amongst these was the head of St Barbara, one of the last Christian martyrs, who was slain by her father during the Roman Persecution. Many pilgrims flocked to the shrine as they also did to that of the boy-martyr, St Kenelm at nearby Clent. St Barbara was one of those recently removed from the calendar by Papal Decree.

Offerings from the pilgrims filled the coffers of the abbey and, if anything, these were even greater at the end of the Middle Ages than they had been at the beginning.

It was very likely that the abbey was responsible for the first exploitation of the mineral wealth of the district. Coal was being mined here in medieval times and was well-established by the reign of Elizabeth. Had the abbey survived the Reformation—or if the Reformation had never taken place—it is interesting to speculate if it would have come to draw its major revenues from the coal and metal industries which were ultimately to replace the local agriculture.

Halesowen is not dominated by any one industry and no great factory has yet arisen to challenge the hilltop supremacy of its parish church. Nail-making, which was the basic metal trade here in the late eighteenth and early nineteenth centuries, is still carried on, together with the manufacture of anchors, rivets, anvils, machine tools and buttons. Conditions in some of the old nailing factories were once poor in the extreme, for this was the epitome of local sweated industries. Nail-making was once carried on all over the region, many people dividing their working life between the domestic forge and agricultural work. Bad harvests in the years immediately prior to the Napoleonic Wars were an important factor in driving many of the casual metal-workers into entering the industry on a full-time basis in the new factories. But the independent domestic forge was to last through-out the nineteenth century and isolated workers still carried on the trade in some regions up to the Second World War.

Until the middle of the last century Halesowen and its neigh-bourhood were included within Shropshire, a situation which had existed since 1100 when it was transferred to the county by the Earl of Shrewsbury, then lord of Hales manor. Some years later it passed into the hands of Emma, wife of Dafydd, Prince of Powys, and it is said that the suffix Owen was added to the original name as a compliment to the manor's Welsh connections.

The parish church houses a number of memorials to the Lyttleton family, the most tragic of which is one to the 14-year-old Edward who died in 1614. He was the son of that John Lyttleton involved in the Essex Plot against Elizabeth I.

Also commemorated within the church is the poet William Shenstone who, besides writing poetry was also a pioneer of landscape gardening and converted the parkland—now a golf course—around his home, The Leasowes, into a place that drew praise even from the taciturn Samuel Johnson. Shenstone's most famous poem was 'The Schoolmistress' in which he celebrated his first teacher, Sarah Lloyd. He attended Halesowen Grammar School and later an academy at Solihull before going on to Pembroke College, Oxford. His poetry was popular at the time and was praised by Robert Burns, but it is now doubtful if it is read by many.

To the north-west of Halesowen is the small hamlet of Illey, lying close to the M5–M6 motorway. Its chief claim to fame is a public house, the 'Black Horse', which is not very old but has been made to look reasonably aged in brewery black and white.

Strange to say I once saw an African crane in fields near here and was later to learn that it was a flyaway from a Coventry aviary.

Nearby is what remains of the old Halesowen–Longbridge single-track railway, one of its stations being formerly located at Hunnington near the local confectionery works. It was closed in 1963 and there is something to be said for developing at least a part of the old track as a linear country-park.

Stretching away to the north-east on the other side of Halesowen is the newly created borough of Warley, comprising Oldbury, Smethwick and Rowley Regis. Until 1966, when the borough was created, Smethwick and Rowley Regis were part of neighbouring Staffordshire but the new borough has redefined the county boundary and is wholly located in Worcestershire.

Warley is almost entirely urban and has been heavily industrialized since the end of the eighteenth century. It was the construction of the Birmingham and Wolverhampton Canal that first made it possible for industry to be established here in a large way and Oldbury became a centre of the heavy engineering trade, producing furnaces and foundry equipment as well as glass and chemicals. Smethwick was almost home to Boulton and Watt's Soho 'manufactory' opened just beyond what, in 1762, was still being described as "an inconsiderable hamlet". In 1790 the Soho Foundry was opened in Smethwick to join its already existing glasshouses.

But, of Warley's three segments, it was probably Rowley Regis that was first associated with heavy industry, for it was in this region that Dud Dudley, an illegitimate son of Edward Sutton, fifth Baron Dudley, made his first efforts to smelt iron-ore with coal. Dudley claimed some success, but much of his work was sabotaged by rival manufacturers who feared that his discoveries would drive their charcoal-burning furnaces out of business.

Yet, with the rediscovery of Dudley's methods by Abraham Darby and the consequent expansion of the iron industry, a tremendous demand was created for coal and, by the early nineteenth century, more than forty pits were in production at Rowley. In the same period the local basaltic stone known at Rowley Rag brought extensive quarrying into the district as the rapid expansion of building in the towns and the creation of new roads throughout the country by engineers such as Telford and

MacAdam brought an unprecedented demand for tough road-stone.

Rowley Regis was an inhabited region in pre-Roman times and Celtic burial mounds have been discovered here. So also have traces of Roman occupation in the form of a horde of 120 silver coins, some bearing the head of the Emperor Galba, which dates the horde reasonably well as Galba ruled for only one year, AD 68–69.

In the thirteenth century the manor was in the possession of the Dudley de Somerys and, on the death of John de Somery, was divided between two female heirs, one part being known as Rowley Somery and the other Rowley Regis. Rowley Somery was to pass to the earls of Dudley whilst, in the mid-fourteenth century, Rowley Regis was granted to Halesowen Abbey.

The oldest building in Rowley Regis is not the present church of St Giles, although a church has stood on this site since the twelfth century, but the Elizabethan Tudor House standing in Hadon Hill Park. The house was, for more than six hundred years, the home of the local Haden family and was purchased by the local authority for use as a recreational centre on the death of George Haden-Best in 1921. The park is now maintained by the borough Parks Department and is large enough to contain an interesting nature trail. Of Rowley's other old houses, Rowley Hall is said to have had associations with the Gunpowder Plotters.

Nearby Smethwick cannot lay claims to such a long period of development and, up until the middle of the last century, was administered as the poor relation of neighbouring Harborne. The manor of Smethwick was in the ownership of the church for many centuries, a situation which was complicated when an area of the original manor was granted to Halesowen Abbey, so that Smethwick now possessed both manor and abbey lands. Following the Dissolution this split in ownership continued so that Smethwick had two lords of the manor down until the mid-eighteenth century.

Ecclesiastically it was administered as part of the parish of Harborne, but in the eighteenth century it became the practice for the Parish Vestry, the forerunner of a local council, to duplicate its officers with one each for Harborne and Smethwick. In 1854 a Local Board of Health for "the District of the Hamlet of Smethwick in the Parish of Harborne" was set up and a School

Board for this district, as distinct from Harborne, followed in 1892. Smethwick became an urban district two years later and, in 1899, was granted the status of a municipal borough by which time its population had grown to over 50,000 from less than 1,000 in 1800.

Smethwick's industrial fortunes were based, like that of the rest of the area, on its mineral wealth and the building of the Birmingham and Wolverhampton Canal which, under the direction of James Brindley, was cut in the years 1768-9. It was the presence of the canal which induced Boulton and Watt to open their new Soho Foundry on the canalside where they were soon to be joined by William Murdock, who was to pioneer gas-lighting. It was at the Soho Foundry that Murdock also turned his attentions to the creation of a steam locomotive. But Watt was unenthusiastic about the idea and effectively discouraged Murdock from pursuing his interest further. Towards the end of the last century the firm was acquired by W. and T. Avery Ltd.

Oldbury dates from Saxon times when it was called Ealdanbyrig, meaning the 'old fort'. Along with so much of the region, including Langley and Warley, it became part of the possessions of Halesowen Abbey in the thirteenth century and remained so until the abbey was dissolved by Henry VIII. Nearby Blackheath, then referred to as Blackley, was then one of the abbey's monastic farms.

During the Civil War Oldbury was briefly involved in events when Queen Henrietta Maria paused here with a train of arms and supplies for the Royalist forces based on Oxford. Local Parliamentarian forces got to hear of this and there was a skirmish on the outskirts of the village. But the Roundheads were too few in number and withdrew without affecting the progress of the supplies. A similar skirmish was to take place two days later when the baggage train was leaving Kings Norton.

After the dissolution of Halesowen Abbey the ownership of the manor passed first to the Dudley and later to the Cornwallis family and the title was not finally abandoned until the middle of the last century. Dating from these more spacious days, when Oldbury was little more than a hamlet surrounded by pasture land, is the Big House, bearing the date 1705 over its door.

Oldbury's first excursion into industrialism seems to have been

via the self-employed nailers, but the coming of the canals opened
up the region to the rest of the country and many manufactories
were soon being set up here. As was so often the case in other
regions, conditions in these local factories were far from good.
I have not been able to trace reports for this precise area of
Worcestershire, but an extract from one on the towns of South
Staffordshire with which it had so much in common, made for a
Parliamentary Inquiry of 1843, serves to give a general impression:

> In Willenhall the children are shamefully and most cruelly beaten
> with a horsewhip, strap, stick, hammer handle, file or whatever
> tool is nearest at hand, or are struck with the clenched fist, or
> kicked.
>
> In Sedgley they are sometimes struck with a red-hot iron, and
> burnt and bruised simultaneously. Sometimes they have 'a flash of
> lightning' sent at them. When a bar of iron is drawn white-hot
> from the forge it emits fiery particles, which the man commonly
> flings in a shower upon the ground by a swing of his arm before
> placing the bar upon the anvil. This shower is sometimes directed
> at the boy. It may come over his hands and face, his naked arms, or
> on his breast. If his shirt be open in front, which is usually the case,
> the red-hot particles are lodged therein, and he has to take them
> out as fast as he can.

One particularly horrifying account of life in these early
factories was given by a 12-year-old boy nailer. In the words of
the commissioners' report he stated that he "knows a boy that
makes scraps [bad nails] and somebody in the warehouse took
him and put his head down on an iron counter and hammered
a nail through one ear, and the boy has made good nails ever
since".

Large-scale industry at Oldbury may be said to date from the
establishment of The Brades works in the late eighteenth century.
Alkali works were established in 1835 and phosphorus works in
1851. More industry came in the latter half of the nineteenth
century and the population continued to expand until, in 1894,
Oldbury was combined with nearby Warley to form an urban
district.

No one can pretend that Warley is the most desirable place to
live, but it is nothing near as bad as many writers have made out.
Its constituent areas have all suffered in the past from coming
under the blanket label of the Black Country, of which they have

never really formed the blackest part, though, certainly, some of
their past industrial history has been of a rather grim shade of
grey. But the Black Country is not what it was, and surprisingly
some people lament the fact. The smoke has largely gone, in
many places only to be replaced by chemical fumes, and the rows
of mean streets have been largely bulldozed to be replaced by
new houses and blocks of flats. We may not all like blocks of
flats and acres of new housing estates, but many at Warley have
been tastefully laid out and are infinitely preferable to many of the
homes they have replaced. Warley is an industrial area and no-one
can get away from the fact. Much yet remains to be done, but it
is at least making the best of the job and after all, it is here that so
much of the work on which not only our county's but our
country's prosperity depends, is carried out.

Almost merging with the new borough, across what was
formerly a thin collar of Staffordshire, lies Dudley which, until
recently, was a detached portion of Worcestershire. It has for so
long formed a part of the county that I am going to disregard the
new boundaries and include it here.

In industrial history Dudley is famous for its connections with
Dud Dudley and Abraham Darby. Dud Dudley claimed, in his
Metallum Martis to have discovered the means of smelting iron-
ore with coal—but he did not reveal his method. His work was
carried out under great difficulties for he was harassed and his
works often attacked by gangs in the employ of his competitors.
But the real disruption to his work seems to have been caused by
the Civil War and after this he apparently gave up his efforts.

Abraham Darby, who was probably born at his father's farm
at Wren's Nest, was 7 years old when Dud Dudley died in 1684.
It is strange that Abraham Darby, whose life's work in the
iron-industry was almost exclusively carried out at Coalbrook-
dale, should have thus indirectly founded the industrial prosperity
of his native town. From the proximity of Darby's birthplace to
the region in which Dud Dudley carried on his own experiments
it has sometimes been argued that Darby did not in fact rediscover
Dudley's method but somehow came across one of the earlier
inventor's original formulae. This is possible, but rather unlikely,
though the fact that Darby knew of Dudley's earlier success no
doubt acted as a spur to his own work. Darby would undoubtedly
have established works near Dudley himself if it had not been for

the absence of means of rapid transportation and it was Coalbrook-dale's nearness to the Severn that was the key to that region's early development as an industrial centre. Once the Midland canal network began to be created it was only natural for the industry to wane at Coalbrookdale and take new root in the Black Country where the mineral resources were more abundant and more easily worked. Up until the close of the eighteenth century most of the iron used in Black Country forges came from Shropshire and it was material supplied by Darby and his Coal-brookdale competitors that originally fostered the North Worcestershire nailing industry and laid the basis of many of the region's metal trades which were later to be almost exclusively supplied from Black Country furnaces.

Dudley's dominating feature, however, is not its industry but its castle, parts of which have stood on its limestone clifftop since before the Domesday Survey. This itself is unusual for not all that many Norman fortresses show up in Domesday and the earth-works of the original motte-and-bailey fortification are still largely intact. Twelfth-century walling, however, shows that soon afterwards the original building was extended in stone and the castle dates principally from the fourteenth century. The fortifica-tions of this period were completed at the direction of John de Somery, who operated a reign of terror over most of South Staffordshire and Northern Worcestershire. De Somery was perhaps the worst local example of the undisciplined and even more unprincipled war-lords of medieval times. Much of his castle was built by forced labour from his own and other people's manors and much of the finance used to obtain the necessary materials was really protection money extorted from his defence-less tenants and neighbours. But this was the reign of Edward I, one of the most brutal of all English monarchs, who rejoiced in his description as the Hammer of the Scots. He apparently thought highly of a man of de Somery's stamp who, in his own small way, could have been called the toffee-hammer of this area of the Midlands, and in 1301 John's brigandage was duly rewarded with a knighthood.

After John de Somery's death the castle passed into the hands of the Suttons who remained in possession until John Dudley took it over in 1533. Dudley had big ideas and made considerable additions to the castle but his ambitions were later to become a little too large and he was executed for attempting to place his daughter-in-law, Lady Jane Grey, on the Throne as the Protestant alternative to Mary Tudor.

Following Dudley's execution Queen Mary granted the castle and its lands to Edward Dudley, a descendant of the Suttons. The Sutton-Dudley's were not to prove the most circumspect of owners and when the last of them died in 1643 the castle was in a bad state of disrepair and the estates were heavily in debt. By marriage it now passed into the hands of the Ward family in the person of Humble Ward, son of a London goldsmith who was Queen Henrietta Maria's jeweller. With these connections it is not surprising that Humble Ward was a Royalist and allowed the castle to be garrisoned for the king.

In the latter months of the Civil War the garrison was commanded by Thomas Leveson, and as Royalist reverses continued, it came to be increasingly isolated. A siege of the castle was lifted when Charles despatched troops from Bewdley in the late summer of 1644, but these had to be recalled and the siege was promptly renewed. After the defeat of Marston Moor, Leveson obviously considered the Royalist cause to be doomed and decided it would be the wisest course to surrender the fortress to the Parliamentarian commander Sir William Brereton. His action undoubtedly saved many lives in what would have been a useless slaughter and incidentally preserved most of the castle intact for another century when it was gutted by a fire that raged for three days.

The parish register records that the fire broke out on 24th July 1753 and that

the folks would not go near it on account of the powder said to be in the armoury, the eastern part of the roof being most lead it ran down the hill red-hot and set fire to the long grass which for a time looked as though the whole hill was in flames and sadly feared the towns foulkes.

Later in the same century some of the castle buildings were rebuilt, but more were left to crumble into those ruins with which all Black Country people are now so familiar. Nowadays the castle grounds house a famous Midland zoo which is a very popular place for local school parties who can mix a little history into their visit to the animals. Facing the zoo entrance, as a sign of the times, is a former cinema turned bingo hall and one of those small night clubs that have proliferated throughout the region over the past decade.

Castle Hill is honeycombed with limestone caverns which link up with those beneath the hill of Wren's Nest. The caverns are largely the result of centuries of mining and Dudley is an area which suffers from the effects of subsidence due to these old workings. Not long ago a local football pitch had to be abandoned when a hole appeared at one corner which, on examination, was found to be several hundred feet deep.

Dudley is still closely linked to the metal trades upon which its late-eighteenth-century fortunes were based. But the town is not smothered by them and the centre of Dudley, at least, still seems to preserve links with its market-town past. New building there is in plenty, but most of the drab streets of the last century have gone. As at Warley and Stourbridge the new housing estates are spreading across what still remains of the open land. But people have to be housed somewhere and cannot all live at Clent, Barnt Green or Malvern. The planners have the most difficult of tasks and seem to be making the best of it. It remains for the future to see if, in their own way, the streets of the new estates become as grim as those of the Victorian gridirons.

VI

NORTH WORCESTERSHIRE AND THE
LOST TERRITORIES

THE Clent and Lickey Hills provide the north-eastern barrier
that divides the rural county from Birmingham and the industrial
area beyond. They have been performing this function for just
over two centuries, ever since the Industrial Revolution first began
to change the face of this part of England.

The area has been subject to many boundary changes over past
centuries, Clent itself, for example, having at various times been
part of both Staffordshire and Shropshire as well as of Worcestershire. Most of the land one can see northward from the eight-
hundred-foot height of Frankley Beeches, which is now mostly
included within the collosus of Birmingham, was once within the
county, some of it until quite recent times. In fact, the county
boundary once ran northward a few miles to the east of this point
to encompass the present-day Birmingham suburbs of Kings
Norton, Moseley and even the distant parish of Yardley. Part
of this area long ago ceased to be a part of Worcestershire, but
that which fell under the administration of the Kings Norton and
Northfield Urban District Council remained in the county until
1911, when it was annexed to Birmingham.

The former capital of these lost territories, as I have called them,
was undoubtedly Kings Norton which, up until the mid-seventeenth century, was a town of far greater importance than
neighbouring Birmingham. In the Middle Ages it was the centre
of a thriving sheep-rearing district and its church of St Nicholas
with its tall spire recalls similar wool-churches to be found in the
towns of the Cotswolds and the West—though the tower and
spire at Kings Norton were not added until the late fifteenth
century. Few reminders remain from this time, but the timber-
framed 'Saracen's Head'—not used as a public-house since the

early years of this century—has claims to date from the period of
the town's early prosperity. Certain it is that the 'Saracen's Head'
was the resting place of Queen Henrietta Maria, wife of Charles I,
who was riding at the head of an armaments train en route to join
her husband at the Royalist capital of Oxford.

The Roundheads were aware that these supplies were moving
across the Midlands and made desperate attempts to prevent them
from reaching their destination. At Kings Norton they were
almost successful, for a party of Parliamentarians stumbled upon
the rearguard of the Royalist escort just after the supply train
had left the town. A fierce skirmish took place with the Roundheads at one point using the church as a redoubt. But the
Roundheads were too few in number to defeat their enemies and
the Battle of Kings Norton must rank as one of the many minor
Royalist victories at this stage of the war. Before reinforcements
could be called up the Royalist arms were well along the Icknield
Way and eventually they and Queen Henrietta succeeded in
getting through to Oxford.

During the period of the Commonwealth the town seems to
have been dominated by its energetic Puritan rector, Thomas Hall.
The son of a small Worcester businessman Hall was a man of
energy and enterprise who had great ambitions to make the town
a centre of learning. This was a time when the Universities of
Oxford and Cambridge were viewed with suspicion by the
Puritans as centres of Royalist sympathy. Though not greatly
interested in universities as such many Puritans certainly wanted
a place of higher learning where they could send their sons to be
educated in the beliefs which they held themselves.

At Kings Norton Thomas Hall was both Rector and Master of
the Grammar School. Even at this date the Grammar School was
an ancient foundation and had been in existence since the fourteenth century. The building which housed it has been restored
and stands in a corner of St Nicholas's churchyard, now being
used for the meeting of local societies. At the time of Edward VI
the school is reported to have had more than a hundred pupils and,
although this number seems to have fallen by the time Hall took
over his own teaching duties, he probably aimed to bring it back
to something approaching its former figure. It would also seem
that the school's pupils came from a wide area, many of them
being boarded out at various houses in the town.

The Tudor House, Hadon Hill Park, Rowley Regis
Brades Lock, Oldbury

Building upon an already existing situation Hall apparently decided to enlarge his teaching activities by the foundation of what amounted to a theological college. His students were drawn almost exclusively from former pupils at the Grammar School and, trained by Hall, secured posts as Puritan ministers with various local families, such as that of Richard Greves at nearby Moseley Hall. Given this basis Hall's activities could have led, ultimately, to the creation of a rival institution to the two established universities and, although there is no evidence to say that this is what Hall himself intended, it would probably have come to pass had not the Restoration of Charles II in 1660 suddenly forced the resignation of Hall and many other Puritan ministers who were unable to accept the new order being established in the English church. Thomas Hall's extensive collection of theological and classical works is now housed in a special section in Birmingham Reference Library.

After the Restoration Kings Norton resumed its existence as a market-town, though industry was soon to put in its first tentative appearance in the form of the iron-splitting mills that were to be set up along the banks of the River Rea. The Rea rises to the north of the Lickey Hills and now, as then, its banks are dotted with factories producing many different products. Today most of the riverside is hemmed in by houses but, until relatively recent years, the factories stood in isolation. The iron-splitting mills were water-powered and the banks of the small river were soon proliferating with these red-brick manufactories and their attendant sluice-gates and mill-ponds. One of these buildings still remains, though long ago converted to other use, at the corner of Camp Lane and Pershore Road near to the Kings Norton Factory Centre. In neighbouring Northfield another, later used as a salt-mill, stood at the corner of Quarry Lane and Mill Lane, later severed from the river by the railway embankment.

Water-power from the Rea was also responsible for the siting of Baldwin's Kings Norton Paper Mills, which were closed in 1965. Until its closure this company continued to maintain teams of dray-horses, which splendidly groomed and arrayed with gleaming horse-brasses, were amongst the few horse-drawn vehicles to survive into the age of automania.

The eighteenth century saw a quickening of the pace of industrialization, though this is a long word to describe the

The 'Talbot', Chaddesley Corbett
Looking across the Stour Valley from Clent

essentially small-scale industry which grew up in the area at this time. From the eighteenth century date the arrival of the paper-mills and the brick-kilns; this, the making of bricks for the expansion of Birmingham and the Black Country towns, now also being a defunct industry. The clay soil of the region provided excellent material for this industry which, apart from Kings Norton, was also carried on at Rubery and Northfield. In Kings Norton the last of the brick-kilns, at the foot of Parsons Hill, were demolished a few years ago to make way for more modern industry.

The impetus for the development of large-scale industry came with the construction of the Birmingham and Worcester Canal in 1815. A lock-basin for on- and off-loading cargoes from the narrow boats was built at Lifford Lane and was well-used, as Kings Norton was the junction point for the Stratford Canal. It also received traffic from the Black Country which had travelled the Dudley Canal via the Lappal Tunnel to enter the Birmingham and Worcester Canal at Selly Oak.

New industry now tended to establish itself around the canal-basin. It was the existence of easily accessible canal transport, more than any other consideration, that led to the original establishment of the present Guest, Keen and Nettlefolds works—a fact which was later to make Joseph Chamberlain no stranger to the area.

Yet the point must be made that Kings Norton had not now mushroomed into a thoroughgoing industrial town. The new industry had roughly divided the town into two parts, the old centre being upon the hill and gathered around St Nicholas's church, with the Rea running beneath its western slopes and the canal lying across the low ground to the north. The factories, and the houses for their workers, lay largely in the areas known as Lifford and Stirchley where the factories, at least, are still mainly located. The exception to this were the mills along the Rea, some of which had already been abandoned, and where later was destined to arise the Triple X glassworks. Taken as a whole the parish was now fairly evenly divided between industry and agriculture. It was a situation that was not destined to remain unaltered.

In the early 1840s the railway line between Bristol and Birmingham was opened and Kings Norton found itself with a station on the line. At first this was seen almost solely as a freight station, handling the goods of the local factories. But it was to prove far more than this. The railway had now opened up the prospect of Birmingham businessmen living not in the city where they made their fortunes, but in more salubrious rural surroundings from which they could reach their city offices in half an hour or less. The age of commuter dawned for Kings Norton with the arrival of its first local passenger train.

At Kings Norton, Northfield and Barnt Green houses sprang up to be tenanted by members of the new commercial classes. New roads of 'villa-type' residences proliferated near the railway stations—Station Road and Middleton Hall Road in Kings Norton owed their creation almost solely to the existence of the railway. In Northfield the same was true of much of Church Road and Church Hill. The green acres began to be gradually replaced by those of red-brick.

This sudden influx of the new middle-class came very near to saving Kings Norton's now decayed Grammar School from oblivion. The rector was now J. M. L. Aston, MA, who, like Thomas Hall before him, had ambitious plans for the school. At this time many of the country's ancient grammar schools were being reorganized to develop into public schools and if Aston's plans had come to fruition Kings Norton may have been amongst them. In 1866 he wrote to the Charity Commissioners that "I desire this school to afford . . . what may be called a middle class education to such of the boys as can go beyond the ordinary subjects." But the Commissioners rated it as a 'commercial school' noting that its 44 day-boys were all taught the three Rs together with history and geography and that the majority of them were the sons of farmers and small traders. Aston's plans foundered, probably because of lack of capital and in 1889 the school was closed following the formation of a parish School Board.

The population of the area had grown to such an extent that it had been largely removed from the control of the recently formed County Council and was now administered by the new Urban District Council of Kings Norton and Northfield. Its area of authority extended not only to the two districts mentioned in its title but also to neighbouring Selly Oak.

Here industrial development was even more firmly established than at Kings Norton, although it had followed roughly the same pattern, small-scale industry having first appeared along the banks of the Bourne Brook, a feeder to the Rea. As in the case of Kings Norton further industry had later been established near the canals and, by 1900, the Selly Oak–Kings Norton region was well on the way to becoming as industrialized as that centring around Oldbury and Halesowen.

The Kings Norton and Northfield UDC were responsible for many of the area's municipal buildings, a large number of which still remain. Indeed the authority seems to have favoured a definite type of civic architecture—which perhaps could be termed Carnegie-Tudor—normally a fusion of red-brick and false black-and-white timbering. Some examples, such as the Selly Oak Institute in Bristol Road and the Northfield Institute, are quite pleasing. Among other buildings the Council was also responsible for the erection of Stirchley and Selly Oak Swimming Baths, Kings Norton Grammar School in Northfield Road, Selly Oak Public Library and also, in 1887, for the opening of Northfield's Victoria Park to mark Queen Victoria's Diamond Jubilee.

At the time the park must have appeared a rather useless gesture, for it was surrounded by countryside criss-crossed by innumerable bridle-paths. Of the three areas controlled by the UDC, Northfield had remained the most rural and scarcely seemed to merit inclusion in the council's affairs at all.

As Nordfeld it had long ago managed to secure an entry for itself in the Domesday Survey. The existent Norman church of St Lawrence is said to be built upon an earlier Saxon foundation, which means that there could have been some sort of settlement around Church Hill twelve or perhaps even thirteen hundred years ago. During the Middle Ages the manor passed into the hands of the freebooting de Somerys, who held Dudley Castle and, on a smaller scale, nearby Weoley Castle.

The centre of the old village was, and still is, on the slopes and crown of Church Hill. Of the original manor-house nothing remains and the site is now occupied by a housing development. Until quite recently, however, the Tythe Barn was still in existence. It was converted into a house in the early 1960s and was later demolished to make way for even more. Its loss is something that many local people still regret.

A number of the cottages on Church Hill date from the

eighteenth century while the nearby Great Stone Inn can trace its existence back considerably further. The inn takes its name from a large boulder which once stood at its corner with Church Hill and Church Road. This was one of a number of such 'great stones' dotted about the Midlands as a remnant of the debris deposited by the retreating glaciers of the Ice Age. In the early 1950s it was considered to constitute a traffic-hazard and was removed to the pound which adjoins the inn, and which once housed stray pigs and cattle rather than large rocks.

Northfield figured marginally in the Civil War for its major families were Royalists hemmed in on both sides by Parliamentarian Bromsgrove and Birmingham. Hawkesley Hall was attacked and burned by the Roundheads while at nearby Frankley, Frankley Hall, the home of the Lyttletons, was defended for a time by none other than Prince Rupert himself. But Rupert came to the opinion that the Hall was of little strategic importance and would be far too costly to defend. In this case the Royalists set fire to the house themselves to prevent it being used by their enemies.

Up until the coming of the railway Northfield remained a typically rural Worcestershire village, dominantly concerned with agriculture—together with Kings Norton it was said to have some of the best wheat-growing land in the county—although brickmaking was also carried out on a small scale. But, by 1715, its population had grown sufficiently for it to be considered to merit a school, which was a one-roomed building erected on Church Hill. This building still stands to just qualify as an unremarkable piece of Georgian architecture. In later years the school was expanded until, in the 1950s, about half its pupils were housed in temporary accommodation both on and off the actual school site. The school has now moved to new premises nearby and the old buildings are in danger of demolition. It will be a great loss to the area if they are entirely demolished for, occupying as they do a prominent hilltop position near to both the church and the ancient inn, I cannot visualize any new building which will not destroy the harmony of the present composition. A solution may be found if the main building, which incorporates the original school-room, could be retained for use as a play-school or some other such activity.

As was the case with Kings Norton the railway brought

Northfield's first commuter settlers but, for some years, even after its official incorporation into Birmingham, it retained a rural rather than an urban identity. Strange as it may seem Northfield, and Rubery and Rednal as well, were not opened up as residential areas so much by the train and infant motor-car as by the relatively new electric tram. In 1922 the Birmingham Corporation tramway was extended through Northfield to terminus points at both Rubery and Rednal.

From Northfield it took only half an hour to reach the centre of the city and it now began to have its attraction for the property developers. This apart, the Austin Motor Works at Longbridge (now part of British Leyland) were expanding and creating more jobs. During the 'twenties and 'thirties ribbon development sprang up along the Bristol Road and the City Council built the first of its great housing estates at Turves Green and Allens Cross. So great were the effects of this local transport revolution that the centre of Northfield shifted from its ancient nucleus to take root along the tramway-served Bristol Road.

By the end of the 1930s almost half the parish was beneath bricks and mortar and the process of urbanization would have continued if it had not been for the economies brought about by the Second World War. Since the end of the war the process has become complete, new housing developments now stopping like a wall at the present county boundary.

Postwar building has not been quite so intensive in the neighbouring suburb of Bournville which up until 1911 was, with neighbouring Selly Oak, also within the administrative area of the Kings Norton and Northfield UDC. This small region is known primarily as the home of Cadbury Bros (now Cadbury-Schweppes) confectionery factory, of the garden-suburb administered by the Bournville Village Trust and as what is certainly the area of modern-day Birmingham that has the largest amount of open space, most of it laid down as parkland and recreation grounds.

Most of Bournville grew up with the factory which was sited alongside the Birmingham–Bristol railway line, though the manor-house, now maintained as a museum, dates from Tudor times. A collection of Civil War weapons and armour is also maintained in a reconstructed seventeenth-century building in the manor-house grounds.

The houses of the Bournville estate were a gradual growth over the years 1890–1939. The idea of a factory creating an estate for its workers was not new, even for Worcestershire, for John Corbett had already done this at Stoke Prior following the earlier examples of such men as Robert Owen at his mills at New Lanark. In its day Bournville was to be paralleled by the Leverhulme estate at Port Sunlight and, a little later, by the creation of Hertfordshire's Welwyn Garden City.

Today much of Bournville seems little different from countless other suburban streets in towns all over the country. But appearances are deceptive, for many of these 'artisans' cottages' are modelled upon an idealized version of seventeenth- and eighteenth-century prototypes. The influence of William Morris and his associates lies heavy here for the Cadbury family really did attempt to create a workers' village on the land to the south-west of their factory and even extended the illusion by buying-up and maintaining a number of farms.

Their concern was not only with the provision of houses—and here they differed from modern-day developers—but with the creation of other amenities as well. Thus it was that a large part of Bournville was given over for recreation with a special style of neo-Swiss architecture—perhaps influenced by Nestles—in the Rowheath Pavilion, the Restaurant at Manor Farm and the Yachting Pavilion at Bournville Yachting Pool. The estate also contains Bournville Village School, originally an all-age school but now a primary school only and tastefully designed in stone and red-brick, as well as the Ruskin School of Art and a College of Further Education, formerly styled the Bournville Day Continuation College. Other features which differentiate this from the normal suburb are the Yachting Pool, opened in the late 1920s, a pigeon house preserved in Woodbourne Road and, of course, the carillon. This latter is a rarity for any part of England, for the home of the carillon is the Low Countries. Playing this instrument is hard work, for although the pedals are operated much the same as those of an organ, the keys are operated, not with the fingers, but by striking with the wrists which have to be specially protected by padding. It must also be said that in the creation of Bournville the Cadburys gave vent to their teetotal prejudices and created an area of alcoholic drought, de-licensing pubs that did exist and turning them into tea-rooms.

Nearby, standing along the Bristol Road, are the Selly Oak Colleges, a loose affiliation offering residential courses, mostly in theological subjects. Westhill College, greatly extended in recent years, is now recognized as a College of Education.

A large amount of new building has recently taken place and the amount of open space has, for some time, been gradually contracting. One notable new building is the Roman Catholic church in Griffins Brook Lane, whose Italianate architecture seems rather out of place here, though in some ways it does twin the rather less exuberant Italian lines of the Anglican church near the Green.

It may be no more than a personal prejudice, but Bournville seems to have become slightly run-down since the Cadburys lost their dominating influence here, and their company became part of the Schweppes group. Undoubtedly, in the past, many people resented the paternalism practised by the company but, in the layout and maintenance of the surrounding area, it certainly had more than just a few good points. Now a forlorn air hangs over Bournville as if it were an abandoned village still mourning the departure of its lords of the manor.

Much of its parkland is now maintained by Birmingham's Parks Department but some still remains in company hands and, at Rowheath, nothing seems to speak more eloquently of changed times than the barred and desecrated Lido, which was once one more feature that made Bournville so unusual. Birmingham has recently declared that it intends to preserve the character of the 'garden village', yet I cannot help feeling that the city will prove a less zealous caretaker than its predecessors.

Nearby Weoley Castle is an area past all caretaking, a region of vast and seemingly unplanned housing estates with the ruins of the old castle as a well-off centre piece. Weoley Castle leads, almost imperceptibly, into California and thence to Bartley Green where the older housing estates give way to the high-rise flats that now hug the present county boundary near Frankley.

Large-scale housing development is shortly to take place at Frankley, this time without any redrawing of the county boundary, though in effect this will be a further extension of the Birmingham annexations of 1911.

The church of St Leonard has origins almost as old as that at Northfield. It was partly rebuilt in the eighteenth century with stones taken from the ruins of nearby Frankley Hall and has been well restored after a fire in the late 1950s.

In days long before the Civil War Frankley Hall was the home of Sir Thomas Lyttleton who was born there in 1422. Sir Thomas found fame as a judge and legal author, his book *Tenures* being for many centuries the major authority on English real property law and it was still being used as late as the eighteenth century.

At Frankley are situated the reservoirs and filter-beds that provide Birmingham's water-supplies. The largest has the appearance of a great lake and, in the Second World War, narrowly escaped destruction by German bombs.

Nearby the motorway linking the M5 and M6 throbs its busy way through this strip of northern Worcestershire and its service station has put the name of Frankley more firmly in people's minds than ever Judge Lyttleton or dashing Prince Rupert once did.

The tree-clad height of Frankley Beeches is an outlier of the nearby Clent Hills, its 800-foot summit presented by the Cadbury Brothers to the National Trust to be preserved, in the words of an inscription on one of the seats "as an open space for ever". Although the view towards the Clents has remained relatively unaltered that towards the north has changed almost beyond recognition since the Cadburys' day and it is almost possible to hear the steady march of 'progress' in the form of vast new housing developments. More is still to come and the day may not be too far distant when Frankley Beeches will be no more than an oasis amid a desert of urban sprawl.

An impressive viaduct once carried the Halesowen–Longbridge single-track railway across the Romsley Valley, midway between Frankley Beeches and the Clent Hills. It had been originally intended that the line should run to Bromsgrove, but a shortage of capital was responsible for its ultimate terminus at Longbridge. There were intermediate stations at Hunnington and Rubery, the latter being more than a mile from the village and situated below the slopes of Cock Hill. Passenger services once carried workers to the Longbridge works and to the confectionery factory at Hunnington. During the latter years of its operation, however, the line carried freight traffic only and was finally closed to make way for the motorway in the mid-1960s.

Romsley is a rarity amongst north Worcestershire villages in that it has no defined centre. From Dayhouse Bank it sprawls for more than a mile along the Bromsgrove-Halesowen road and if it possesses a centre at all this would appear to be the Rising Sun Inn. The parish church is that of St Kenelm which lies on the approach to the main hills of Clent and Walton and stands about a mile beyond Romsley. The church is reputed to stand on the spot where the child-king Kenelm of Mercia was murdered on the orders of his sister Quendryda. The story has been retold many times and once in verse by Francis Brett Young who once lived near here—though I do not think his poem will ever enter the ranks of immortal verse.

Kenelm succeeded his father Kenulph at an age which has been variously computed at between seven and eleven. Quendryda, whose eye had been on the throne for some time, bribed one of her retainers Askobert, to take the young king on a hunting expedition to Clent and to ensure that Kenelm did not return alive. Pausing to rest for the night in the shelter of the hills Kenelm went to sleep while Askobert busied himself in digging a grave. According to the story Askobert had almost finished when Kenelm awoke and related to him a dream which had revealed Quendryda's intentions and Askobert's part in her plan.

No doubt Askobert was rather shaken by this. But there were great things at stake, for he was in love with Quendryda and hoped to share her throne. Kenelm now began to sing a hymn and, Askobert by now probably in a state of panic when faced by such composure, struck off the boy's head with a stroke of his sword. Afterwards he buried the young king and rode back for Winchcombe, then the Mercian capital, as fast as he could.

Legend has it that a shining light now appeared to illuminate the place of Kenelm's grave and that a white cow came down to graze there and would not be moved from it. Later it was said that cows who grazed here gave a double supply of milk for the ground was hallowed. Although Quendryda naturally tried to keep the affair quiet she was unprepared for the intervention of the supernatural. In Rome a white dove appeared before the Pope as he was celebrating Mass at St Peter's, and placed a scroll, telling where Kenelm's body lay hidden, upon the high altar.

The Pope relayed the information to Wulfred, Archbishop of Canterbury who, in his turn, informed the monks of Winchcombe Abbey. A party of monks came from Winchcombe to Clent where they removed the body of the king from his grave and later buried him beside his father at their abbey.

At the burial service Queen Quendryda was in a furious rage and, in an attempt to subvert it began to sing the 108th Psalm backwards. But, according to the Douce Manuscript which is said to be based on the account of a monk at Worcester about a century after the event, when she reached the words "Let this be the reward of my adversaries" her eyes fell out on to the page. Her blood-spattered psalter was said to be in existence at Winchcombe a century after the event.

Not unnaturally Quendryda died soon afterwards and, as no church would accept her body for burial, it was at length thrown into a ditch. Just what became of Askobert is not known. Although many details of the story have undoubtedly been added over the centuries it can hardly be doubted that the young king was murdered at Clent and very likely at the instigation of his sister.

Within the tiny church Kenelm is portrayed in the work of a number of centuries, the oldest being a carving which is so crude a representation as to almost rank as a piece of abstract art. Gladstone, who was a friend of the fourth Baron Lyttleton and sometimes worshipped in the church, gave the east window which also depicts Kenelm. There is also a figure of Kenelm in the lych-gate. But the most recent memorials to his memory are a series of glass windows showing the main incidents of his life and which were given in 1915 by the Camm family in memory of child victims of the Great War.

The church was once the centre of a thriving village, Kenelm-stowe, which grew up as a result of the pilgrimage-trade centred upon the martyr-king's shrine. There are now no visible remains of this and the village had ceased to exist by the end of Tudor times.

Less than a mile away, at the end of a narrow road through the hills, is Clent's church of St Nicholas. But whereas St Kenelm's is a small, rather cramped place, its twelfth-century structure being partially modelled upon an older Saxon one, St Leonard's, dating from the mid-fifteenth century, is a much more expansive building. The church is tucked so closely into the slope of a nearby hill that its chancel is several feet higher than the rest of the building and has developed a pronounced sideways tilt. Like so many other churches the restorers paid it a visit in the last century, but much of the original work remains.

For many years the Clent villagers made a great celebration of Oak Apple Day—as the day of Charles II's Restoration on 29th May 1660 was known, as a gesture of remembrance that the fugitive king had eluded his Roundhead pursuers after the defeat at Worcester by taking refuge in Boscobel Oak. The day was once celebrated in many other parts of the county, but the tradition seems to have lasted longest at Clent. Here the houses were decorated within and without by oak boughs and the villagers sported oak-apples in their hats and lapels. The tower of St Nicholas's was also adorned with oak-boughs so that, from a distance, it must have looked like a great oak tree itself. The marks worn in the sandstone parapet by the ropes used to haul up the boughs can still be seen.

The old heart of the village, containing the church, the Vine Inn and a tea-shop which must be known for miles around judging from the amount of custom it attracts, is no longer the real centre of population. This has largely shifted to Lower Clent with large houses and the village school lying along the hillside road linking the old and new villages. Part of this road borders a stream which could be quite attractive if it were not now used as an unofficial rubbish tip.

Mid-way along this road is the Fountain Inn—once, I believe, in common with many inns in hilly districts, more appropriately bearing the biblical appellation of the Rock and Fountain Inn—and from here a short road reaches to the foot of Clent Hill. Here the lower slopes have been blighted by the erection of a garish amusement arcade and the situation is not improved by the discovery that the main path up the hill has been badly broken up by trains of horses from local riding schools.

But the ascent is well-worth it for all that. From its summit on a clear day there are superb views across to Malvern and the distant peaks of Wales. To the north are the factories and tower-blocks of the Black Country forever hazed in a grey mist which no amount of smokeless zones or pollution control has yet been able to dispel.

The ridge of the hill is lined with a bristle of trees and at its summit stand the Four Stones. These are no prehistoric remnants of an ancient civilization, but mock standing stones erected, at the end of the eighteenth century, at the direction of George, Lord Lyttleton at a time when Gothic romanticisms of this order were all the rage. It may safely be assumed that Sir Walter Scott would have drooled over them. They are afforded scant respect these days for they seem to be alternately splattered with paint by skinheads or, as evidence of higher education, daubed with rag slogans by students. If the Lyttleton Standing Stones are less than genuine comfort may be taken in the fact that their inspiration was not. Wychbury Hill is crowned by the earthworks of a pre-historic camp with double ramparts and, though there is no direct evidence to say that the camp fell to the Romans in their forward advance to the north-east, it doubtless did. Evidence of Roman activity hereabouts has been found in the form of coins both near Wychbury and on Clent Heath.

Clent has fared rather well in the realms of legend for besides that of the boy Kenelm there is the even more inexplicable tale of Harry Ca Nab. Harry and his ghostly hounds are reputed to hunt at night over the Clent and nearby Lickey Hills hunting not animal, but human prey which he bears to an, as yet, undiscovered lair. But Harry has not been seen for a long time now and presumably rode his last before the advancing horde of excavators which provided the new motorway.

Isolated on the Clent side of the motorway is the Bell Inn—an old coaching-house which has, unfortunately, been chintzed almost out of recognition. The inn, though it stands at Bell End, is generally referred to as the 'Bell at Belbroughton'. Belbroughton, however, lies some distance away and now, as if to emphasize this, the motorway slices between them.

Belbroughton is a village where a local craft has survived in its original location against all efforts for it to be sited elsewhere. For centuries this has been a specialized industrial centre producing scythes with, until recently, water-powered machinery. The small scythe mills at once recall descriptions of the vanished splitting-mills at Kings Norton and Northfield for these two were situated along the banks of a small river. Local expertise has triumphed here over the early efforts of the agricultural machinery combines to grab the industry for themselves. Many different types of scythe are made, for different work and different localities, and it is a job which automation could not now tackle economically. Electricity is now the main source of power, but the industry's resistance to standardization has ensured that it will remain at Belbroughton for a long time to come.

To the south-east of Belbroughton lies black-and-white Chaddesley Corbett, one of those untypically typical English villages that rank almost as collectors' items. It secured a mention in the Domesday Survey and was one of the few manors to remain in Saxon hands. Even more unusually it remained in the hands of a woman, Eddive, who may have been the widow of the defeated King Harold. The village has a further distinctive claim to fame for its church, dating from the twelfth century, is the only one in England to be dedicated to St Cassian, one of the early Desert Fathers. Saxon culture must have hung on here later than in many other parts of Worcestershire for St Cassian's twelfth-century font is of Saxon design.

The village once stood in the heart of forest-land and it was from here that much of the forest was administered. In such a relatively inaccessible place pagan superstition and ritual lingered for many centuries and, until the end of the last century, one of these ancient ceremonies persisted in altered form when a company of local foresters, calling themselves Robin Hood's Men, would dance their way through the village and the surrounding district calling at various houses for beer and food. One of the few survivals of this type of ritual is the Horn Dance at Abbott's Bromley across the Staffordshire border.

The Corbetts, who added their name to that of the original village, became lords of the manor in the early thirteenth century and there are a number of memorials to members of the family in the church, the earliest being to Sir William Corbett who died in 1275. But Chaddesley, in all but name, is now Corbett-less, its chief attraction to the visitor being its main street of half-timbered houses, one of which, the Talbot Inn, can always be entered during licensing hours. The interior of the inn has recently been renovated with fine care for the original structure.

About a mile beyond the village stands historic Harvington Hall, honeycombed with hides which are reputed to have sheltered a fair number of human bees in the days when religious persecution was an unpleasant part of the English way of life. Harvington's hides are thought to have been constructed by 'Little John', or to give him his true name, Nicholas Owen, who built similar refuges for Catholic patrons at many of Worcestershire's great houses. But there is some mystery surrounding those at Harvington, some authorities claiming that Humphrey Pakington, the owner of the Hall, was a Protestant at the time of Owen's death in 1606. Owen, by the way, was still very much in business earlier that year and would have carried on his secretive trade much longer if he had not been forcibly retired by the executioner following his discovery at Huddington Hall in the company of Father Garnett in the wake of the abortive Gunpowder Plot investigations.

From the evidence it would appear that Sir Humphrey was either a Catholic masquerading as a Protestant—which is unlikely but not impossible—or that he considered that, even as a Protestant, the possession of a few hides at Harvington could prove a good investment for the future.

Four hides have been discovered, the last not being found until as late as 1897. Of the other three, one is behind the dining-room wall and was made by lowering the ceiling of the adjoining pantry. Another is sited behind the wall of the entrance gateway and is reached by a trap-door from the floor above. The third, and most elaborate, is a combined hide and bolt-hole situated beside the kitchen chimney. The bolt-hole from this opens into a shaft running the whole height of the building and would have brought anyone using it on to the roof. There is no record to say that the bolt-hole was ever used, but records of this type are hardly likely to have been made.

To the north-west lies the isolated village of Broom standing on the upland plain beyond the Clent Hills. It occupies a rather exposed position and in the winter months receives the full blast of the season's gales. Broom was once part of the medieval manor of Clent and its church dates from the eighteenth century. A twelfth-century church once occupied the site and a font from that time was discovered some years ago holding flowers in a nearby garden and now stands in the present church.

Looking northward from Broom it is difficult to realize that, beyond the further slopes of the Clent Hills, lies the ever-encroaching sprawl of Birmingham and the Black Country. So far the hills have proved a fairly effective barrier against the further spread of mass urbanization, but the neighbouring range of the Lickeys can hardly be said to have been so successful in the same task.

Geographers seem confused as to just where the Clents end and the Lickeys begin. I would, however, include both Waseley Hill and Cock Hill, which lie immediately to the west of the M5 approach road, as part of the latter group. Rubery Hill was once the site of extensive quarrying and what is left of it is now largely covered by housing. Cock Hill is still being systematically blasted out of existence and if houses are ever built here the site will then presumably be known as Cock Hollow. Below Cock Hill stands the vandalized and rubbish-tip remains of the abandoned Rubery Station and the level-crossing points of Holly Cross and Frogmill.

Rubery, which occupies the valley between Waseley and Cock Hills on the west and the main Lickey range on the east, is now by-passed by the M5 approach road—though it is stretching the language to describe a road which cuts almost through the centre of a village as a by-pass. It is a place of no antiquity and, apart from its nearness to the hills, has little to recommend it. It is a sprawling place, half in Birmingham and half in Worcestershire, being almost entirely a dormitory suburb of the former. New Road is an object-lesson in how not to plan a suburban main-street and has recently exchanged its monstrous down-at-heel cinema for a hardly less distasteful shopping block. But, perhaps to be charitable to Rubery, mention should be made of the church of St Chad, also on New Road, which is a reasonable example of modern parish church architecture.

For the masochistically-inclined walker or the hill-climb motor enthusiast the best approach to the highest of the Lickey Hills, Beacon Hill, is from Rubery via Monument Lane. I once met an old woman here who, nodding at the nearby Girl Guide company, described it as "a camp of keen young hussys", but declined to expand the remark.

Not long ago the Lickey Hills were no place to recommend to the serious walker and, in the height of summer they are still not. Two decades ago any weekend would have found the hills teeming with day-outers from Birmingham who had taken a tram-ride from the city to enjoy a day in what Birmingham officials rather unpleasantly described as its 'south-west lung'. No doubt they well deserved their recreation and to profit from this sudden influx two fairgrounds were established, one dangerously sited on the slopes of Bilberry Hill, together with amusement arcades and a host of teashops which all did a roaring trade. Teashops are

Halesowen Parish Church
Kings Norton Parish Church

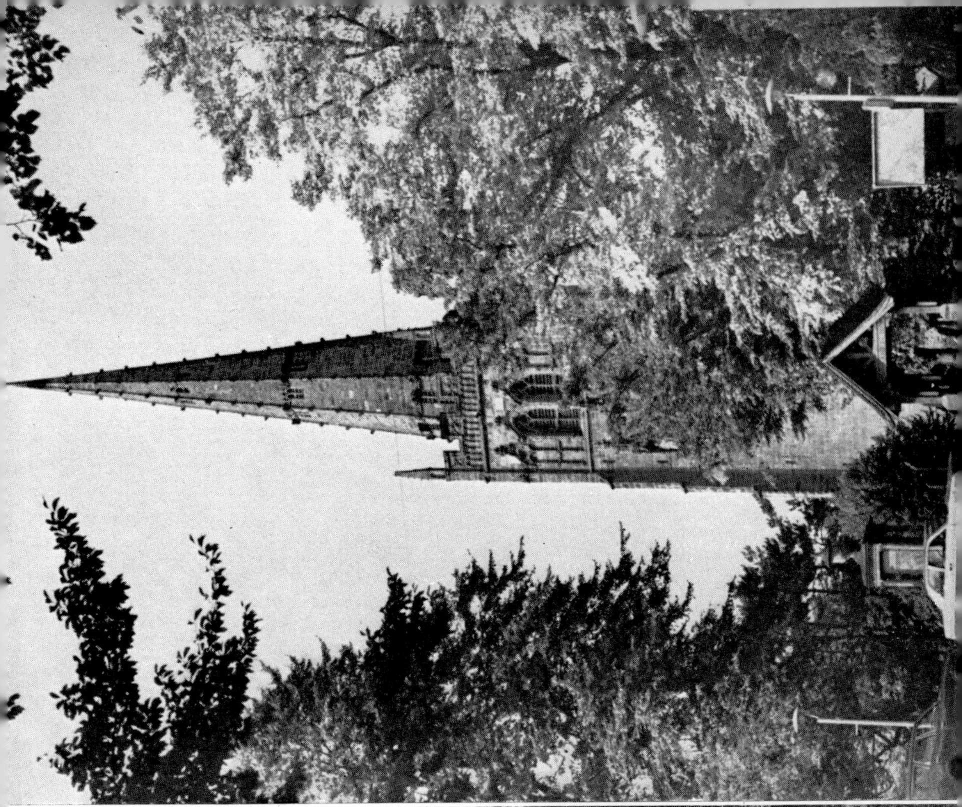

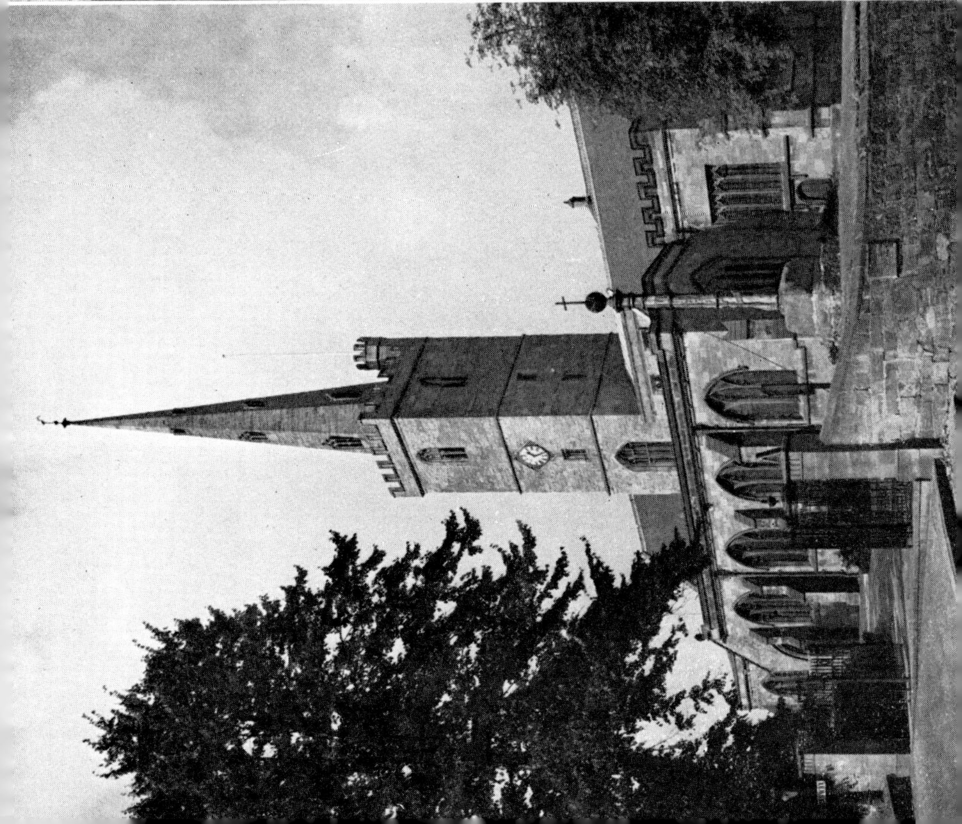

still something of a local craze and even the Rose and Crown Inn, which apparently would offer stronger stuff, is unlicensed. Today the fairgrounds have disappeared though the amusement arcades have become even more firmly established. The age of four-wheels-for-all has taken much of the pressure off the hills and it is now possible, at most times of year, to walk from Beacon Hill to Bilberry Hill and through the woodlands down to Barnt Green in comparative solitude.

Beneath the eastern slopes of the hills lies Cofton Hackett with the Longbridge Motor works forming part of its northern boundary. Here, too, are some of Birmingham's reservoirs whilst in the church lies William Leycester, who died in 1508, and whose two wives and two children are buried with him.

Longbridge is really an outlying part of the expansive suburb of Northfield with the motor works as almost its sole claim to fame. Once known simply as the Austin Motor Co., it has latterly been part of the now-defunct BMC and is at present included in the British Leyland group. Longbridge does, however, possess a fine modern church, dedicated to St John the Baptist and, until recent demolition, a strange, Gothic pumping-station stood near the motor works on Bristol Road (South).

At nearby West Heath the agricultural past is hidden beneath acres of recent housing developments. But this too, can claim its prizes, notably for a Roman Catholic church equipped with a converted theatre organ, a public house quaintly styled 'The Man In The Moon' and as the home-ground of the Midland pop-comedy group, The Rockin' Berries. From 'The Man In The Moon' a road leads eastward to the Peacock Inn, built in 1837 and being almost the last of the old coaching-inns to be built in the county before the railways came to drive the four-horse teams off the road.

Near here is Goodrest Lane in which stands Goodrest Farm, one of the places where Charles II is said to have rested on his flight from Worcester. It may be only a traditional story, but it seems as good a place as any for the weary monarch to have grabbed a few hours sleep.

Beyond the Peacock Inn the old Roman Icknield Way narrows to take the steep incline to Weatheroak. Until recently the road was unmetalled along this stretch and it can still hardly be de-scribed as the average motorist's idea of a good road. Almost at

Wythall Parish Church
Bournville Carillon

the foot of the slope stands the Coach and Horses Inn where Midland wagoners used to pause on their journeys to the West. Even in their day this part of the road caused its problems and, because two wagons were unable to pass each other on the steep track, they carried warning bells by which they could signal their approach. Moor Green Hall has associations with Richard Baxter, the Puritan divine, who is dealt with at length in reference to Kidderminster. Weatheroak village stands in the shadow of Weatheroak Hill which is topped by a sail-less, red-brick windmill. Nearby Windmill House is now used as an adventure centre for Birmingham youth clubs.

Nearby is Wythall, largely strung out along the Alcester Road. It has become one more commuter suburb of Birmingham with its railway station, on the North Warwickshire line, seemingly under the ever-present threat of closure. In 1086 Wythall was a bailiwick of Bromsgrove and it remained a chapelry of Kings Norton for more than seven hundred years. Its nineteenth-century church is a redoubtable piece of Victorian Gothic standing in isolation from the main village and from it a field-path leads to the once double-moated Blackgraves Farm. Close to the Horse and Jockey Inn the Warwickshire border edges across the Alcester Road in the direction of Hopwood where pleasure-craft now ply the northern section of the Stratford Canal.

Hopwood can hardly be said to have blossomed into commuter-suburb status though its near-neighbour, Barnt Green has some claims to being the oldest-established of north Worcestershire's commuterized villages. It has earned some recent fame as the birthplace of the late Godfrey Winn, the well-known author and broadcaster, and recent notoriety as the dumping ground for chemical waste which caused some anxiety to the officials of the East Worcestershire Water Board. Barnt Green has almost ceased to exist as a village being largely composed of substantial houses, though, it must be said, with fenced and hedgerowed gardens often quite as large as pastures. But it does possess a half-timbered manor-house as well as, more prosaically, a thriving cricket club and the Lickey incline.

The Lickey incline, over which trains from the West to Birmingham have to travel, rises one inch in each yard and is the steepest railway gradient in Britain. In the days of steam extra engines were kept in readiness at Bromsgrove to help in pushing the trains up the slope, but since the coming of diesel traction, this is an expedient only rarely resorted to.

Lying in the shadow of the hills are a number of villages, some of which, like that of Lickey itself, have long ago lost their character. But it would certainly be an omission not to praise Burcott, a hamlet which has succeeded in maintaining its charm even in the face of the misguided attempts of some individuals to 'improve' it. Nearby are Wildmoor, Catshill and Fockbury, the latter being the birthplace of A. E. Housman who was born at Valley House and later lived at the Clock House, a gabled, half-timbered building with a bell-tower and carving which declared that it was built in 1600. Surely more than a hint of his native county crept into his Shropshire poetry, and certainly in his youth he would have heard "the bells of Bromsgrove town" more frequently than he was ever to hear those of Ludlow.

VII

FECKENHAM FOREST

MENTION of Housman must include Bromsgrove, where he was educated at Bromsgrove School and spent much of his younger life at Perry Hall. Perry Hall, standing on the Kidderminster road, is now a hotel and until recently was the home of a popular jazz club which may have rather upset the poet's delicate shade.

Leland described Bromsgrove as "all in a maner in one very longe strete, standynge on a playne ground", which could be said to smack rather of a heraldic description. The town has now spilled out from its "longe strete", though that remains— somewhat altered, however, since Leland's day.

Bromsgrove makes some claims to be a rural town, though the claim is quite untenable as it is an uneasy fusion of both rural and urban, with the urban greatly predominating. It is by-passed by the M5, but this does not prevent its main street being traffic-clogged at most hours of the day and plans are now afoot for the creation of another motorway which the planners optimistically hope will ease the congestion.

The main A38 Birmingham–Worcester road runs through the centre of its town and for some miles either side of it extends Bromsgrove in a wavering line of piecemeal ribbon development. If Chadwick Manor Estate did not have the good fortune to be a National Trust property there is little doubt that housing would now line the A38 for the whole of its course from Birmingham to beyond the western fringe of Bromsgrove.

It was at Bromsgrove that Charles II, on his flight from Worcester, paused to have a horse shod at the local blacksmith's forge. Charles was disguised as a footman in the service of Jane Lane and carried on a conversation with the Parliamentarian smith in which he berated the royal fugitive to such good effect that the smith was sufficiently moved to declare that he was an "honest man". But it can hardly have been a pleasant experience for Charles to have paused in Bromsgrove at all, for almost alone amongst Worcestershire towns, it was fiercely for the Parliament cause and if Charles had been caught the wrath of the townsfolk would probably have been so great that they would have killed him before more sober men could have taken him to London.

Bromsgrove and the surrounding area was once a centre of the domestic nail-making industry. Numerous cottagers had small forges attached to their houses and, receiving the split-iron which was their basic material from suppliers in the Black Country and along the River Rea, made the nails at home. Wages were poor and hours of work excessive, children being put to work by their parents as early as six years of age. The last of the local nailers was working until comparatively recently, but now the trade has died out altogether. In its place arose Garringtons Ltd, whose factory has the largest output of forgings of any in Europe. Until recently this was Bromsgrove's major employer, with a large proportion of the town's working population having to find their employment in nearby Birmingham. Recently, however, it has been announced that the town's industrial estate is to be expanded which, it is hoped, will somewhat ease the local employment situation. But, with the urban district's population expected to top the 100,000 mark by 1980, this seems a rather optimistic prediction.

Bromsgrove's church has a spire dating from the fourteenth century and its approach is fortunately from a relatively secluded part of the town standing away from the traffic-thronged A38. There is a monument here, the oldest in the church, to Sir Humphrey Stafford of Grafton who, together with his brother William, was killed in the Jack Cade rebellion of 1450. This rebellion was largely a re-enactment of parts of the more widespread Peasants' Revolt of the previous century and the murder of the two Stafford brothers was later incorporated by Shakespeare in *Henry IV* Part II. Sir Humphrey's son, another Humphrey, backed the loser at Bosworth Field fighting for Richard III against the Lancastrian-supported Henry Tudor. Humphrey survived the battle only to be executed afterwards for treason. Henry VII now awarded the manor of Grafton to Sir Gilbert Talbot, whose first wife is buried in the church.

In the churchyard of St John's are two tombstones erected in

memory of two railwaymen, Thomas Scaif and Joseph Ruther-
ford who lost their lives in a railway accident on the Lickey
incline in 1840. Both men were employees of the Birmingham
and Gloucester Railway Company and both tombstones depict
locomotives of the period with verses then considered suitable for
railwaymen who died on duty.

Bromsgrove School has been expanding steadily since the
mid-nineteenth century and is now a hotch-potch of buildings of
unrelated styles. In common with many other public schools it is,
in the wake of the general implementation of comprehensive
education, going through something of a boom period. Additional scholarships are now being offered, but I have a feeling
that many such schools are riding for a very heavy fall. At the
moment there is a danger that they are merely offering an
alternative form of education rather than one that is basically
different or of a higher standard than can be obtained within the
state system. If an alternative is to mean no more than a different
means of control then, legal niceties about their education
being offered free while their boarding facilities remain chargeable
notwithstanding, their eventual absorption into the State system
seems assured. It is rather to be doubted that Bromsgrove School,
and many others like it, will survive as an independent institution
beyond the end of the present century. Besides having had
Housman as a pupil Bromsgrove School has seen one of its more
recent old boys, David Rudkin, make his entry into the literary
world, his play *Afore Night Come* making a considerable stir in the
London theatre in the mid-1960s.

Bromsgrove is another of Worcestershire's growing band of
'festival' towns and, with Birmingham so close at hand, failure is
hardly likely. The festival was founded in 1950 under the direction
of Joseph Stone and is one of the few small-town festivals which
have managed to steer clear of financial difficulties. The festival,
with a marked bias in favour of musical events, is staged annually
in mid-April.

Nearby is the Avoncroft Museum of Buildings where buildings
of many historic types have been brought from many parts of
the Midlands to be re-erected at the museum site. They include
barns, windmills and numerous examples of domestic architecture and draw visitors from all parts of the country. It is a rather
sad place though one of Bromsgrove's older buildings that has

not yet been considered for a place in this architectural graveyard is the William and Mary house known as The Steps forming a part of Bromsgrove School.

Bromsgrove was once an important administration centre for the royal Forest of Feckenham. It possesses a relic of those days in its Court Leet which meets annually for an election of officers with much ceremonial. The Court Leet is a picturesque survival, but today it is totally without powers, providing no more than a few hours' amusement for those who like to dress up, or to watch others dressed in fancy costumes.

Around Bromsgrove, especially to the east, are extensive orchards and, moving out of the town in the direction of Redditch, Tardebigge is almost surrounded by them. This is basically apple and pear country, though other crops are grown and some of the most delicious honey I have ever tasted came from local hives. The land hereabouts was once cultivated by the monks of the Cistercian Abbey of Bordesley which was founded by the Empress Maud, wife of Geoffrey, Duke of Anjou, in 1136.

There was a church at Tardebigge as early as the twelfth century, but this was pulled down to make way for the present eighteenth-century building. Perched on its hilltop, the church with its tall spire is a perfectly proportioned Georgian master-piece and its galleried interior is one of the most beautiful in all Worcestershire. Close by is the huddled village school, parts of which are considerably older than the church.

Within the church are memorials to the Archer family who, as Earls of Plymouth, resided at Hewell Grange from 1542 until quite recent times. Two of the monuments were re-erected here after the demolition of the old church, the oldest being that to Henry, fifth Lord Windsor, who died in 1605. The other monument to survive from the old building is that to Mary Cookes, who was a daughter of Thomas, Earl of Plymouth. She was the wife of Thomas Cookes who endowed Bromsgrove School in 1693. Thomas Cookes also founded Worcester College, Oxford, at which Bromsgrove scholars still have special entrance facilities.

Below the hilltopped church runs the Birmingham and Worcester Canal and, long before the canal was dug, the road which Catesby, Rookwood and the other Gunpowder plotters took on their flight to Holbeach House, ran near here.

Hewell Grange, the former home of the Earls of Plymouth and

once the centre of one of the largest estates in the Midlands, now provides for the rehabilitation of juvenile delinquents. Up until 1542 the family held the manor of Stanwell near Windsor but in that year Andrew, Lord Windsor, was compelled by Henry VIII to exchange his old home for lands at Tardebigge and the site of the recently dissolved Bordesley Abbey.

The present house was built in Tudor style in 1884 to replace an earlier building which had fallen into partial ruin. The house has some splendid rooms, fifty-one in all, an oak staircase and a private chapel with a lapis-lazuli floor. It fully justifies the modern contention that the Victorians could produce work of an artistry comparable to that of any of their predecessors.

Tardebigge was once quite a bustling place for it was an important stop on the Birmingham–Worcester Canal, its wharves being the nearest for both Redditch and Bromsgrove. The Tardebigge Tunnel, the longest on the canal, was opened from Birmingham to Tardebigge in 1798, although it was not finally carried through to Worcester until 1815.

The men who worked on the canal's construction, the navigators, must have turned the village into a hectic place. Two public houses were opened for their use, but these no longer remain, one having disappeared, the other now being a private house. Until the early 1960s a survival from this period, 'The Halfway House', stood a little further along the canal near Lower Bentley. The inn had existed almost solely to cater for the barge-crews using the canal and had remained unaltered since the days when it would have been one of their favourite ports of call. The one-room bar-parlour was equipped with trestles and high-backed wooden benches while decoration took the form of framed samplers and a large Victorian oil-painting entitled 'The Village School' by an artist named Townsend, though I have failed to discover if he was a local man. When I was last there it was a blisteringly hot summer's day and, although the room was as cool as a cave, I was the only customer. The landlord doubled as a chimney-sweep and, with hens clucking about the yard, no-one would have suspected that it was an inn at all unless they had happened to espy a very faded advertising sign. Since then 'The Halfway House' has been de-licensed and converted into a private house.

Tardebigge is the site of the deepest lock in England and also of one of the longest locked sections of canal, the thirty locks being known as the Tardebigge Flight. It was originally intended not to use locks at all but to bring boats up from the low land of the Severn Valley by means of a vertical lift. The lift, designed by John Woodhouse, was installed experimentally on the site of the present top-lock in 1811. It consisted of a wooden caisson—or chest—into which floated a narrow boat. The caisson was connected by pulleys and chains to counterweights in the form of wooden boxes filled with bricks and rubble. Similar chains were hung from the bottom of the caisson to counteract the effects of the suspension chains. Guillotine gates operated at each end of the caisson and at the upper end of the caisson-pit.

The lift was given a public trial between 25th February and 10th March 1811, its best performance being 110 boats in twelve hours. But the canal committee was not thoroughly convinced of its efficiency and called in John Rennie, the famous canal and bridge engineer, to give his opinion. Rennie considered that Woodhouse's lift, while obviously workable, would require a lot of maintenance due to its many moving parts. While the committee was still pondering over its final decision the lift was severely damaged by floodwaters in the aftermath of a local cloudburst. This seems to have made up the committee's mind for them. The go-ahead was given for the creation of the Tardebigge Flight and Woodhouse's lift was never repaired.

This decision to use locks instead of the vertical lift created a pressing problem in the provision of water-supply. It was later solved by the erection of a pumping-station which pumped water from a 100-foot deep well into a brick chamber on a higher level. From here it travelled via a culvert to the summit of the flight. The pump and beam engine were a Newcomen unit improved by James Watt and worked until 1914, although the construction of the Bittal reservoirs in 1832–3 had made them largely redundant for many years. In 1915 the engine and its equipment went for scrap to aid the war effort and now all that remains is the tall building beside the canal in which they were housed.

Tardebigge Wharf is still a comparatively important centre of the British Inland Waterways who maintain workshops here responsible for dealing with the upkeep of a large section of the canal. It is also one of the few places in England where the massive lock-gates are still made.

To the east of Tardebigge is Redditch, a town of relatively

recent origins which first rose to prominence in the early years of the last century. Its first tentative appearance, however, was as long ago as 1300 when, as Le Red Dych, it was included in a perambulation of Feckenham Forest as one of the many sites marking the forest boundary. A picturesque legend links the town's name with that of its village-suburb of Headless Cross and asserts that here was once fought a great battle, Le Red Dych being so called because, in the aftermath, the waters of the little River Arrow ran red with blood. It is an unlikely tale—but perhaps it does contain a vestige of truth, and a town with so little history as Redditch could do worse than cherish such legends.

For many centuries the small settlement was totally dwarfed by the importance of neighbouring Bordesley Abbey. After the abbey's dissolution it was not considered important enough to be provided with a parish church and, for more than two centuries, the inhabitants had to be content to use the gatehouse chapel of the old abbey. This gradually deteriorated to the point of near ruin and in 1805 a church was actually built in the town, later being replaced by the present parish church.

Modern Redditch, which is practically all of it, is a true off-spring of the Industrial Revolution. In the late eighteenth and early nineteenth centuries mills grew up here using the water-power of the Arrow to produce needles, nails and fish-hooks. It is still, as its local newspaper declares, the centre of the Midland needle trade. One of these old mills has recently been restored and preserved, though the industry, together with the manufacture of cycles and other light industry, is now located in the town.

Redditch is linked to Birmingham by the Barnt Green loop-line, another section of our railway system that British Rail officials alternatively declare they are closing down or going to improve. At the moment passenger facilities on the line are woe-fully inadequate, especially as Redditch is expanding rapidly as the centre of a New Town development.

North-east of Redditch is Beoley, a village which, to me, always seems to be clouded in a strange sadness—a relatively modern sadness, too, with its war memorial recalling those who fell in the Great War, and its village institute to which they never returned. Before 1914 Beoley could easily have been a maypole-dancing place, afterwards it seems a village in which no-one ever danced again.

Beoley was once the home of the Sheldon family whose mansion has long since vanished from the scene. William Sheldon was a man who anticipated some of the techniques and methods of the Industrial Revolution by more than two centuries. He was the grandson of John Sheldon of Rowley and the family originally came from northern Warwickshire where they have given their name to the Birmingham suburb that now adjoins Solihull.

It was William Sheldon who in 1509 first introduced tapestry-weaving into England at Barcheston just over the Warwickshire border. Sheldon had earlier sent his overseer William Hickes to the Low Countries on what would nowadays be described as an industrial espionage expedition. When Hickes returned, his head full of the skills he had learned from Dutch and Flemish weavers, Sheldon appointed him as master-weaver at Barcheston.

William Sheldon fought for Henry, Duke of Richmond, at the Battle of Bosworth Field and this action seems to have assured the family a permanent place in the affections of subsequent Tudor monarchs. When Bordesley Abbey was dissolved William Sheldon took it over and converted a large part of it into what amounted to a factory. Many fine and beautiful tapestries were woven here and both the workers and the Sheldons prospered.

Beoley church, whose Sheldon chapel was built at the direction of William's son Ralph, contains numerous memorials to members of the family ranging from the sixteenth to the eighteenth centuries. The Sheldon's own tapestry collection was sold at the end of the eighteenth century when the family fell on hard times. Some exhibits from it can be seen at Birmingham University's Barber Institute while others are housed in the Victoria and Albert Museum.

Not far away is Alvechurch, now threatened by proposals to build a new motorway nearby. It was once the site of the episcopal palace of the Bishops of Worcester, and described by Leland as "the byshope of Wircester's fayr manor place". It was given to the bishops as long ago as the ninth century and had earlier been in the possession of the monks of Bredon. Nothing now remains of the palace though it is possible to trace the site of its moat. The village contains many half-timbered houses, the sixteenth-century Old House, perched on a nearby hillside, being especially outstanding.

In the realms of Elizabethiana Alvechurch is something of a

frontier-post of the 'Shakespeare country' being one of those villages that the guide-books often declare the 'Bard' may have visited. The 'maybe Shakespeare was here country' takes in a large slice of the eastern portion of the county and, if all the claims are true, he was something of a marathon-champion as well as a dramatist.

Lying to the south of Redditch, on the other side of the town from Alvechurch, is the village of Ipsley. This was once involved in the iron-ore smelting industry, using timber from the forest as fuel. There are no signs of the industry today, but it is remembered in the name of Forge Meadow which lies near to the fourteenth-century church.

The manor-house here was the eighteenth-century boyhood home of the poet Walter Savage Landor. Landor was the friend of Wordsworth and Southey, though Byron, who had little that was good to say about anyone, made some particularly caustic references to him. Landor was born in 1775 and inherited Ipsley Court through his mother. Much of his youth was spent abroad and when he returned he bought an estate at Llananthony Abbey. But he never forgot Ipsley Court, which more than once crept into his verse. Although he lived into his eighties he never fitted the description of an old man for all his life he was said to have retained the attitudes and outlook of a typical English public schoolboy. Dickens is said to have based his *Bleak House* character Boythorne closely upon Landor's personality.

Ipsley was once a true forest village and the surrounding area is still well-wooded. But it was Ipsley's iron-industry, together with that of other villages, that was partly responsible for the de-forestation of the region. Feckenham Forest was once the largest area of forest land in the county, taking its name from the village standing roughly at its centre. It was from Feckenham that the main business of forest administration was conducted by the Wardens of the Forest, amongst whom in the fourteenth century was none other than Geoffrey Chaucer, having their official residence here. In medieval times the forest was badly managed, experiencing what today would be termed an ecological disaster, as trees were felled for fuel for the Droitwich salt-industry with no thought of replanting by the forest officials. The wardens were also guilty of illegally selling large tracts of forest land which was converted to agricultural use. By the close of the Middle Ages the forest timber supply was severely depleted and what remained was largely destroyed in the seventeenth century to provide for the military needs of both sides in the Civil War.

The forest region has, however, remained a wooded one, at least when compared to the nearby Forest of Arden large parts of which were probably never timbered at all. Vestiges of the former forest can be found in the great trees which line some of the existing hedgerows and in the many small woods and thickets that abound in the region. These remnants still give the area a feeling of density which is found elsewhere in the county only in the Forest of Wyre and the neighbouring slopes of the Lickey Hills.

The villages here, including that of Feckenham itself, have their origins as forest-clearings which, at first, probably consisted of no more than a primitive homestead and a few acres of laboriously-tilled land.

One such forest village is Bradley standing close to the River Himble, though this is something of a glorification for the Himble is more correctly described as a brook. Bradley is another black-and-white village, the farmhouses of Upper and Middle Bearhall being fine examples of half-timbering. Middle Bearhall was once the seat of the Hanburys and the house is a fusion of sixteenth- and seventeenth-century work. Nearby is Himbleton set at the foot of a wooded hill and almost islanded by the stream from which it takes its name.

For those who delight in black-and-white buildings a visit to the monochrome splendour of Mere Hall is a must. Here the magpie timbering can only be equalled by the contorted confusions of some of Cheshire's great houses and Mere Hall, for me at least, always conjures up pictures of that strange foray into the world of Tudor baroque, Moreton Old Hall.

The date 1377 above the entrance does not refer to the building of the Hall but to the grant of the land in that year to the Bearcroft family. The central portion is the oldest section and dates from the early sixteenth century, though some claims have been made that it is more than a century older. The section was partly reconstructed in the seventeenth century and was later enlarged by a Georgian wing and further early nineteenth-century additions.

A by-road from Himbleton leads to the three old forest villages of Warndon, Tibberton and Crowle. Warndon church, with its black-and-white timbered tower which only just tops the roof of the nave, is one of the ancient 'forest churches'. The village now stands near a junction with the M5 and has recently been developed as a suburb of Worcester.

Tibberton has suffered something of the same fate as Warndon, though here development has been of a more gradual nature. The old village now clusters around its church, which was entirely rebuilt in 1868 together with its timbered bell-turret. The main street is the chief area of new development which has brought new life to this once basically agricultural village.

Crowle was once a manor in the possession of the priors of Worcester, though nothing now remains of their manor-house which was first raised here in the thirteenth century. The main street is set on a ridge giving expansive views over the surrounding countryside and contains a mixture of black-and-white and Georgian cottages. Like its neighbour at Tibberton, Crowle church was completely rebuilt during the last century and all that now remains of the earlier building is the fourteenth-century archway incorporated into the present tower. The church does however possess a valuable treasure in the form of a marble lectern that lay abandoned in the churchyard until 1845. In that year it was brought within the church and mounted on new shafts and base. It is profusely carved with vine leaves which cover the old capitals and the lectern itself. It has been suggested that the lectern may be that which Thomas de Marleberge, Abbot of Evesham, provided for the abbey in 1216. But, if this is so, just how it came to be resting in Crowle churchyard must remain a mystery.

A little to the north is Oddingley, now sandwiched between the M5 to the west and the railway and the Birmingham–Worcester canal to the east. It is a scattered village lacking a true centre, a fact which betrays its origins as a piecemeal forest settlement which very possibly grew up from a collection of squatters' cottages. The church is another to have felt the hand of the nineteenth-century restorers, though here some fourteenth-century work was allowed to remain. But the pride of Oddingley church is the late medieval stained glass which is deservedly regarded as some of the finest of the period and, without doubt, is a wonderful possession for so small a place as this.

Oddingley lies in the heart of Gunpowder Plot country for to the west is Hindlip Hall while to the south-east is Huddington Court, both of which houses played a prominent part in the efforts to blow James I through the roof of his Parliament. Huddington Court remains much as it was in those days of well-meaning treason, but the old Hindlip Court was pulled down in the last century and replaced by the present building. Shortly before its demolition a contemporary writer described the Hall in the following terms:

> Its every room had a recess, a passage and a trap-door or secret stairs, the walls were in many places hollow, the ceiling false, several chimneys had double-flues, one for the passage of the smoke, the second for the concealment of a priest, no-one—except those immediately concerned—having key or clue to the whole maze of secrets.

Even before the Gunpowder Plot Hindlip Hall had been the centre of a conspiracy against the Crown. This earlier affair was known as the Babbington Conspiracy and aimed at the murder of Elizabeth and her replacement by Mary Stuart, Queen of Scots. Thomas Habbington had inherited Hindlip from his father and he and his brother Edward were amongst the most important people involved in the plot. The plot was ultimately discovered and both brothers were arrested, Edward being executed and Thomas spending six years in the Tower.

But Thomas remained pro-Catholic and upon his return to Hindlip he employed Nicholas Owen, a local carpenter, to construct the hides which were soon to turn the Hall into a haven of refuge for persecuted priests. Nicholas Owen led a busy life in Worcestershire. His hides were designed in a distinctive manner and, besides those at Hindlip, he also worked on those at Harvington Hall and nearby Huddington Court.

When the Gunpowder Plot failed Father Henry Garnett and Father John Oldcastle took refuge at Hindlip. Soldiers were twelve days searching the house and would probably never have found the two priests who were forced to surrender themselves due to a mixture of hunger and lack of air in their cramped hiding places.

Thomas Habbington had remained aloof from the plot—though he had been sympathetic to its aims. But, in the panic of the time, he was arrested along with the others for concealing traitors. He would probably have been executed on this charge if it had not been for the intervention of Lord Monteagle, one of the king's advisers. But Habbington was not to escape entirely without punishment. He had already been involved in one plot against the Crown and here he was on the fringes of another. James I seems to have considered that he was too dangerous a man to be allowed to move freely about the country, probably helping to foster further conspiracies. Thomas Habbington was therefore forbidden to leave the boundaries of his native Worcestershire and the remaining forty years of his life were to be spent entirely within the county. These years he devoted to investigating the history of the county, many of his notes being published during his lifetime. His work has been extensively used by later historians and Dr Treadaway Nashe, Worcestershire's eighteenth-century historian, was particularly indebted to him.

In the nineteenth century the manor came into the ownership of the Allsopp family and, in modern times, has become the headquarters first of the Worcestershire Constabulary and, more recently, of the West Mercia Constabulary. It is now conspicuous, not so much for its turrets, but for the mass of radio-communication masts that have sprung from them.

Huddington Court was once the home of the Hodingtons, in the mid-fifteenth century coming into the possession of the Wyntour family. The mansion is built in classical Elizabethan style in the shape of a T and incorporates some building from the preceding century. The Court is moated and within the grounds are two dovecotes, one standing on the lawn at the approach to the house.

Huddington was the home of Thomas Wyntour and it was here that he discussed with his cousin Robert Catesby and the other plotters just how they would rid Catholic England of King and Parliament at one explosive blow. Huddington was almost certainly the headquarters of the conspiracy and was the centre of the activities of Father Garnett, who is now considered to have master-minded the plot. When their plot to dispense with James and his Parliament with the aid of four tons of gunpowder was discovered Catesby, the Wyntour brothers and the other conspirators hid here for a time before deciding to make their dash into Staffordshire and their final stand at Holbeach House. This was to have been a death and glory affair but, fording the River

Danzey Green Mill and Temple Broughton Granary at the
Avoncroft Museum of Buildings
Chateau Impney, Droitwich

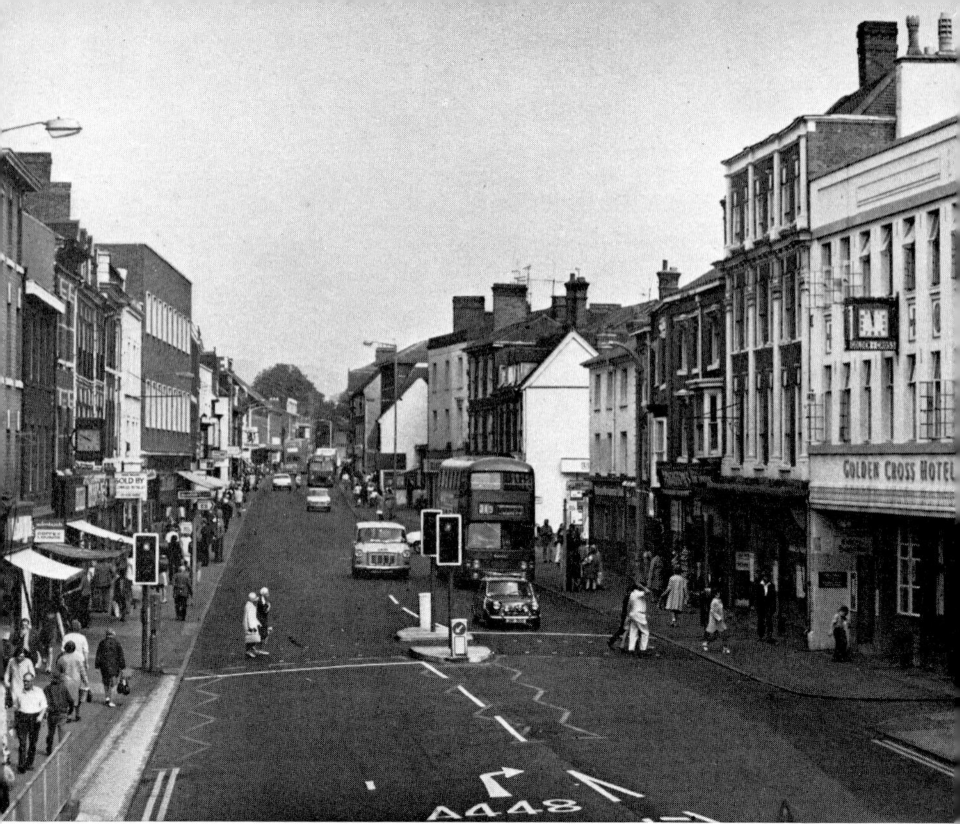
GOLDEN CROSS HOTEL
SOLD BY
A448

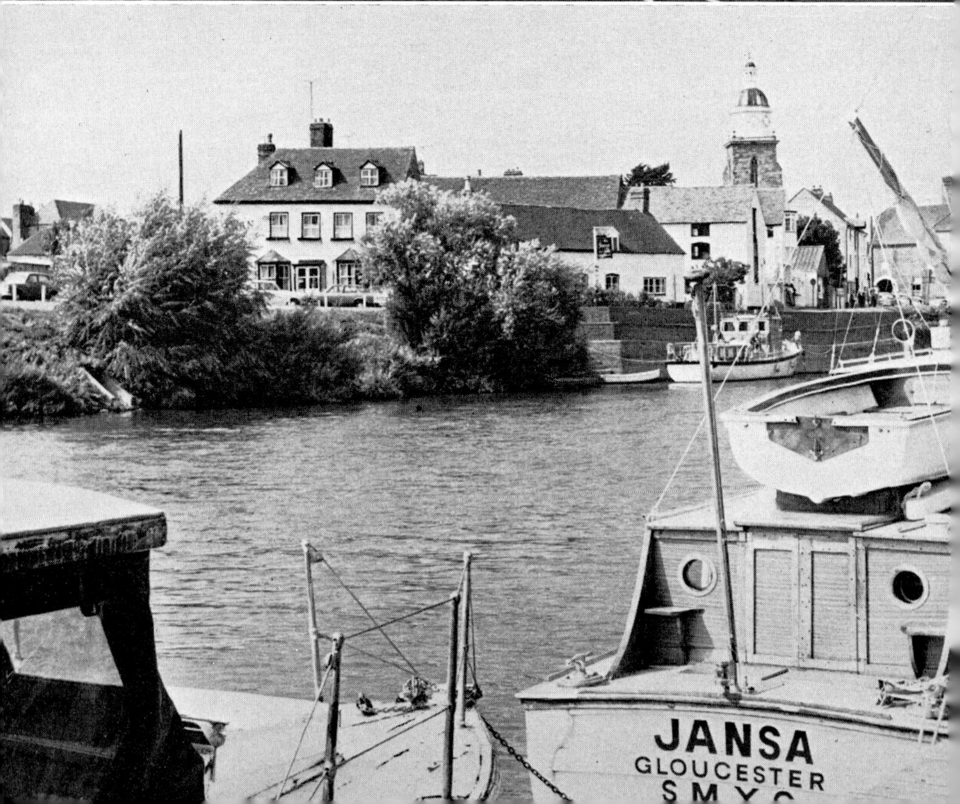
JANSA
GLOUCESTER

Stour, the fugitives' gunpowder became wet. Trying to dry it out at Holbeach it blew up in their faces and Catesby and Rookwood were seriously injured. By the time the skirmish took place with men led by Sir Richard Walsh, the Sheriff of Worcestershire, most of the fight had gone out of the conspirators and their lot was to be the inevitable journey to London and execution.

Unlike many churches in the region that at Huddington largely escaped the attention of the nineteenth-century restorer. The building dates largely from the fourteenth century, but two Norman doorways survive from the time of its original foundation. Within are monuments to the Wyntours, but much else is older still, the font alone dating from the thirteenth century.

Both the delightfully named villages of Grafton Flyford and Flyford Flavell lie on the Worcester–Stratford road which points a well-worn finger through this southern section of the forest region. Grafton Flyford is the projected centre of a new village which, it is planned, will have the thirteenth-century village church as its centre point. The church, occupying a small hill off the main road, has a battlemented tower, topped by what must be the most diminutive of church spires.

Flyford Flavell is more compact than its somewhat straggling neighbour. An avenue of cypresses leads to the oak porch of the church which, like that at Grafton, stands on a slight elevation. The church was drastically restored in the last century and most of it dates from that time. Like so many other churches it once possessed a churchyard cross, but this was destroyed at the Reformation and now only its base is to be seen.

From the point of view of its church at least Dormston has fared better than Flyford Flavell and may consider itself fortunate to have escaped the Victorian standardization of so many rural churches. Dormston church is one of the original 'forest churches' with a gabled, half-timbered tower erected in the fifteenth century, though over the years it has been in danger of becoming a local rival to that of Pisa, for it has developed something of a list. The elms amid which the church stands are at the present time threatened with the virus known as 'Dutch elm disease' and which has already wrought so much havoc among the county's woodlands. The effects of the disease are much more apparent in the former forest region for, of those trees that have survived from afforested times, the elm has been the predominant species.

Bromsgrove High Street
Quayside, Upton on Severn

It would seem that Dormston's church has probably suffered from the effects of geological faulting for not only is the tower out of alignment but the windows in its fourteenth-century nave are also at a list. Part of the old churchyard cross has been built into the chancel wall and on the wall of the nave survive fragments of medieval wall-painting. The roof timbers have queen-posts and the ancient font still has the staple-holes which once secured the font-cover.

Nearby is gabled Moat Farm with the date 1663 carved upon its timbering. There is a timber-framed dovecote here and there are two others at Bag End Farm, eloquent reminders of the days when fresh meat was virtually unobtainable in the winter months and when doves were kept as much-prized delicacies for the table.

Kington, like many villages in the more immediate neighbourhood of Worcester, has been the scene of considerable development in recent years. But this cannot be said to have marred the old village which, like Dormston, is proud of its possession of a 'forest church'. The fifteenth-century half-timbered bell-tower stands upon a stone base. Although the church was the subject of some restoration work, parts of the thirteenth-century nave and chancel survive and the pulpit contains fragments of the medieval rood screen.

Close to the Warwickshire border lies Abbots Morton, a small black-and-white timbered village which, although it stands at the eastern extremity of the county, is typical of rural Worcestershire. The church dates from Norman times and more than once gave sanctuary to the villagers in the distant days when Feckenham Forest was the home of outlaws. In fact, most of the forest villages were attacked by outlaw bands with almost monotonous regularity for, judging by the records that have survived, almost a third of the county's medieval population once lived outside the law. In those times many a man charged with an offence seems to have decided that, rather than turn up for trial, he would evade the law and the forest proved a perfect haven. After a time he would be legally declared an outlaw—which really meant that he could not be found. Banding themselves together these fugitives from justice lived a predatory existence, raiding the forest villages in war-parties sometimes up to a hundred strong. Accounts of these events make this area of the county appear like some local version of the later Wild West.

At Abberton, which lies a little way to the south-west of Abbots Morton, the church once had a spire which was known as a landmark for miles around. However, the spire has been removed at the request of the RAF who considered it presented a hazard to aircraft using RAF Pershore. Both village and church stand upon a hill, the church occupying the highest point. The old church which once occupied this site was demolished in the last century and the present building was erected in 1881, many of the stones used being from the former church.

A by-road from Abberton leads to Naunton Beauchamp which, like so many villages in the area, now stands amid orchard country. Even though the ancient forest is now largely a thing of the past the wooded landscape remains, though now it is more commonly composed of the regular rows of fruit trees than of the broad oaks and tangled thickets of primeval forest. Naunton Beauchamp is another of the county's half-timbered villages and possesses a rare treasure in the half-timbered Naunton Court. The Court is a splendid example of an Elizabethan manor-house and, unlike its peer at Huddington, is designed in the shape of an L. The house was once the home of a branch of the Lyttleton family and within the village church is a tablet commemorating Sir Humphrey Lyttleton who died in 1624. The tablet declared that Humphrey had earlier arranged a tomb for himself and his first wife at Kings Norton "long ere he gasped forth his dying breath". But when Humphrey died his second wife seems to have taken umbrage at Humphrey's previous arrangement and decided that he should be buried at Naunton.

The church stands close by a small brook fringed by willow trees. It was largely rebuilt in the eighteenth century and is none the worse for that, for eighteenth-century restorers did their work with taste and style. The fifteenth-century tower, however, remains, its buttresses carrying the remnants of medieval carvings which have weathered to the point where they can no longer be properly identified.

Nearby are the small villages of North Piddle and Bishampton both of whose churches were heavily restored last century. North Piddle lost its ancient manor-house more than two centuries ago and in a field near the church are the remains of a long-dry moat which is all that now marks the former site.

Upton Snodsbury, lying west along the Worcester–Stratford

road, is a name which many authors have conjured with. The village skirts the main road, but its true centre lies around the church which is neighboured, in almost obligatory Worcestershire fashion, by a group of black-and-white cottages. The manor here was once in the ownership of the Lyttletons but the half-timbered house, lying a little distance from the church, is now a farm almost surrounded by later buildings. A pun on the Lyttleton name is to be found within the church where one of the capitals of the arcade has been decorated with a small barrel—a little tun. A Restoration chest is carved with the names of the church-wardens on its top, the artist evidently mis-spelling one of these worthies and not bothering to remove the evidence of his correction.

From Upton Snodsbury a by-lane leads almost directly south between wooded hedgerows to Peopleton, which has the restored remnant of a 'forest church'. In the last century the original timber-framed tower was replaced by a brick one and the overall effect of this is by no means discordant. The main building dates from the thirteenth century and the priests' doorway from this time remains with its oak lintel. Indeed the timbering within the church, as with so many in the forest region, speaks eloquently of the forest's former glory. But even if timber were somehow miraculously to again become a major building material it is very much to be doubted if the craftsmanship of the carpenters of those days could be restored as well.

Within the church is a monument to Mark Dineley who bought the manor of Peopleton in 1682 and, having moved in, died in the same year. Another Dineley was rector here for 58 years and died at the age of 93. Both these men were ancestors of the Dineley-Goodere brothers who both came to a rather sticky end in the eighteenth century in the affair which has entered local history as the 'Charlton Fratricide'.

South of Peopleton, on the Worcester–Evesham road, is Drakes Broughton, a scattering of houses, mostly nineteenth-century cottages and modern houses, strung out along the main road. Drakes Broughton hardly ranks as a village at all, but it is set amid some of the finest orchard country on the edge of the Vale of Evesham and some of the best plums in the county are grown about here.

White Ladies Aston was once known as Aston Episcopi. This

was back in the dim days before the thirteenth century since when most English place-names have undergone more than a little alteration. From then until the Dissolution it was in the possession of the Worcester Cistercian Nunnery of Whitstones, the nuns being the White Ladies of the present name. During the Civil War Cromwell—making a pleasant change from King Charles—stayed here on the eve of the Battle of Worcester. His host was an old friend named Symonds and some years later Thomas Symonds, of the same family, carved out an unenviable reputation for himself as a local gangster and thief. Upon his eventual execution his estate was forfeit to Bishop Lloyd of Worcester, who put Symonds' ill-gotten gains into trust for the education of needy children.

One of White Ladies' past vicars holds the record for the longest ministry in Worcestershire. H. M. Sherwood is commemorated within the Norman church by a brass recalling that he ministered here for seventy-one years, living to the age of 99.

Almost running into White Ladies on the north is Churchill—not to be confused with the other Worcestershire village of the name which lies just off the Kidderminster–Birmingham road. Its church stands on a small hill and dates largely from the fourteenth century, though much restoration has been carried out. A tombstone in its churchyard recalls the panic-stricken days of the French Revolution for it states that:

Here reposd the bodies of English nuns of the Order of Poor Clares, who, when banished from Dunkirk by the fury of the French Revolution, about 1792, found a refuge at Churchill.

Also buried here are their chaplain and a priest who accompanied them from France. At Churchill the nuns lived at Manor Farm, which was lent to them by Robert Berkeley of Spetchley. On the farmhouse roof is a brick and timber dovecote containing more than six hundred holes for the birds. The birds from this and other dovecotes must have created havoc with the crops of local farmers who heartily detested the dovecotes maintained by the large landowners.

Nearby is Broughton Hackett, once in the possession of the abbots of Westminster and to the west, on the Stratford–Worcester road, is Spetchley. Spetchley Park has been the home of the Berkeley family for more than three centuries and before this it was associated with Sir Thomas Lyttleton. The first of the Berkeleys to hold Spetchley was Rowland Berkeley who bought the manor from Phillip Sheldon in the late sixteenth century. But the most famous member of this family was Rowland's son, Robert, who was to become a judge and to support Charles I in the Crown's case against John Hampden's refusal to pay Ship Money. Such sympathies made him many enemies in this bitter time and three years later he was impeached by Parliament for "endevouring to . . . introduce an arbitrary and tyranical government against law". Parliament was determined to have its revenge on the man it considered had so barbarously treated Hampden and Judge Berkeley was deprived of his office, ordered to pay a fine of £20,000 and lodged in the Tower until it was paid. He may have been destined to stay there for a very long time if it had not been for Parliament being in need of ready cash to subsidize the army of its ally, the Scottish Covenanters. Berkeley was released after only six weeks upon his promise to pay half of his fine there and then. He was now fated to live the rest of his life in retirement—but it was hardly to be a pleasant one. Cromwell's men used the house as a garrison and practically destroyed the rest of the village. Later it was captured by the Royalists who, deciding they could not afford to hold it, burnt it to the ground to prevent it again being used by the Roundheads. When Judge Berkeley returned to Spetchley he found his house gutted and the village a wasteland and was compelled to live out the few years left to him in what remained of his stables. The present house is a Regency mansion built in 1810 with a massive Ionic portico. It is approached by a mile-long avenue of elms which are under dire threat from Dutch elm disease.

Numerous Berkeley monuments are housed in the fourteenth-century church, two brass plates from the last century, resplendant with heraldic art, depicting Robert Berkeley (who died in 1897) kneeling at prayer with his wife while his predecessor, another Robert, is also kneeling at prayer, his arms resting on his mantle. But the Berkeley most splendidly commemorated here is that Rowland Berkeley who was the first of the family to make his home at Spetchley. Rowland and his wife Katherine lie beneath an arched canopy supported by pillars and emblazoned with coats of arms. The effigy of Rowland is clad in doublet and breeches and at his feet lies a bear.

On the outskirts of Worcester, Whittington forms a triangle with nearby Spetchley by its position on the Worcester–Evesham road. The nineteenth-century church is attractive, as indeed most nineteenth-century churches are. The Victorians knew how to build churches from scratch, but their ideas of restoring old ones tended to verge on the disastrous.

The dominant landmark here is Crookbarrow Hill, site of an ancient British camp and standing alongside this stretch of road. The Romans apparently made use of it after dispelling its Celtic inhabitants, for Roman coins have been unearthed here. It is possible that they fortified the site, but it is more likely that they used it as an observation post providing a signal link between Worcester and their riverside camp at Kempsey.

A mile or so on from Whittington is Stoulton sitting astride the main road and lying amid rich orchard country. The church is largely Norman with Norman walls, two Norman doorways, a tub font and an imposing chancel arch. Members of the Acton family are commemorated here and the family has been associated with the village since 1585. Stoulton was the birthplace of William Derham who was chaplain to George II and a Fellow of the Royal Society. He was evidently a man of wide interests for he wrote books on theology, natural history and mechanics.

A lane to the right leading from the Worcester–Evesham road leads first to Wadborough and then to Pirton. The latter is a scattered village straddling a number of lanes. The church stands on a hill removed from the main village and has a conspicuous black-and-white Tudor tower. Some of the walling of the old Norman tower which it replaced remains at the east end of the nave. At the other end of the village is Pirton Court, a long, half-timbered building which is one of the most outstanding examples of half-timbering to be found in this part of the county.

Following Pirton's lanes through the hamlet of Clifton leads first to the Worcester–Gloucester road and then to the Severnside village of Kempsey. Lying so close to the main road into Worcester it is not surprising that, of recent years, the village has attracted the attentions of the property developer so that Kempsey is now, in common with many other Worcestershire villages, really in two parts. The new development is strung largely along and off the main road whilst the old village is centred around the church above the Severn. Positioned along a small lane the church stands on a small rise and is relatively remote from the clangour of the nearby road, whose traffic has now reached a level higher than that known before the construction of the M5. The church stands partly on the site of an early British earthwork which was subsequently used by the Romans, one relic of those times which has been discovered here being a stone inscribed to the Emperor Constantine.

It was at Kempsey church that Simon de Montfort and his prisoner Henry III came to hear mass on the morning before the fateful Battle of Evesham, though it is doubtful if de Montfort would recognize much of the present building for the church has been twice restored in more recent centuries. The night before de Montfort had stayed at Kempsey as guest of his ally Bishop Cantelupe.

A tree figured in Kempsey's local fame in the last century. A choirboy, so the story goes, decided to munch a chestnut during service, but was unfortunate enough to be spotted by the parish clerk. Evidently quite put out by this irreligious behaviour the clerk seized the offending chestnut and threw it so that it came to rest behind the tomb of Sir Edmund Wylde. The clerk obviously did not bother to retrieve it later for, in time, a chestnut tree was to grow from a crevice behind the tomb and, for more than ninety years, it continued to blossom and leaf within the church.

Buried here is Sir Richard Temple, once Governor of Bombay in the days before the British Empire entered the league of lost civilizations.

The church also contains an eighteenth-century riddle tablet set in the wall which reads:

Underneath the corruptible parts of a vicar, one husband, two helpmeets, both wives and both Anns, a triplicity of persons in two twain but one flesh, are interred.

Nearby is Court Farm, an L-shaped Elizabethan house, its porch having an overhead room. Half-timbered Manor Farm is partly medieval with a rectangular, timber-framed dovecote.

At the Ketch Inn Samuel Butler is said to have written part of his satirical masterpiece *Hudibras*. This reach of the Severn was once busy with traffic moving to and from Bristol. That sort of commercial activity is now of the past, but Kempsey is now the home of the Severn Yacht Club and still seems to maintain its links with the days of sail.

It must be said that Kempsey and the nearby villages do not really lie within the bounds of the former forest of Feckenham. They were, however, forest villages with an origin and pattern of life little different from that of their Feckenham neighbours, though here the forest was that of Horewell whose boundary with the southern extent of Feckenham was never clearly defined. Deforestation here was occasioned, apart from the gradual spread of husbandry, largely by the requirements of Severn boat-building and not so markedly by the expansion of industry which was greatly responsible for the eventual denuding of Feckenham.

As I have mentioned earlier the forest took its name from the village standing roughly at its centre and it was here that its administration was centred.

Almost alone of the forest villages Feckenham benefited by the extension of the forest area in the reign of Henry II. At this time the forest was extended to cover almost a quarter of the county and the application of the stringent forest laws meant that many villages were drastically depopulated, some ceasing to exist completely. But, Feckenham itself, as the centre of the enlarged forest, expanded as a direct result of the depopulation of its neighbours.

There are few vestiges of Feckenham's former importance to be seen today, though on the south-west side of the church are the remains of the ditch which once surrounded the prison in which offenders against the forest laws were housed. The now-vanished prison must once have been quite a crowded place for the laws forbade not only the hunting of royal game within the forest but also, amongst a host of other things, the gathering of any but fallen timber, the grazing of pigs or cattle on forest ground, the ownership of a dog which had not been rendered incapable of hunting, the tilling of forest land or the erection or extension of a house without the prior permission of the forest wardens. But even the ferocious forest laws could not protect Feckenham. Corrupt officials enclosed large tracts for agriculture and sold off timber to supply fuel for the local iron-smelting and for the Droitwich salt industry so that, in the absence of any policy of regular replanting, the forest area continued to contract throughout much of the later Middle Ages.

The once-great forest had largely disappeared by the time that

Feckenham's greatest son, John de Feckenham, was appointed by Queen Mary to be the last Abbot of Westminster. He had been educated at the monastery of Evesham and, after the Dissolution, was domestic Chaplain first to the Bishop of Worcester and later to the Bishop of London. In this time of religious upheaval John de Feckenham remained a firm Catholic, being imprisoned by both Henry VIII and Elizabeth I for those religious convictions which, in the reign of Mary, made him one of the most powerful clerics in England. But John de Feckenham was not a man who was interested in power for its own sake and, in an age of great religious strife and bigotry, he was outstanding for his tolerance and humanity. Entrusted with the task of reconverting many Protestants to the Catholic faith, he was moved by pity to intercede for those who found it impossible to renounce their beliefs and undoubtedly saved a great number of his fellow men from the stake.

After the accession of Elizabeth he spent many years in prison, but was later released and allowed to spend his remaining years ministering to the poor. In these later years he did not confine himself to religious matters but also offered medical aids to those in need. A manuscript in the Sloan collection is prefaced with the following:

> This book of sovereign medicines against the most common and known diseases, both of men and women, was by good proof and long experience, collected by Mr De Fickmann, late Abbot of Westminster, and that chiefly for the poor, which hath not at all times the learned physicians at hand.

John de Feckenham died in 1585 and perhaps his best epitaph is to be found in the words of a contemporary writer who states that he was "stout and round-faced, of pleasant countenance; his manners affable, his charity to the poor acknowledged by all".

At Feckenham a portrait of Abbot John forms a window of the twelfth-century church. This received a visit from the Victorian restorers who were not so zealous as to remove the traces of some medieval murals which still remain on the thirteenth-century arcade. Within the church is an inscription to Martin Culpeper who died in 1604 having lived at the nearby moated Astwood Court.

To the east of Feckenham are ruins which recall the days of

religious ferment in which Abbot John lived. These are the ruins of the Cistercian Nunnery of Cookhill, standing close to the Warwickshire border. Founded in the thirteenth century, the nunnery was another of Worcestershire's religious houses that fell under the heavy hammer of Thomas Cromwell's commissioners. In 1783, the chapel, which is substantially all that remains of the former building, was rebuilt and most of the original structure was replaced. However, some of the original walling remains and within is an alabaster Assumption dating back to the fourteenth century.

Close by is the drowsy village of Inkberrow where the harassed Charles I left his maps on his way to the disastrous Battle of Naseby. Charles spent a restless night at the village vicarage and the incident is one more reminder that Worcestershire was, more than any other part of England, the real heartland of the Civil War. Local legend has it that Inkberrow is the home of the Arkubs, of whom modern preservationists would seem to stand in need. The Arkubs are the reputed guardians of Inkberrow church and when, in 1840, it was decided to rebuild the church on a different site they are said to have frustrated the efforts of the workmen by moving the building materials to the old site under cover of darkness. This they did so persistently that it was eventually decided to rebuild the church on its original site. Unfortunately they do not seem to have been heard of since and there is little likelihood of pressing them into service to remove a few shopping precincts and grain silos as well.

On the other side of Feckenham from Inkberrow both Hanbury and Hadzor are forest villages, the latter now tending to link up with Droitwich. Hanbury Hall was once the home of the vanished Vernons, many of whom are commemorated in the Norman church. The 'z' in the name of Hadzor always seems reminiscent of similar Cornish names, but it would appear to be a relatively modern mutation for I have seen old maps where the village name was more usually spelt as Hadsor. Both Hanbury and Hadzor still stand amidst woodland and a road from Hanbury leads southward to the Domesday village of Shell.

These three villages stand close to the outskirts of modern Droitwich, the town which was so largely responsible for Feckenham's gradual fall from greatness. The importance of Feckenham declined in direct relationship to the withering of its forest and it was the furnaces of Droitwich that, from Roman times and probably even earlier, almost literally ate the forest away.

Domesday records show that Droitwich was, even in Saxon times, an industrial rather than an agricultural centre, its salt-pans providing salt for manors throughout the Midlands and, in some instances, as far south as Buckinghamshire. Because salt-production required such vast amounts of timber as fuel, the industry, in medieval times, was confined to a relatively small number of centres in an attempt to conserve the national timber supply. Droitwich, or Wyche as it was anciently called, was one of the few towns allowed by royal licence to involve itself in the industry.

Just when salt was first discovered in the valley of the Salwarpe is not known, but its existence was certainly well known to the Romans. Fragments of Roman pottery and pavements have been unearthed in the town as well as innumerable Roman coins. Although the Romans well knew the medicinal advantages of brine-baths it is rather unlikely that they established anything at Droitwich that resembled the splendours of Bath. Whereas Bath was a social and administrative centre Droitwich was a purely industrial one, its Roman population being almost entirely composed of a few legionaries and officers who heartily detested being posted to this remote area of the countryside to supervise the labours of a group of disgruntled and sweaty Celts.

Succeeding the Romans the Saxons normally left Roman things well alone, even to the extent of siting their villages away from the roads their predecessors had laboriously established. But salt was one thing that the Saxons could not do without and as early as 717 a Saxon charter mentions 'Saltwic', a name which is identifiable with Droitwich. They also made use of the old Salt Way to transport the salt southward, and this is a road which was probably a well-used highway in days long before either Saxon or Roman came to the region.

The town was well established by the reign of Edward the Confessor, with three hundred salt houses occupying this part of the Salwarpe valley, and secured a borough charter as early as the twelfth century. It was Edward III who was responsible for the town being prefixed with the word 'Droit' to demonstrate that it was authorized by royal licence for the manufacture of salt.

In the thirteenth century one of the town's three principle salt-springs is reputed to have dried up and was not restored to production until Richard de la Wyche, Bishop of Chichester, made a spiritual intercession. After this the Droitwich salt-workers annually celebrated the event by hanging banners at the well and generally giving the day over to festivities.

Richard de la Wyche is commemorated in the chantry chapel of St Andrews Church. As his name implies he was born at Droitwich and after his death he was canonized. During the time that he was Bishop of Chichester he led a life of great simplicity and, after his death, it was found that he was clad in horsehair bound about him by iron bands. But the most striking memorial to Droitwich's St Richard to be found in the town is in the Roman Catholic church of the Sacred Heart and St Catherine which stands to the south-west of the old town. The church is a splendid example of Italianate architecture and within the walls are covered by brilliant Venetian mosaics. Somehow this startling decoration seems to suit the church but, despite the fact that most English churches were once considerably decorated, I do not feel that such elaborate art would now transplant well to the majority of older churches. The English tradition in such matters has for too long been one of austerity for such a radical change to find a general acceptance. But, with modern church buildings, the example offered by this Droitwich church could perhaps be followed with profit. Too often modern churches do little more than reflect the urban environments in which they are largely built, an environment of uniformity where buildings are reduced to the most economic of geometric lines. In such places a church with a beautiful interior could act as something of a counterpoise to the functionalism of the everyday world.

In the sixteenth century Leland recorded that at Droitwich

There be at this present tyme 3 salt springs in the towne of Wiche, whereof the principall is within a but shot of the right ripe [bank] of the river that there cummithe downe; and this springe is double as profitable in yeldynge of salte liquer as bothe the other.

At the time of the Civil War the town opted for the Royalist cause and was attacked and partly destroyed by the Roundheads, much to the advantage of its Parliamentarian rivals at Nantwich. Originally the brine reached the surface via natural springs but in the early eighteenth century the first of a number of bores were made and the brine pumped up from below ground. This had the effect of increasing both the quality and the quantity of pure salt obtained but it also created underground caverns of considerable size beneath the town. These, in time, led to a sinking of parts of the town so that many houses have now been affected by subsidence, one in High Street being aptly known as the Crooked House.

It was the salt-trade which, in 1767, led to the construction of the Salwarpe Canal linking the town to Bristol via the Severn and later to Birmingham. Much of the salt carried on this canal came from the salt-grinding mills set up along the little River Salwarpe, some of which still remain though converted to other uses.

Aside from its ancient connection with the salt-industry Droitwich is also known as a health resort and first developed as a spa town following an epidemic of cholera in 1832. Various treatments were prescribed, amongst which was the frequent use of hot baths. These had some success, but were generally beyond the reach of the town's poor, who decided to take hot baths of their own by bathing in the hot brine of the salt vats. These proved even more curative than the hot bathing in normal water recommended by the town's doctors and it was from this modest and accidental beginning that Droitwich's fame as a spa town can be said to date.

The Royal Baths were opened in 1836, in the last year of William IV, the 'Sailor King', and it was largely due to the later work of John Corbett that their facilities were extended and that Droitwich ultimately changed from an industrial town almost exclusively concerned with salt-production to one whose main functions were those of a well-patronized spa.

Of Droitwich buildings which pre-date the spa-revolution pride of place must go, I think, to St Peter's Church which lies to the south of the town. Here, in the eighteenth century, its rector was Dr Treadaway Nashe, whose *History of Worcestershire* ran to two very bulky volumes. Within the originally Norman church, which is now a fusion of many architectural styles, are memorials to the Wyldes and to the Nashes who succeeded them as lords of the manor.

An entry in the parish register records the birth, in 1595, of Edward Winslow, leader of the *Mayflower* pilgrims and is all that this remarkable man possesses by way of memorial in his native town. Winslow was the first governor of the New England colony of New Plymouth and his son Peregrine was the first white child to be born in New England. Although the New England was essentially isolated from the mother-country Winslow returned to England a number of times, largely on trading missions. At the close of the Civil War he came to England to hold office under the Commonwealth, in which he primarily concerned himself with colonial matters. In 1655 he was the head of the Commonwealth Commission sent to the West Indies, but he died on the voyage and was buried at sea. In many ways Edward Winslow could be regarded as the architect of England's first Colonial Empire and it is surprising that his native town has made no effort to honour, however belatedly, one of her most famous sons.

The church at Dodderhill, now a suburb to the north of the town, is positioned on a hilltop. The walls of its tower are more than six feet thick and are said to have been so solidly built as a precaution against subsidence which was thought to have caused the toppling of the former tower in 1700. Nearby is Chateau Impney, now a restaurant and conference centre, but originally built in 1869 at the direction of John Corbett for his French wife who desired to live in something that reminded her of home. It was modelled on one of the Loire *châteaux* and designed by a leading Parisian architect. It was in this rather eccentric mansion that John Corbett lived whilst he was revolutionizing the town's ancient trade.

Corbett was to be called 'The Salt King' in his own lifetime and it was he who was responsible for the greatest expansion in the local industry. But it was also as a result of his rationalization of the trade that salt ceased to be produced in the old town, the industry being relocated at his new works at Stoke Prior.

Corbett was born at Brierley Hill, Staffordshire in 1817 and his first venture into the world of commerce involved the acquisition and running of a small fleet of canal boats. It was not until 1852 that he moved in on the Droitwich salt-workings having developed a greatly improved method of extracting the brine using improved boring techniques. As the Droitwich brine springs had been used almost continually for more than a thousand years it was decided to site the new Corbett borings nearer to the source of their supply to obtain a mineral of greater quality. The new borings were so successful that it now became only a matter of time for the industry to be run-down at Droitwich and re-established at Stoke Prior, a process which, however, was not finally effected until 1922.

Partly in compensation for depriving the town of its ancient industry Corbett now turned his efforts to expanding Droitwich as a spa-centre and, amongst other things, improved the facilities at the Royal Baths and built the now-demolished Salters' Hall. It is to Corbett that the town owes much of its present appearance for, with the spa established by the latter decades of the last century, the architects moved in to graft a new town of villas and hotels on to the older settlement. Other Worcestershire towns to benefit by the 'Salt King's' generosity were Bromsgrove and Stourbridge where he provided the money for new hospitals while he also contributed substantial funds to Birmingham's new university. Corbett later moved to Towyn, where he was largely responsible for providing the funds that went to making the sea-wall and esplanade.

Not far from Chateau Impney the straggling village of Wychbold lies athwart the main Worcester–Birmingham road. The site of the original Domesday manor is now the location of the BBC's long-wave station, Radio 2, and, in the thirties, in the hey-day of what was then almost universally referred to as a wireless, programmes were actually put out from here.

A little further along the road a lane leads off to Upton Warren where the River Salwarpe edges close to a Norman church which was heavily restored in the eighteenth century. Within is a memorial to John Sanders who bequeathed ten pounds a year so that those poor boys of the village who had somehow found the time to learn to read and write, could be sent to London as apprentices where, hopefully, they could take their first steps to fame and fortune. Part of the present village once formed the separate manor of Cookesey. The manor-house seems to have been replaced in the seventeenth century by the black-and-white timbered Badger Court which was once the home of the Wyntours and like the manor-house at nearby Grafton has associations with the Gunpowder Plot.

The Staffords of Grafton have already been met with in connection with Bromsgrove. Before their day the manor was given by

Malvern Priory Church

the Conqueror to the freebooting Urso d'Abitot and, in much later times passed to Sir Gilbert Talbot as part of his reward for backing Henry Tudor at the Battle of Bosworth. In the eighteenth century the house was considerably rebuilt and enlarged but a lot of the earlier work was retained so that it is now a mixture of styles running from Tudor to Georgian times. Although the eighteenth century witnessed a positive craze for the razing of old English manor-houses in favour of the creation of Classical palaces the Talbots of Grafton were not guilty of succumbing to this fashionable passion for ostentation and the house would probably have remained unaltered if it had not been for a disastrous fire which gutted a large section of it in 1710.

A chapel has existed here since at least the thirteenth century for, in 1218, the tithes of Grafton Chapel were used to provide for the maintenance of the candles around the tomb of King John at Worcester Cathedral. The roof of a subsequent chapel near to the manor-house was destroyed in the fire of 1710, but the walling and the west bellcote still survive.

Grafton and Upton Warren can still stake some claim to being rural villages but nearby Stoke Prior cannot for, from the middle years of the last century, this was the centre of the Worcester-shire salt trade. Of course, Stoke Prior did not owe its creation entirely to John Corbett who sited his salt-works on the edge of the village. As long ago as the eighth century the manor had been granted to the church of Worcester and there has been a church here since Norman times. Within is a window commemorating Corbett's action in forbidding the employment of women and girls at the brine pits. In an age when women were still working in the mines and at the ironstone quarries of Staffordshire this was little short of a revolutionary step and was probably resented by many of the women who now had no way of adding to the family income. Stoke Prior also had a sixteenth century 'man of fortune' of its own for within the church is commemorated Robert Smith who left the village to become a merchant and citizen of London and was later to marry the daughter of the Lord Mayor of London.

Corbett's Stoke Prior works echoed his concern for the condition of England's nineteenth-century workers. He built model houses for his workers, provided them with on-site baths and showers, reading and recreation rooms and a school for both

Tenbury Wells Pump Room
Edgar Gateway, Worcester

adults and children. There was also a club-house and lecture room and a dispensary where treatment was provided free of charge almost a hundred years before the introduction of the National Health Service. Corbett was so well loved that when he returned to the village after a long absence in the 1860s he was carried shoulder-high to the works by his employees.

But Corbett was a businessman as well as a philanthropist. By the use of improved techniques he increased the output of salt from 26,000 tons per annum to over 200,000 tons within a period of 25 years. It was the work of Corbett that was partially responsible for salt ceasing to be almost a luxury item and becoming instead a cheap everyday commodity that was within the reach of all.

In later years, however, the output of the Stoke Prior works was severely restricted for Corbett sold out his interest to the Salt Union which exercised a virtual monopoly of salt manufacture throughout England. This may have been an error on the old 'Salt King's' part, for he would not himself have allowed the high unemployment which followed the implementation of the Salt Union's policies. In Droitwich an attempt was made to reopen one of the old brine springs, but the Salt Union had a stranglehold on the town and local initiative was no match for the great monopoly which successfully resisted the efforts to revive the industry in the town. But, by then, the great days of John Corbett were past and he, along with the other great men who have left their mark on the county, was already passing into history. Whether Chateau Impney or the Stoke Prior salt-works are his greatest memorial must depend entirely upon one's point of view.

VIII

MALVERN CHASE

SOUTH-WEST of Worcester the county was once largely forest land which passed under the general name of Malvern Chase. The Chase extended roughly from the eastern slopes of the Malvern Hills to the west bank of the Severn, although across the river much of the eastern bank was also forest land, being part of the royal forest of Horewell which ran in a dense wedge from Worcester to Tewkesbury.

Indeed, in medieval times the county was one of the largest afforested shires in England. Not until the Tudor period did it begin to assume its present pastoral character which makes it, for me at least, the most typically and traditionally English of all our counties.

As was the case with early settlements in Feckenham Forest those in Malvern Chase had their beginnings as little more than woodland clearings. But settlement here was slower than in the Feckenham region for not only was it impeded by the operation of the harsh Forest Laws but also because the nearby Severn was a tidal river with an ill-defined channel. Large areas on both sides of the river were for long an uninhabited region of salt-marsh frequented only by the occasional wild-fowlers who eked out precarious livings there. In fact this part of the lower Severn valley must have closely resembled the undrained Fens of East Anglia and the lives of its scattered population can have been little different from that of the old-time Fenmen.

This combination of forest and marshland made the Chase an ideal refuge for those wishing to escape from either justice or injustice and from the time of the Roman Occupation until the late Middle Ages the Chase gave shelter to innumerable fugitives.

There is little evidence that the Romans attempted to enter this wilderness and in their time the area survived largely as a Celtic redoubt on the fringe of Roman England. Their Saxon successors must also have found the area difficult to control and, as was the case with the Forest of Dean, Celtic influence and religious beliefs lingered here longer than in many other parts of the country.

In Saxon times, as now, Upton on Severn was the major settlement here, standing at the eastern edge of the great Chase. At the Conquest the manor was granted to the de Mariscoes but, by the fourteenth century, it had passed into the hands of the Beauchamps and ultimately came into the possession of Richard Neville, 'Warwick the Kingmaker'.

Neville was the last of the great medieval war-lords to hold the manor of Upton and, although he controlled a large slice of the Midlands as well as numerous estates in the North, Upton was of particular importance to him. Its possession gave him a considerable measure of control over the Severn traffic in days when the river carried more commercial traffic than any other English waterway and certainly much more than any of the roads of the period.

The town was passingly involved in some of the events of the Wars of the Roses but later, in Tudor times, it settled down to a more peaceful existence. It was a peace that was only mildly disturbed by the activities of one of its Tudor rectors, John Dee, who held the living from 1553 until his death in 1608.

John Dee has been called both a genius and a fool and from all accounts he apparently lived up to both contradictory descriptions. Dee lived in credulous days and he acquired an unenviably sinister reputation as early as the age of 19. Then an undergraduate of Trinity College, Cambridge, he produced there a Greek comedy with such ingenious stage-effects that many thought they could only be possible if he had been in league with the powers of darkness. The enlightened few undoubtedly thought that Dee was no more than a clever young man, though even some of these Tudor sophisticates would probably have said that he was too clever by half. But the mass of people who heard of his activities considered that Dee had acquired supernatural powers. Although he was to vehemently deny the rumours they never died out completely and his youthful activities at Cambridge were to provide the basis for a reputation that was to remain with him for the rest of his life.

Most of John Dee's life was spent in what would nowadays be

termed scientific research. He became a mathematician with an international reputation and drew up a plan for a reform of the calendar, as well as collating discoveries in the New World and drawing up maps and projections of the newly discovered territories. But he was also drawn to the ancient art of necromancy and seems, out of a spirit of genuine inquiry, to have dabbled in the occult, something which ordinary people then regarded not with scepticism but with a fearsome dread.

It was John Dee's interest in the occult which was to prove his downfall. In 1581 he met Edward Kelly, a Worcester apothecary whose main stock-in-trade was quack medicines which he advertised as being able to cure virtually every disease known to man—and quite a few that have never been known to any living creature. Kelly was not a complete rogue, but he had certainly discovered that it was only too easy to make a living out of other people's gullibility.

He was, however, seriously interested in discovering the elusive elixir of Life; something which he, like many others of the time, seriously thought was possible. He also believed in the existence of what others had called the Philosopher's Stone—a medieval concept of a magician's crystal ball by which it would be possible to see into both the future and the past and thus be able to discover both the secrets and destinies of men.

As an apothecary and part-time alchemist Kelly was almost a natural to be influenced by these ideas. When he became acquainted with Dee he obviously considered that here was a man who was likely to solve these ancient mysteries. Dee was now 54 and much of his life had been one of disappointment, for there had been few who had taken his earlier work seriously. Kelly's ideas and enthusiasms appealed to someone who had become an embittered and isolated man and Dee seems to have thought that here was at least one person who would appreciate his own interests.

Kelly soon discovered that Dee could produce neither an elixir nor the Philosopher's Stone. This was certainly a disappointment, but Kelly was not unduly downhearted. After all, he had not been an apothecary for nothing and if Dee could not produce these things his reputation was such that people could be persuaded to believe that he could. Somehow Kelly convinced Dee that he was working along the right lines and at the same time managed to persuade the public that Dee's work was producing great results.

Dee found himself the centre of an awesome adulation and, caught up in a fraud from which he could see no way out, began to visit not only places all over England but also to make visits to the Continent. But Edward Kelly's confidence trick could not last indefinitely. Finally, on a visit to Germany, he was revealed as an impostor and thrown into prison. Trying to escape from the building he fell to the courtyard below and was killed.

Back in England John Dee's reputation was in tatters. Not only were his recent activities now discredited but so too, by association, was all the serious work he had done earlier. When he died he had been living in extreme poverty for some years entirely neglected by those who had once regarded him so highly.

One of the oldest and most attractive buildings in Upton is the White Lion Inn. It is here that Henry Fielding set a number of episodes in his novel *Tom Jones* and Upton is just the sort of town what one could imagine Tom and his friends turning inside out with their merrymaking. It is said that in the churchyard there was once a tombstone commemorating one of the inn's landlords in the following words:

> Here lies the landlord of the Lion
> Who died in lively hopes of Zion;
> His son keeps on the business still,
> Resigned unto the Heavenly will.

There is no trace of this tombstone in the churchyard now—but it would certainly be a sour-hearted person who did not care to believe that there was once.

Upton was once an important river-port, vying with Bewdley and Worcester for the position of being the premier port on the Severn. Like its sister ports its great days were in the late seventeenth and eighteenth centuries when the Severn carried an immense volume of trade to and from the port of Bristol. Today little remains of those days of hectic and adventurous commerce, though they largely account for the many inns still to be found here.

In those bustling times Upton bridge was the meeting-place of what was locally known as the Bridge Parliament. The river trowes were generally laid up around Upton bridge, which became the accepted meeting-place of all who used the waterway. This bridge survived until 1853 when it was replaced by one of more modern lines which made the old practice no longer possible. In 1938 this was replaced by the present single-span bridge.

Yet, even before 1853, the old Bridge Parliament had shrunk to a shadow of its former self. By then much of the formerly man- and horse-hauled traffic had been replaced by steam tugs which did not need to stop at the Upton quays and even these were to decline rapidly in numbers as cargoes deserted the river in favour of the newly built railways. By the mid-nineteenth century, Upton had suffered an almost complete reversal of its fortunes; its warehouses were empty and derelict, its quays largely deserted and much of its remaining population was unemployed.

Upton's way of life now became that of a small agricultural town, though naturally agriculture had played an important part in its affairs even in the hey-day of its commercial prosperity. In medieval times the townsfolk had enjoyed rights of pasture in the Chase, retaining them until the seventeenth century when a large area of the Chase was sold by Charles I and subsequently enclosed. The announcement of the royal intention at first led to serious riots in the town, but then, as now, the ordinary people did not come off very well against the force of organized authority.

As was the case with Bewdley, Upton's development tended to freeze after the loss of the river-trade and there remain a considerable number of buildings dating from the time of Anne and the Georges. Especially noteworthy is the group on the western bank of the Severn composed of the ancient Swann Inn and the Georgian Waterside House, the red-brick of the latter pleasantly mellowed in the fading sunlight of a summer day.

Until the advent of the Tudors Upton's importance was largely over-shadowed by that of neighbouring Hanley Castle. This is another Worcestershire village whose name commemorates a fortress that long ago ceased to exist. But if present-day Hanley Castle is without its castle it is certainly not without its past which once intruded the turbulent affairs of kings into the steady flow of rural life.

The castle was originally built in the late twelfth century by

Gilbert of Clare, the Red Earl of Gloucester and it was here that he married Joan of Acre. This was the age of the war-lord and Gilbert was one of its most unruly representatives. For many years he was engaged in a legal wrangle with the Bishop of Worcester over the extent of his own landholding in the Chase. Gilbert does not seem to have put great store by the eventual outcome of the dispute and sent in his private army to occupy large areas of the disputed territory. It was the kind of action with which even lawyers could not argue and when the boundary of the Chase was finally drawn up along what is now known as the Red Earl's Dyke, Gilbert's possessions had been extended much further north than their original line.

In the later Middle Ages the castle passed into the hands of Richard Beauchamp through his marriage with Isabel, the heiress of the powerful Despencers. Ultimately Richard was to succeed to the whole of the Despencer inheritance and to become one of the most powerful men in England. In acknowledgement of his position he was later created Earl of Warwick, the first person to be so created as, up until then, the title Earl had been an hereditary one associated only with those families whose ancestors had played a prominent part in the Conquest.

In the mid-fifteenth century the castle came into the possession of Richard Neville, who had succeeded to the Beauchamp estates and title by marriage. It now became a hotbed of intrigue as The Kingmaker made his various alliances, first within the dissentient House of York and later with that of Lancaster. Warwick used the castle primarily as a hunting-lodge where he could relax from affairs of state and it was here that he brought his wife Anne and their young children.

George, Duke of Clarence, was one for whom a visit to Hanley was to prove fatal, for it was here that Richard of Gloucester drowned his younger brother in the famous butt of Malmsey wine. Clarence's son, Edward, also met his end here, again on the orders of Richard who had now succeeded in getting the crown on his head. Richard was concerned that someone might take into their mind to set the young boy upon the throne in his place and behaved with predictable ruthlessness in removing yet one more potential rival.

With the coming of the Tudors Hanley Castle's importance rapidly waned and it was one of many fortresses throughout

England that was now allowed to crumble into decay. Henry VIII was later to grant the castle to Sir William Compton of Compton Verney who had most of it pulled down and the materials used for other buildings. A gateway tower, however, stood until 1795 when it was dismantled and its stones used for the reconstruction of Upton bridge. The castle has now completely vanished, though traces of its moat may still be seen.

Before the castle was first ravaged by the dismantlers Edward Bonner was born in the village. Bonner was later to become Bishop of London under Queen Mary and has secured a bad place in most English history books on the grounds of his harsh treatment of Protestants at the time of England's Counter-Reformation. Yet Bonner occupied the most difficult of positions and had to face criticism from Mary, not for his severity in dealing with 'heretics', but for his mildness. It was a harsh, even barbaric, age in which the spirit of compromise was a rare and fragile flower. Criticism of Bonner is really criticism of the bigoted times in which he lived.

In the churchyard lies a man whose activities excited controversy of a far different sort from those of the Marian Bishop. This was Thomas Attwood, the social, political and monetary reformer who was the first Member of Parliament for Birmingham. Attwood was a radical and was elected following the 1832 Reform Act. He was a leading member of the early Chartist Movement, but came of a group which believed more in the power of economic than political reform.

Hanley Castle has a diminutive village green and a medieval church with a churchyard cross. The grammar school is an ancient foundation, though modern buildings have been added to the original timber-framed structure.

For more than seven centuries Hanley Castle and neighbouring Hanley Swann, Swan End and The Rhydd have been associated with the Lechmere family. The Lechmeres are first mentioned in a taxation roll of Edward I and it is probable that members of the family were once Constables of Hanley Castle under the Earls of Warwick. Numerous Lechmeres are buried in Hanley Castle church, their main seat for many generations being at nearby Swan End. At the time of the Civil War the head of the family, Judge Richard Lechmere, aligned himself with the Parliamentarians, his wife being the sister of the Cromwellian Colonel

Edwin Sandys of Ombersley who was killed in an engagement with Prince Rupert's cavalry.

Shortly before the Battle of Worcester Judge Lechmere was unwilling host to the Royalist Major-General Massey and in his diary he recorded that Massey, "with about 130 Scottish horse quartered in my house at Hanley, hee treated my people civilly but threatened extirpation to me and my posterity bycause I was joined to the army of the Parliament".

A few days later the Judge was to record his account of the battle. He describes it as beginning "about one of the Clock, and lasted till night. I was present at it, in pursuit of the victory. The City of Worcester was taken by storme, and all the wealth in it became booty to the souldier."

At the Restoration Judge Lechmere secured the favour of the hard-up Charles II on payment of a fine of £200 and continued to practise at the Bar. It may appear strange that such a convinced Parliamentarian should have managed to gain the royal favour on any count; but Judge Lechmere had played no part in any of the more violent episodes of the war and his legal mind was one that even Charles II would have been loath to lose.

One of the Lechmeres was to give Hanley Castle an association with the New World for Thomas, a grandson of the Judge, was Surveyor General of Customs for the New England colonies. During his term of duty there Thomas sent home some young oak tree shoots. These were planted on a piece of land henceforth known as New England and grew into a fine crescent of trees which, unfortunately, were felled in recent years. Thomas Lechmere died at Boston in 1765.

In general the Lechmeres were content to live quietly on their estates, Anthony Lechmere, who was born in 1776, probably typifying this more than any other member of the family. He was something of a real-life Sir Roger de Coverley, well-loved by all. He lived until his ninety-fifth year, dying in 1870, revered as the epitome of the English squire.

To the south-west of Hanley Castle lie the villages of Queenshill and Bushley tucked in against the Gloucestershire border. But the village of Longdon is reached before either, though its timber-framed manor-house, Eastington Hall, stands some way from it. The house was built in the early sixteenth century at the direction of William Brugge who named it in honour of his wife Alice, whose maiden name was Eastington. Both William and Alice are buried in nearby Longdon church. The fourteenth-century church and village of Longdon stand in high ground above the levels of Longdon Marsh, where it is still possible to discover maritime plants which survive from the days when so much of the area was covered by the flat waters of the tidal Severn.

In Queenhill's twelfth-century church is a memorial to Henry Field who died in 1584. Field purchased the manor of Holdfast from the Lygons, whose best memorial is probably the inn of that name at Broadway. Holdfast is one of those villages which can hardly be said to exist at all and its church has long ago crumbled to dust.

Great families once played an important role in this area of the county and at Bushley are buried many members of the Dowdeswell family. One of these, William Dowdeswell, fought in the eighteenth-century wars against the French, was appointed Governor of the Bahamas and was later Commander in Chief in India. A later William Dowdeswell was responsible for the nineteenth-century restoration of Queenhill church.

Bushley is said to have been the place where Queen Margaret of Anjou, wife of Henry VI, sought refuge after the defeat of the Lancastrian army at the Battle of Tewkesbury in 1471.

On the opposite side of the Severn, in the narrowing triangle of land between the 'High Streame' and the Avon, stands the village of Ripple. Its Norman church, built upon the site of an older Saxon foundation, has acquired a national reputation for the carving of its misericords, or choir-stalls, which are of such quality and workmanship that they surpass that of many to be found in some of the country's leading cathedrals. The fifteenth-century carvings depict rural life through the twelve months of the year with ploughing, sowing, reaping and threshing all shown along with many other activities some of which have changed only in technique since the misericords were first carved.

At the time of the Civil War Ripple was the scene of a minor battle that was to prove to be the last of the Royalist victories. Royalist hopes were then centred upon the defence of Worcester and it was necessary for them to hold the area to the south of the city to prevent the Parliamentarians gaining control of the river-crossing at Upton. At the Battle of Ripple Field the Parliamentarians, who had advanced from their stronghold of Gloucester, were routed largely by Prince Rupert's cavalry. No doubt the cavaliers justly celebrated their victory—they were not to know that it had been their swansong.

Nearby, and still on the eastern bank of the Severn, though now moving back in the direction of Upton, are the Croome villages, Hill and Earls Croome. Samuel Butler once lived in the manor-house at Earls Croome when he was private secretary to its owner, Thomas Jeffrey, in the days of the Commonwealth. Both Thomas Jeffrey and his father Leonard are commemorated in the twelfth-century church.

Hill Croome is generally associated with Baughton which has a cluster of half-timbered houses and a church standing at a slight remove from the main village. One theory advanced for this off-centre position of the church is that the village once was centred about it but at a later time, probably in the years immediately after the Black Death, gradually moved to its present position. In conflict with this is another theory that the original settlement here was so well-established in early Saxon times that when the church was built it was not possible to give it a central site and so it had to be placed on the periphery.

Much of the land here, and indeed a large area of southern Worcestershire, was once in the possession of the Earls of Coventry. At Croome d'Abitot—whose name recalls Worcester's first Norman earl—stands their eighteenth-century seat of Croome Court, now in the hands of a religious order. Both the Court and the church within its grounds were amongst the few buildings designed by Lancelot, better known as 'Capability', Brown who also laid out the extensive gardens and parkland. Croome Court reveals Brown as one of the leading eighteenth-century architects and although the Court contains work by Adam, Sanderson Miller and Chippendale its overall design is now generally attributed to Brown. Within the gardens is an urn and pedestal with the following inscription:

To the Memory of
LANCELOT BROWN
who, by the powers of his indomitable and creative genius,
formed this garden scene out of
A MORASS

It is a just enough description for, before Brown's arrival, the region was a mixture of heath and bog and apart from his land-scaping activities, Brown's work here was really land-reclamation on a grand scale.

The Earls of Coventry were not aristocrats in the old tradition with fortunes founded in the great carve-up of England following the Norman Conquest. They were typical examples of the new Tudor upper class and were, in origin, a merchant family, one of them, John Coventry, becoming Lord Mayor of London in the turbulent days of Henry VI. It was this John Coventry who was the friend of another London merchant whose rags to riches story is still enacted on Christmas stages as the tale of Dick Whittington and his Cat. Whittington remains one of Gloucestershire's favourite sons and, whatever may be the truth about his begin-nings, he, like John Coventry, died a very wealthy man and was three times Lord Mayor of London himself.

The first of the Coventrys to enter the ranks of the peerage was Thomas Coventry, born at Croome d'Abitot in 1578 and created Baron Coventry by Charles I. Thomas Coventry was Keeper of the Great Seal in the days of the Civil War and is commemorated in the church by a white marble effigy, one of the most outstand-ing of all the family memorials.

Beyond Longdon, on the opposite side of the river, are the twin communities of Rye Street and Birt Street and south of these is Berrow which has some fame in geological circles as the source of rare fossils. As early as 875 Berrow was a manor in the ownership of Worcester's Cathedral-Monastery and, unlike many other Worcestershire villages which neighbour the Gloucestershire border, has never formed a part of that county. The village takes its name from The Berrow, an isolated hill which is really an outlier of the Malverns and upon which there may or may not once have been a Celtic camp.

In the church, which is mostly of fourteenth- and fifteenth-century work but which dates back to the twelfth century, the Nanfan Sermon is preached once a year, the Nanfans being the Tudor occupiers of nearby Birtsmorton manor. It is said that the sermon owes its origin to the benefaction of a local spinster whose lover had been killed in a duel with her brother. She is alleged to have subsequently left the vicar two pounds a year on condition that he would annually preach a sermon against the evils of duelling. It is a romantic story but, unfortunately, one which seems to have little basis in fact. The sermon is not directed against duelling and was first preached in respect to the wishes of the will of a local farmer. Yet such a duel very probably did take place in the neighbourhood, though it would seem not so much because of the love and honour of a lady but largely because the two participants had chosen opposing sides in the Civil War.

Neighbouring Berrow is Pendock which also has a church dating from the twelfth century and enriched with Elizabethan linenfold panelling. A nineteenth-century rector here was W. S. Symonds whose historical romances *Hanley Castle* and *Malvern Chase* achieved considerable popular acclaim. Symonds, however, was primarily a geologist and was a founder-member and first President of the Malvern Naturalists' Field Club. He undertook a great amount of original research into the rock formations of the Malvern area and was one of the men first responsible for turning the study of geology from being a rich man's hobby into one of the most important of the natural sciences.

Lying to the south almost on the Gloucestershire border is Eldersfield which has associations with Richard Whittington of Cat and Fortune fame mentioned earlier. Amongst a collection of armorial bearings on the octagonal font of the largely Norman church are those of the Whittington family, who are said to have once held land in the parish. If Sir Richard Whittington was indeed a descendant of the Whittingtons of Pauntly Court, just over the Gloucestershire border, the story may well be true and would also account for his close association with John Coventry.

Like Berrow, Eldersfield is neighboured by a hill, Gadbury Hill, which lies a little to the north-west of the village and is crowned by an ancient earthwork. To the west is Redmarley d'Abitot, once the seat of Worcestershire's hated Norman overlord, Urso d'Abitot.

North of Redmarley begins what could be called the Malverns proper and in their foothills nestles Birtsmorton Manor, for long the home of the Nanfan family.

The most famous name associated with Birtsmorton is that of Thomas Wolsey who is said to have been given refuge here by Richard Nanfan who appointed him to be tutor to his young children. But some doubt has been thrown on this story by recent research and there is now some uncertainty as to whether Henry VIII's great cardinal was ever in the area in his younger days. The Nanfans' association with Birtsmorton goes back to the reign of Henry VI when the king granted the manor to the Cornish knight, Sir John Nanfan. It was probably this Sir John who sheltered Sir John Oldcastle, the Lollard martyr who, with other of Wycliff's adherents, fled to the fastness of the Chase to avoid persecution. Sir John's successor, Sir Richard, was Captain of Calais and a firm supporter of the Lancastrian cause.

The Nanfan line lasted until 1737, when Catherine, the last survivor of the family, died. She lived to be over 70 and married four times. Her first marriage was to the Earl of Bellamont who was later to be appointed as Royal Governor of New England. It was the earl who decided to recruit the notorious Captain Kidd as a high-seas officer of the royal peace. Bellamont's logic was that Kidd, as the most successful of English pirates, should also prove to be equally successful at tracking down his rivals. Kidd was fitted out with a special ship—but Bellamont's plan misfired, for the 'terror of the Spanish Main' now proceeded to ignore his royal commission and, instead of capturing other pirates, carried on his own piratical activities with increased zeal. It was at Bellamont's orders that Kidd was finally captured and sent for trial and execution in London in 1700.

The following year the earl died and Catherine, now stirred by the adventurous life of the sea, promptly acquired a new husband in the form of Admiral William Caldwell. Caldwell was rarely on land, but he did come ashore to die at Birtsmorton in 1718. His monument, on which there is a bas-relief of his three-masted ship, declares that he was "Rear Admiral of ye Red Squadron in the Brt. Fleet in the Baltick".

Following the death of the Admiral Catherine now married, first, Edmund Pytts and, later, William Bridger, a leading London merchant who was afterwards to become Lord Mayor of London.

In 1771 Birtsmorton was to pass into the hands of the Huskisson family in the person of William Huskisson. His son, also named William, held parliamentary office under Lord Liverpool in the 1820s where he introduced a number of tariff reforms and was an early exponent of 'free trade'. In 1830, however, he earned the unenviable distinction of being the first man to be killed by a railway train, being knocked down at the opening of the Liverpool and Manchester Railway.

In the realm of legend and local lore Birtsmorton is also said to have sheltered Queen Margaret of Anjou after the Battle of Tewkesbury. She is also said to have sought shelter in the Bushley area and just what did happen to the unhappy queen in the days immediately following the battle will probably now be never known. The Nanfans, however, were firm Lancastrians and, lacking evidence to the contrary, it would do no harm to suppose that she did spend some of those days at their house.

Castlemorton is now generally spelt as one word, though in the seventeenth century it was more generally referred to as Castle Morton and in even more distant days was known as Morton Foliot. Like Worcestershire's other two southerly 'castle' villages —Hanley Castle and Elmley Castle—Castlemorton once possessed the fortress still implied by its name. It has long crumbled, but the church of this widespread parish, containing Norman and later medieval work, has better withstood the blasts of time.

From Castlemorton the common stretches away towards Little Malvern, with the straggling village of Welland a little way to the north-east on the main road between Upton and Little Malvern. Little Malvern is the most southerly of the chain of Malvern settlements with origins going back to the twelfth century when a cell of the Benedictine monastery of Worcester was established below the main escarpment. In later years the religious community expanded leading to the building of Little Malvern Priory.

Life at the priory was relatively quiet for a medieval monastic institution, its monks being content to pursue an untroubled existence until, with the rest of their religious brothers, they were dispersed at the Dissolution. The priory, however, hovered on the fringe of great events in the latter part of the fifteenth century. At this time considerable rebuilding was undertaken at the direction of Worcester's Bishop Alcock who was often in residence at the priory.

Alcock was a supporter of the Woodville faction at the Yorkist court of Edward IV, the Woodvilles being the family and kinsmen of Edward's wife Elizabeth. The older Yorkist aristocracy, and especially Edward's brother Richard, Duke of Gloucester, bitterly resented the growing influence of the Woodvilles, whom Edward appeared to be appointing to high positions in the kingdom whilst ignoring his old colleagues who had helped him overthrow the House of Lancaster. While Edward lived the growing rivalry of the Woodvilles and the older Yorkist warlords remained as an

The Guildhall, Worcester, built by Thomas White in 1721

undercurrent of intrigue and growing resentment. But, when Edward died at the beginning of 1483, it emerged with increasing violence as Richard of Gloucester made the Woodvilles' unpopularity a stepping-stone in his own ambitions to achieve the crown.

Bishop Alcock now found himself in the midst of a power-struggle. Earlier he had been appointed tutor to Edward's son and heir Edward, Prince of Wales and to the prince's younger brother Richard, Duke of York. He was at Ludlow with the two princes and their mother when word was brought that the king was dead and that Prince Edward must now journey to London for his coronation. London was firmly in the hands of Duke Richard and the Yorkists and, as the symbolic head of Woodville influence, the young King Edward V, when he left Ludlow for the capital that fateful day in May was riding, not to his coronation, but to his death.

Alcock probably knew this—or, at least, realized that, now that the young king's father was dead, the power of the Woodvilles was no match for that of the Yorkists and the popularity of Duke Richard. Richard had already pursuaded Parliament to appoint him Protector for the period of Edward's minority and, seeing how things were shaping, it is likely that Alcock now changed his allegiance.

At all events he did not accompany the king on his ride south-ward and probably knew that the Yorkists intended to take Edward into their own control once he reached Stony Stratford. It was a control that was to be finally exercised as a strangle-hold.

Alcock's complicity in the events leading up to the murder of the boys who had now become the Princes in the Tower is apparently borne out by the fact that he did nothing to aid what was later to be known as the Duke of Buckingham's Revolt, the main events of which were almost entirely confined to Worcester-shire. This occurred in the autumn of the same year and was led by Henry Stafford, Duke of Buckingham, who had been the man largely responsible for Richard of Gloucester at last becoming the wearer of the English crown. But Buckingham seems to have developed second thoughts, especially over the alleged illegiti-macy of the two princes who had now been declared by Parliament to be plain Edward and Richard Woodville.

Buckingham accordingly raised the standard of revolt, not in

Worcester from the west bank of the Severn

his own name, but in that of Edward V. His motives were
certainly mixed ones, for if Richard fell then Buckingham would
certainly have assumed the position of Protector and would have
ruled as virtual king in his own right. But at the same time he was
prepared to fight to end what a growing number of people were
coming to regard as an injustice against the heir of Edward IV.

The revolt was planned to be a four-pronged affair, with
risings in East Anglia, Kent, the West Country and the Midlands
all aimed to converge on London. Those in East Anglia and Kent
were quickly put down while that in the West Country, which
was successful though essentially small-scale, ultimately joined up
with the Midlanders, so that Herefordshire and Worcestershire
became the main theatre of action.

Buckingham raised his standard at Brecon and then, in the
company of Bishop Morton of Ely, began to move eastward at
the head of a largely Welsh army. Recruits also came in from
Shropshire and Herefordshire and by the time he reached the
southern slopes of the Malvern Hills where he was joined by the
West Country contingent headed by the Marquess of Dorset and
the Bishop of Salisbury, the 'Army of Edward V' was several
thousand strong and soon to be augmented by many more
volunteers from Worcestershire manors.

Although Buckingham's army included three bishops, those of
Ely, Salisbury and Exeter, Bishop Alcock of Worcester made no
move to join those fighting for the freedom of his former pupil.
Either, it must be assumed, he had determined not to break his
peace with Richard or that he knew more than many others at the
time—namely that the two princes were already dead. Yet this
was only mid-October and there are reports that the princes were
still alive at this time, though gradually dying from starvation
in the confines of the Tower.

On the face of it Buckingham had a good chance of defeating
Richard for his army was considerably larger than the king's
hastily assembled force, though it was obviously not as well
trained as Richard's seasoned troops. When Buckingham heard
that Richard had arrived at Coventry and was advancing to meet
him he was all for speeding up the eastward march and joining
battle as soon as possible.

This was not merely out of eagerness to get at Richard—for
Buckingham now had other problems on his mind. Ever since

the revolt had been launched the weather had been appallingly bad. Most of the march from Wales into Worcestershire had been through storm and continual rain, conditions which had now begun to wear down his men. This apart, the army was now being attacked from the rear by forces led by the Earl of Devon which had pursued the West Country rebels northward as they had journeyed to join up with their leader. This running fight was finally to end with the Earl of Devon capturing the rebel baggage-train.

Emerging from the woodland of Malvern Chase, Buckingham's intention was to take his army across the Severn at Upton and to force a battle with Richard as soon as possible, probably in the vicinity of Stratford. But when Upton was reached it was found that floodwaters had risen so high as to make the bridge impassable. In fact, the Severn had overflowed to such an extent that all the low-lying ground was under water and the Lower Severn Valley had taken on the appearance of a great lake.

Buckingham now turned northward, skirting the floodwater and with the hope of crossing the river at Worcester. He was now in desperate straits, for the storms were still raging and, with his baggage-train gone, supplies were running low and hungry and exhausted men were deserting his ranks in droves. Yet, if he could cross the Severn at Worcester, he would still have most of his army intact and would be able to requisition supplies from the city.

But the situation at Upton was to be repeated when Buckingham's army reached the Severn crossing before Worcester— floodwaters had again made the river impassable. There was nothing to be done but to retire to high ground and hope that they would soon subside.

Buckingham's army retired north-westward and encamped on Woodbury Hill. They must have been a dismal sight, these ragged remnants of the 'Army of Edward V'. For some days they hung on in rain-lashed, makeshift tents with everything so wet that they could not even light their fires. Under cover of darkness many began to slip away and, when Bishop Morton of Ely finally decided to make a break for it as well, the rebel Duke must have realized that he no longer had an army with which to fight. Now he, too, fled, riding for the Shropshire border where, three weeks later, he was captured, soon to journey to London and the well-honed axe of Richard's headsman.

It was probably Buckingham's Rising which, ostensibly at least having been on behalf of the two young princes, was ultimately responsible for their deaths. After the defeat of Buckingham Richard could not be sure that they would not be made the pretext for further risings and it was to prevent any such possibility that they were now removed from the scene. In a roundabout way Richard's fears were later to be justified in the reign of his successor Henry VII when twice revolts occurred centred around pretenders to the throne who claimed to be either of the two princes who had somehow managed to escape from the Tower. The rising which had Lambert Simnel at its head as 'Edward V' was so ineffective that Henry VII was able to treat it largely as a joke, but the later ones, with Perkin Warbeck as a dangerously re-incarnated Richard, Duke of York, gave him headaches in the super-migraine class.

Buckingham's Revolt came at the tag-end of the Wars of the Roses, and undoubtedly many fugitives from his sodden and dispirited army sought a temporary refuge at Little Malvern's Priory, the remains of which have been partially incorporated into its parish church. More than a century earlier the priory had been home to the youthful William Langland and it was here that he received his early education and took minor orders. For many years there was considerable doubt as to William's connection with the area, but modern research has cleared up most of the mystery and if it cannot be fully claimed that he is Malvern's most famous son then I am sure there will be few to quarrel with the description of him as her most famous foster-son.

William was born near Ledbury as the illegitimate son of a prominent supporter of the Despencers, Eustace de Rokayle who held land in Oxfordshire and it was the influence of de Rokayle and the Despencers which was largely responsible for his being accepted at the priory. Just whether he wrote any of his famous allegorical poem *The Vision Concerning Piers the Plowman* at the priory before he later moved to London cannot be said with any certainty, but the Malverns were certainly not to be without their influence in its writing. Along with Chaucer, Langland stands at that bridge of time when English was to re-emerge as a written as well as a spoken language. Since the Conquest the old Saxon tongue had been largely driven underground as a source of literature, its place having been usurped by Norman-French. By the fourteenth century, however, the two tongues had begun to coalesce and Langland is important not only as the author of his great poem, but as the forerunner of the revival of the literature of the English language that was later to blossom in the sixteenth century in the hands of Spenser, Shakespeare and Marlowe.

Midway between Little and Great Malvern lies Malvern Wells, now very much a residential area and once a favourite haunt of Lord Byron, after whom one of the hillside walks is named.

Great Malvern, as its name implies, is the largest of the Malvern group. The original Saxon settlement was for many centuries known as Baldenhall, the Celtic mutation Malvern being reserved to refer to the neighbouring hills and Chase. Gradually, however, Malvern came to be accepted as referring to the town as well and the old name dropped out of usage.

Malvern remained a quiet backwater of the county until the mid-eighteenth century when Dr John Wall of Powick began his promotion of the beneficial effects of Malvern waters which, within a few years, had turned the hitherto small and virtually unknown village into one of the most famous of English spa towns.

Wall was born at Powick in 1708, the son of a prosperous Worcester merchant. He was educated at Worcester College School and Worcester College, Oxford, returning to Worcester in 1736 where he soon established a thriving practice. But medicine was only one of his interests. He was one of the first 'Sunday painters' and, on the strength of his 'historical' paintings, Dr Treadaway Nashe, in his *History of Worcestershire* went so far as to declare that he was one of the best artists of his age. Yet, although Wall was certainly a man of many parts, his artistic skills were hardly the best among them and good historian though Nashe may have been there are no grounds for holding that he was an equally good art critic.

Wall was predominantly a scientist and apart from his pursuit of general medicine he also took a serious interest in chemistry that was later to lead to his discovery of a new process for the manufacture of porcelain. As such he became the leading founder of the Worcester Tonquin Manufactory, the original of the Royal Worcester Porcelain Company.

In 1745—the year of Prince Charles Edward's abortive rising

when Wall's Jacobite sympathies were finally dashed—he was one of the promoters of the new Worcester Infirmary, with which he was to be closely associated for the remainder of his life giving generous professional and financial support.

It was Wall's connection with the new infirmary that was to lead him to promote Malvern as a health centre. The waters of St Anne's Well had been reputed to contain medicinal properties since the Middle Ages and Wall appears to have decided to put them to the test with some of his infirmary patients. The results were so good that the doctor set about popularizing the beneficial effects of Malvern waters with such success that the town was soon experiencing the eighteenth-century equivalent of a revival of its medieval pilgrimage trade. Malvern's spa-town boom had begun—yet for some years it was to be a spa-town with a difference. The fashionable spa-towns, such as Bath and Cheltenham, had long ago grown to become more of seasonal social centres than health resorts. Under John Wall Malvern was, for many years, to scorn the more frivolous side of spa-town life and, by comparison with most other English spas, was to be relatively austere.

After the doctor's death his writings were collected and published by his son, Dr Martin Wall, who also published his own *Treatise on Malvern Waters*. All this very serious propaganda had the effect of bringing people to Malvern who were not merely suffering from social jaundice but who were actually infirm. These traditions were later to be continued by Dr Wilson and Dr James Gully who, in the following century, were to establish separate hydros for men and women.

Yet the provision of entertainment could not be ignored for ever and, in the course of time, the Winter Gardens Pavilion was to put in its appearance. Some writers condemn this as an incongruous building, yet without it, I think the town would lose much of its atmosphere.

It was John Wall, too, who started the Malvern water-bottling industry by sending bottles of the St Anne's Well water to those of his patients who were too ill to make the visit to the town themselves. By the mid-nineteenth century, however, Malvern, as was the case with most spa-towns, was becoming primarily a residential town for the prosperous and retired and it is largely this Victorian town that exists today.

Dating from these Gothic and red-brick years of Empire is Malvern College and a number of lesser schools, many of which have mushroomed from premises in private houses. In fact, if Malvern has largely ceased to be a health resort then it seems true to say that it has become a school resort, though to be fair, many of the brochures of the private schools do mention that the atmosphere is healthy as well as educational. Few towns in England, for their size, could boast quite as many preparatory schools as Malvern now possesses—all, I am assured, doing a roaring trade as parents remove their children from the 'threat of comprehension' which hangs over the State system. On a week-end summer morning one of the sights of Malvern is not so much its hills, but the gaudily-uniformed school-party crocodiles ascending and descending on their weekly outings—this, presumably, being the health part of their curriculum.

In the realms of higher learning Malvern is remembered as having been home to Dr Peter Roget, who undertook much important medical research here, but who is now best known as the author of his *Thesaurus of English Words and Phrases*, a work for which generations of writers have since had cause to be grateful.

Elgar was, for many years, closely associated with the Malvern Festival and is buried in the churchyard of the Roman Catholic church of St Wulfstan. Born at Broadheath, a small village just beyond Worcester, Sir Edward was destined to become one of the most famous of all English composers, his music to portray not only the pastoral landscape of his beloved native county but also the bright visions that in his day lent so much colour to the Imperial dream. Malvern Festival still preserves a fitful existence, though its great figures, Elgar and Sir Barry Jackson, have long since departed.

Malvern had associations with great music even before Elgar began his long association with the town. In the 1880s it was at the house known as Wynds Point that Jenny Lind, 'The Swedish Nightingale', made her home and where, in 1887, she died— surely, from all accounts one of the most truly popular of great singers of all time.

Malvern, too, was once the home of Elizabeth Barrett, before she at last eloped with Robert Browning to become part of a literary duo whose story has already inspired the film-makers and television-producers. As yet I am not aware that it has formed the basis of an ice-spectacular, though a rock-musical version must, by now, be long overdue.

But Malvern is not all associations with well-known figures of the recent past. It is a town which is also quite firmly rooted in the present, nothing epitomizing this more than the fact that it is the home of the Radar Research Establishment. It is also a redoubt of the British—as against the American—motor-car industry, for at Malvern is a small, independent company which, against all the odds, has managed to survive the cut-throat competition of the motor-industry giants.

Yet the name Malvern seems only passingly to refer to the line of small towns and much more to the hills below which they are set. The hilltop British Camp is just what it says it is—and there are some authorities who would claim that it was here, and not on Shropshire's Caer Caradoc, that the British leader Caractacus made his final, last-ditch stand against the advancing Roman army. I rather doubt this, but it is quite possible that Caractacus was here and made a strategic withdrawal in order to fall back upon the hills of the Shropshire highlands.

From nowhere else but the heights of Malvern is it possible to obtain such an impression of Worcestershire's predominantly pastoral character. Looking out across the Worcestershire Plain it is strange to realize that four centuries ago this would have been a far different prospect, and a land which now seems almost evenly divided between pasture and the related husbandry of arable and market-gardening would then have been almost entirely smothered by dense woodland. Only the Severn and the great religious houses would have substantially pierced the forest which, as Malvern Chase, would have rolled up to the very slopes of the hills in the spent waves of an exhausted sea. Yet, then as now, it would have been possible to see the great monastic houses in the distance, Worcester, Pershore, Evesham, Gloucester and, on the edge of the Cotswolds, the now vanished monastery of Winchcombe. All these places, and many more, can be identified with the aid of an indicator set upon Malvern Beacon. It is only fair to add that the indicator is neighboured by a cafeteria-restaurant together with attendant ice-cream cartons, fizzy-drink cans and confectionery wrappings.

Almost in the shadow of the hills is Newland where church and almshouses were rebuilt last century at the direction of the then Earl Beauchamp. Together with nearby Madresfield this section of the Malvern country has for long been associated with the Lygon family, whose home is the Tudor Madresfield Court. In the Civil War the house was held for the Parliamentarian cause by Colonel Lygon and was alternately occupied by Royalists and Roundheads.

The Lygons always paid the greatest attention to their land and in the mid-nineteenth century were one of the first of Worcestershire's landowning families to put steam to work in cultivation. In 1864 Henry Allsopp of Hindlip Hall set up as a steam-ploughing contractor and, purchasing an engine and set of ploughing-tackle from the Bedford firm of J. and F. Howard, exhibited this at Malvern's Beauchamp Hotel. A contemporary report stated that "After inspecting the engine, which bore the appropriate name of 'Centaur', Mr Allsopp inaugurated the venture by throwing a bumper of champagne over it and drinking to its success. It then moved along to Madresfield where, by request of Earl Beauchamp, it will be set to work for the benefit of the Madresfield tenantry."

Beyond Madresfield lies Callow End and nearby, on Severnside, is Powick standing just below the point where the Teme joins forces with the larger river. The bridge here is renowned as the spot where the first Civil War engagement took place, resulting in an early victory for the Royalist cavalry which prevented the Royal plate from falling into Parliamentary hands. The church, which dates from the twelfth century, contains a monument to William Cookes who died in 1672 and who was the younger brother of Thomas Cookes who founded Worcester College, Oxford. As mentioned earlier the village was the birthplace of Dr John Wall and, by association, of Malvern Spa and the Royal Worcester Porcelain works.

IX

THE TEME VALLEY

THE valley of the Teme is that area of Worcestershire least visited by the stranger, though its two main roads, both leading to junctions with the South Wales–Chester road (A49) are, despite the advent of the motorway, still well-used by traffic from Kidderminster and the Black Country. Through traffic apart, anglers, who rank the Teme high on their list of Midland rivers, are virtually the only invaders of the valley. This is despite the fact that it is criss-crossed by innumerable footways which could afford almost endless pleasure to the walker and that its villages are amongst the most interesting in the county. Somehow this north-western salient seems fated to be overlooked though the inhabitants of the valley apparently view this as a good rather than a bad thing.

Agriculturally the Teme Valley is distinctive as being the last remaining of Worcestershire's once extensive hop-growing districts, the hop-yards and their attendant oast-houses spilling over the county boundary into neighbouring Herefordshire. Although the area given over to hop cultivation has declined greatly during the present century it still remains one of the largest hop-growing districts in England.

Hops are thought to have been first grown here in the sixteenth century, though they did not become a large-scale crop for another two hundred years. The great days of the growers' prosperity were in the middle decades of the last century, after which prices began to fall following the increasing importation of foreign hops. To combat this foreign competition the Teme Valley growers, together with those in other parts of the country, unwisely embarked on a policy of greater production which, naturally, only had the result of further depressing prices. For some years the disastrous effects of this over-production were not appreciated by the growers and crops were so large that hops had to be temporarily stored at Worcester's Guildhall, the Worcester Skating Rink and other large buildings.

The situation in the industry became desperate and attempts were made, with little success, to persuade a government wedded to the principles of free trade, to limit the importation of hops. The Hop Growers' Conference was formed, with Worcestershire growers well represented on its committee, in an effort to draw government attention to the state of the industry. The manual workers also had their own organization, the Hop Pickers' Defence League, which aligned itself with the growers agitation for a limit on imports.

The representations of these two bodies having had little effect it was decided to organize a mass-demonstration in London in May 1908. Three trains packed with workers, many of whom had their fares paid by the growers, left Shrub Hill, whilst two further trains left Leominster. In London they were joined by contingents from Kent and Surrey and a march through the city streets ended with a massed meeting in Hyde Park. Here the marchers heard speeches by some of the leading growers including T. Lawson Walker of Tenbury, John Stokes of Evesham and Henry Hill of Worcester, the Chairman of the Growers' Conference.

But the demonstration, impressive though it was in illustrating the plight of this section of the nation's agricultural workers, produced few results. In fact the prevailing condition of rock-bottom prices now began to produce the natural result of many hundreds of acres of hop-yards going out of cultivation, a process which at least kept prices for those hops that were produced from falling any further. The industry did not begin to recover until the First World War, when imports were severely restricted and the home industry was allowed some measure of expansion.

Although lean times were destined to return after the war they were never to be as bad as in the years 1895–1914. Today the industry is much smaller than in that black decade for new processes in the brewing industry have resulted in a fall in the demand for hops. Nevertheless, the taste of our traditional pint would undoubtedly be even more that of a mysterious chemical compound if it were not for Teme Valley hops.

In the latter years of the last century, in the period immediately prior to that which produced the disastrous over-cultivation of the hop, the Teme Valley briefly became one of the most intensively cultivated parts of the county. This was largely due to the formation of a steam-ploughing contracting company which went by the long-winded title of the Tenbury and Teme Valley Steam Cultivation and General Implement Company Ltd.

Operating on a larger scale than Henry Allsopp of Hindlip the Tenbury company also used machines and tackle manufactured by J. and F. Howard of Bedford, whose most renowned engine was known as 'The Farmers' Friend'. Unfortunately, although the company's machines did much good work in opening up new land for cultivation, they were faced by serious competition from the already existing Hereford Steam Cultivation Company. Founded in 1866 the Tenbury company struggled for no more than four years before being driven out of business by its more powerful rival. When cheap foodstuffs began to reach England from Europe, America and the Colonies in the latter part of the next decade even the Hereford company found itself in difficulties as much of the arable in the area went over to pasture.

Tenbury Wells is the market-town centre of the valley, perched on the very edge of the Shropshire border. Its suffix was added at the beginning of the last century when the water from its mineral wells were promoted to the point where, somewhat belatedly, it was able to enter the spa-town league.

Tenbury became a spa almost by accident when its saline springs were first discovered in 1839 during a search for a domestic water supply. This was far too late a date for the town to assume the proportions of a health and social centre on the lines of Bath and Cheltenham and it was Tenbury's fate to assume the aspect of a serious health resort more reminiscent of neighbouring Malvern. Its Pump Room and Brine Baths were built in 1862 and the building housing them, rather resembling a small oriental temple, is one of the architectural features of the town. The waters were reputed to cure liver diseases, scurvy and glandular swellings while bathing in them was said to relieve gout and rheumatism. In 1911, when the inland health resorts were still well-patronized places, the Pump Room was renovated and plunge and steam baths were added.

After the First World War the spa-trade declined and Tenbury's Pump Room gradually fell into disuse. Today it still remains—but its future is uncertain. Much of its interior is in a dilapidated and dangerous condition and there are plans for it to be purchased and preserved by the County Council. At the moment the Pump Room remains in the hands of a local brewery while the council decide what use to make of it should they purchase it. So far the only generally acceptable proposal has been that it should be converted into use as a small museum, though this has been rejected on the grounds that it would not give a sufficient return on the proposed purchase price. Perhaps, however, some museum use could yet prove a solution with the Pump Room as a survival from the great days of the Worcestershire spas, housing exhibits from Malvern and Droitwich as well as from Tenbury.

Tenbury is an ancient settlement and there was probably a church here in Saxon times, for during nineteenth-century restoration work part of a Saxon cross was found incorporated in the chancel wall. The church is now a fusion of Norman and eighteenth-century work, for, in 1770, the floodwaters of the Teme rose so high as to undermine one of the nave pillars which collapsed bringing down a considerable portion of the original fabric. During the subsequent restoration the height of the tower was increased, the old Norman windows being inserted in the topmost section.

St Michael's College and church, both founded in 1856 by Sir Frederick Ousley, the composer of church music, lie just two miles south of Tenbury. The college is a rarity amongst public schools in that it is more famous for its library than for its scholars. It is primarily a school of music founded as it was by one of the most prolific, if not most well known, of English composers. Its library, of more than 8,000 volumes, contains many famous original manuscripts including the copy of the *Messiah* which Handel himself used at the first performance of the oratorio in Dublin. Other unique manuscript treasures include works by Byrd and Purcell. Ousley was vicar here from 1856 as well as being principal of the college. Scholars from the college now sing in the church in which the founder once preached and delight the ear with impeccable renderings of some of the most intricate of English devotional music.

Bockleton near Tenbury, is the most westerly village in Worcestershire with a Norman church to which has been added some thirteenth-century work. Within is a monument to William Prescott who died in 1865 at the age of 21. He was a keen lover of

field-sports and died from a fever contracted whilst tending his
dying gamekeeper.

Nearby Kyre Magna is dominated by Kyre Wyard House
standing amid parkland a little way beyond the village. The house
has seen a whole series of rebuildings and restorations since it was
first erected as Wyard Manor House in the early fourteenth
century. A fragment of the original manor-house has been
incorporated in the present building and parts of the structure
date from the first reconstruction in the sixteenth century. But
the house as it now stands is dominantly the work of the eighteenth
century and its design was probably due, in part at least, to
Lancelot 'Capability' Brown. It was Brown who was responsible for the landscaping of the park with its ponds and banks of
trees and it would seem that, as at Earls Croome, he also extended
his designing abilities to the house.

Kyre Magna once had what could perhaps be claimed as the
longest-lived vicar in English history. This was Hugo Thomas
who held the living here for sixty years and who died in 1693 at
the reputed age of 107. Perhaps this accords some measure of
comfort to the present occupants of Kyre Wyard House, for it
now functions as a convalescent home.

Stoke Bliss church is one of many along the valley that is set
upon a hill overlooking the swiftly flowing Teme. The valley
appears to be positively guarded by hilltop churches, amongst
them being those of Knighton-on-Teme, Lindridge, Stockton-
on-Teme and Stanford, whilst further downstream in the direction of Worcester, Clifton-on-Teme is set so high above the river
that it scarcely seems to belong to the valley at all.

Though Stoke Bliss church occupies an ancient site it is of little
antiquity though within is a Norman font removed from an
earlier building. More eye-catching is the early seventeenth-
century pulpit and reading desk, the latter bearing the words
"Roger Osland Churchwarden 1635" and carved with two
dragons and an array of human figures, a local example of the
short-lived Laudian revival.

At nearby Rochford the church defies the general rule in that
it is at low level whilst most of the houses are ranged on the hills
above. Knighton-on-Teme is a name largely without a village
and its Norman church must house an almost entirely ghostly
congregation.

Eastham and Lindridge both border the river as it moves towards its junction with the Severn. Both are ancient settlements and Eastham is one of the numerous places where the Teme is bridged. In respect of bridges the inhabitants are more fortunate than their counterparts along the Severn and the Avon for the bridge here is only one of several that knit both sides of the Teme into one whole. There is, I feel, even in this day of the urban underpass and flyover, nothing quite so divisive as a rural river which cannot be crossed.

Clifton-on-Teme stands so high above the river that it would more justify the type of Welsh place-name that would probably translate as 'the village above the steep cliff overlooking the swift river'. But, as it is not Welsh, it must be content to be described in a mis-statement. Its church is one of the few to be dedicated to St Kenelm, the child-king martyr who, as king of Mercia, was murdered at Clent on the orders of his elder sister. Clifton preserves its village green, with a scattering of chocolate wrappers, whilst its church contains much work of the thirteenth and fourteenth centuries.

Nearby lie Stanford-on-Teme and Stockton-on-Teme. All the Teme valley bridges are relatively modern structures, but that at Stanford stands upon the site of one which once carried the inscription:

> Praye for Humphrey Pakington Esquyer, borne in Stanford, whiche payed for the workmanshepe and making of this brygg the which was rered and made ye fyrst yere of ye rayne of Kyng Edward ye VI.

Tudor spelling tended to be something of a matter of personal taste, such licence now only dubiously claimed by young schoolchildren.

For more than two hundred years Stanford was the manorial home of the Salweys and at the time of the Civil War Humphrey Salwey took up the Parliamentarian cause. In 1649, as a member of the Long Parliament, he declined to sit in trial on Charles I, maintaining that Parliament did not have a legal right to pass judgement on the actions of the king. As a man who could aptly be described as one of Cromwell's "men of tender conscience" his views were respected though, of course, they did not prevent Charles from losing his head.

In time the Salweys of Stanford Court gave way to the Winningtons and, at the departure of the latter in relatively recent times, the house has been converted into a factory. This may be rather a sad fate, but at least it has helped to alleviate the local employment problem, which in the past has often been acute.

Nearby are the villages of Hanley William and Hanley Child, both standing on high ground and facing away towards the tangled hills of Shropshire. These, together with most of the small Teme valley villages, are predominantly associated with the cherry orchards and hop-yards that fill so much of the landscape in this westernmost corner of the county. With hops being grown in such profusion, though on a smaller scale than in former years, it comes as some surprise to discover that beer is not the traditional local drink and that valley locals favour, when they can get it, a local brew of mild cider. But then, hop-growing has not been introduced into Worcestershire for all that long and large-scale cultivation dates only from the last century. Before that cider was produced on local farms, excess production going to the local cider-house, most of which have long since been either delicensed or converted into beer-houses.

The fringe of the valley has also had its share of the effects of the Industrial Revolution, for Mamble and some of the surrounding villages, once formed part of a small, thriving coalfield. The pits were mostly of the smaller type and in some ways may have resembled those of the Forest of Dean though the rights of that region's 'free miners' did not, so far as I have been able to discover, have their equivalent here. The pits are closed now and there remains little to tell anyone that Mamble was once a mining community.

Woodbury Hill, which neighbours the Abberley Hills on the eastern side of the valley, is a far cry from thoughts of the Industrial Revolution and was once the encampment of a Franco-Welsh army led by Owain Glyn Dŵr. Under the terms of an agreement he had reached with Henry Percy (Shakespeare's 'Harry Hotspur') and other English nobles in their revolt against Henry IV, Glyn Dŵr was to assume the title of Prince of Wales and to extend the boundaries of the Principality south of Shrewsbury to include all the land lying to the west of the Severn. To aid him in his campaign he was generously helped by the French who placed a large army at his disposal. If this combined Franco-

The interior of Worcester Swimming Pool
Choral Scholars of King's School in Worcester Cathedral cloisters

Welsh force had been able to link up with Hotspur's own northern troops Henry might have been in real trouble and it was his strategy to keep them apart. When Glyn Dŵr moved out of Wales he was too late to prevent Henry inflicting a decisive defeat on the English rebels at Shrewsbury, after which Hotspur and most of the English rebels were executed.

Glyn Dŵr now drew back to encamp on Woodbury Hill while Henry's army made camp across the valley on the Abberley Hills. Henry obviously hoped for a pitched battle—but Glyn Dŵr was having none of that. Some days were spent while individual knights from opposing sides took part in single combats on the low ground between the two camps. But then Glyn Dŵr and his French allies withdrew westward into the Welsh hills. The invading army had been able to do little more than attack the outskirts of Worcester, notably St John's, and had been compelled to withdraw largely because their supplies were running low. But the event does at least deserve mention as being the time when an invading Welsh army penetrated most deeply into England.

Around the hills stand the once-great houses of Abberley Hall and Witley Court. The mock-Italian Abberley Hall is now shorn of much of its former grandeur while Witley Court has, for more than thirty years, stood as a burnt-out shell which has so far proved far too costly even to be considered for restoration. Plans are, however, at present under review for a restoration of a part of the building. The Court was bought in 1850 by the Earl of Dudley who spent an enormous fortune in making it one of the largest and most sumptuous of private palaces. The family had moved to Himley Hall a few years before the great house was gutted by fire in 1937. Now only the church standing in the grounds remains intact, its windows and painted ceiling having been brought from Cannons in Middlesex when that great mansion was demolished in the mid-eighteenth century. It was at Witley Court that Queen Adelaide, widow of William IV, lived for a short time.

Not far away is Astley Hall, from which Stanley Baldwin used to delight in the view towards the Abberley Hills. No doubt they made a refreshing change from views of the ironworks at Wilden.

South of Woodbury Hill the two Shelsleys stand guard on either side of the Teme, Shelsley Beauchamp on the eastern bank

Worcester Cathedral—floodlit—from the west bank of the Severn

and Shelsley Walsh on the western. Around Shelsley Beauchamp
the hop-yards spread away across the red soil almost to the slopes
of Woodbury. While Shelsley Beauchamp takes its suffix from
the family who ultimately sired the first Earl of Warwick,
Shelsley Walsh is associated with a local family who seem to have
been content to live on a less exalted plane. The last of the Walsh
line, however, Sir Richard, was High Sheriff of Worcestershire
at the time of the Gunpowder Plot and helped to capture the
plotters at the skirmish at Holbeach House.

Travelling from the direction of Tenbury it is not until I reach
Shelsley Walsh that I feel that I am about to enter the real
Worcestershire. I am sure that the people of the Teme valley will
not take my words amiss for in many ways the valley is so
different from the rest of the county. In scenery and feeling it
really belongs to Herefordshire and the Welsh border, this
upland valley whose river, unlike the more placid Severn and
Avon, is still charged with the unpredictable spirit of its mountain
origins. There is a theory that the county boundary here owes its
existence to some distant Saxon campaign against the Welsh, a
campaign which resulted in the Saxons gaining control of this
important gateway into the Severn Plain. This is certainly
tenable for neighbouring Herefordshire was to remain largely in
Welsh hands long after the rest of the West Midlands had fallen
to the Saxons and it was not until the campaigns of Harold
Godwinsson in the latter years of the reign of Edward the
Confessor that Herefordshire was finally incorporated into Saxon
England.

Downstream from Shelsley Walsh is the largest village in the
valley, Martley, whose church has an interior bright with the kind
of wall paintings that so delighted our medieval ancestors. This
fact alone makes Martley well worth a visit while the nearby
rectory has retained a fine example of an Elizabethan hall. Within
the church is a memorial to Lettice Lane, sister of Jane Lane who
helped Charles II escape after the Battle of Worcester. Martley
was also the birthplace of Charles Stuart Calverley—a Royalist
name if ever there was one—who was born here in 1831 and was
later to achieve fame as a poet, scholar and wit.

A little southward lies Berrow Hill, an outlier of the nearby
Malverns, which the Teme sweeps around before it reaches
Lulsley and the steep cliffs of its western bank. To the south-west

lie more Malvern-offspring, in this case the Suckley Hills. Suckley village lies close to the Herefordshire border set amid the hop-yards and oast-houses which are so common a feature hereabouts. Nearby is Alfrick and both villages are close to the Leigh brook which flows down to meet the Teme at the village from which it has taken its name.

Leigh's church dates from the twelfth century and within is to be found an heraldic monument to Sir Walter Deveraux who bought the manor from Edmund Colles in the early seventeenth century. Sir Walter was later to become the first Viscount Hereford.

Between Leigh and Lulsley is Broadwas, a black-and-white village with its church standing almost at the river's edge. It is here, in this fertile stretch of country where the Teme is about to join forces with the Severn, that Sir Edward Elgar was born. His home at Broadheath is now preserved as a museum. There is no doubt that his intense feeling for the pastoral county helped inspire some of his finest work and it is, in imagination, to the strains of his 'Nimrod' Variation, that the Teme Valley is left behind for across the meadows rises Worcester and, on its eminence, the majestic height of its great cathedral.

X

CIVITAS IN BELLO ET PACE FIDELIS

Civitas in Bello et Pace Fidelis, the city faithful in peace and war, Worcester's motto at once declares its associations with the Royalists and the Civil War. Together with Oxford it could claim to have been the most Royalist city in England and, in the years after the Battle of Worcester and the flight of the un-crowned Charles II, its Royalist associations acquired more than a hint of the romantic. This was to be somewhat reinforced when Thomas White, a local architect of great merit, designed the Guildhall and had its entrance flanked by statues of Charles I and Charles II while Cromwell's head appeared nailed by its ears above the doorway.

Yet Worcester could not live on its Royalist past forever and, by the time White's Guildhall was erected the events of the mid-seventeenth century retained only a dim significance. Six years before the Guildhall's opening Worcester played no part in the Jacobite Rising of 1715, and although some of its leading citizens had Jacobite sympathies, the city, in common with most other English towns, did nothing to aid the heir of the Stuarts, Prince Charles Edward, when he entered the Midlands in the summer of 1745 en route, had he but known it, for the rout of Culloden Moor.

It was now a century since the upheavals of the Civil War and Worcester, like most other towns, had long ago accepted England's marriage of convenience with the Hanoverians. If the city had remained faithful it was not to the Stuarts but to itself.

Worcester's origins probably go back well before Roman times when it was the site of one of the major fording points of the Severn which was then tidal well beyond here. Later the Romans built a fort here, but Worcester was not to achieve any prominence until the latter part of the seventh century when it was chosen as the centre of a new see, embracing most of modern Gloucestershire and Warwickshire as well as our own county.

The ecclesiastical significance of Worcester was soon turning it into quite a thriving community, which occasionally paused from thriving to accommodate the members of a Danish free-booting excursion trip. These early day-trippers usually stopped off at Worcester on their way up the Severn to indulge in a little seasonal rape, pillage and arson. After a time the people got a little accustomed to these visitations and tended to forsake the city while the Danes tore hither and thither, looting before burning it to the ground. The citizens generally dug themselves in on Bevere Island in the midst of the Severn and on one memorable occasion after refusing to pay Danegeld to Hardicanute, son and successor of Canute of running-water fame, they defied the armed forces of the three Saxon earls Leofric of Mercia, Siward of Northumbria and Godwin of Wessex who had dutifully come to subdue them on Hardicanute's behalf. The earls had to offer very favourable terms before the citizens of Worcester agreed to call off their insurrection.

The original inhabitants of Worcestershire and more particularly of Worcester seem to have been a more than usually independent brand of Anglo-Saxon. The region was occupied by the Saxons in the late sixth and early seventh centuries and, although the original invading force was headed by Caewlin, the leader of the West Saxons, the fact that those who came to settle in the area of the Worcestershire Plain came to be known as the Hwiccans may indicate that they had a separate and unified identity before their arrival. In time the Hwiccan kingdom became absorbed into the vast Midland kingdom of Mercia which eventually fell to the invading Danes. It was not until the West Saxons first contained and then reduced the Danes that England became in any way unified and the shire system was adopted which first brought the county into being.

The shire system of administration was adopted in the reign of King Edgar, King of Wessex and Overlord of England. But Edgar was also a zealous religious reformer and it was due to him that under St Dunstan and St Oswald the Benedictine Rule was established at Worcester. It was Oswald who obtained from the king a charter granting the Bishops of Worcester the right of civil, as well as ecclesiastical administration, over more than a third of the county which, as the Hundred of Oswaldslaw, survived into the eighteenth century.

At the Conquest Worcester was the only diocese in England which, in the person of Wulfstan, was to retain its Saxon bishop. It was during Wulfstan's episcopate that plans were drawn up for rebuilding the cathedral and he was also to be responsible for the foundation of the Commandery as an Augustinian house. Worcester's secular administrator was the Norman Urso d'Abitot but, although Urso was no better than most of his gangster associates, his rule was at least moderated by the presence of Wulfstan whose influence was largely responsible for this remaining the most Saxon of England's post-Conquest shires.

It has even been claimed that the county had associations with the dispossessed royal House of Wessex. At Chaddesley Corbett the Saxon woman Eddive, who was one of the few Saxons to be holding land in England at the time of the Domesday Survey, may possibly have been Emma, who was successively wife of Gruffydd, King of Powys and of the defeated Harold of England. Certainly there is no logical explanation why this Saxon landowner should have been allowed to retain such extensive possessions while most of her race was systematically dispossessed by the conquerors.

Under Bishop Wulfstan Worcester continued to flourish as a centre of Saxon learning and culture and it was here that both the monastic chronicler, Florence of Worcester, and the poet Layamon received their early education. Florence remaining at the monastery for the whole of his life while Layamon became the parish priest at Areley.

In the years after the death of Wulfstan the city suffered a train of natural disasters in the form of floods, fires and even earthquakes. But Worcester was still very small, most of its buildings, apart from the cathedral-monastery and the castle, being of wood and thatch and rebuilding was soon affected. Fire was a permanent hazard in all medieval English towns and Worcester was twice gutted during the disastrous reign of King Stephen de Blois, a period which historians have generally dubbed 'The Anarchy'. The events of this chaotic Civil War, which engulfed most of the country, have been eloquently expressed by an anonymous monastic chronicler of Peterborough who declared that violence and destruction were so great that "Christ and all his saints slept".

Worcester's double visitation of destruction was largely the responsibility of Waleran de Beaumont, her first earl. Waleran began by siding with Stephen in his struggle against Matilda, the daughter of Henry I and wife of Geoffrey, Duke of Anjou. In the early years of the war Waleran was cooped up in Worcester castle with Matilda's army besieging the city. When he refused to hand over the fortress the town was fired in reprisal.

In 1141 Stephen was defeated and captured at the Battle of Lincoln and Waleran, of the opinion that Stephen's cause was lost, changed sides. But the loyalists then succeeded in capturing one of the major rebel leaders, Robert, Duke of Gloucester, who was handed back to Matilda in exchange for Stephen who promptly undertook a campaign to avenge himself on all those who had deserted his cause after Lincoln. At Worcester Waleran again had to shut up himself in the castle and to bear the mortification of seeing the city reduced to ashes for a second time, this time by Stephen's army.

The Civil War dragged on and was all but ended in Stephen's favour when his son and heir, Eustace, was killed. If legitimacy had then been a recognized principle of inheritance Stephen's brother, Henry de Blois, Bishop of Winchester, would now have been next in line to the throne. But, in theory, the crown was still elective and, beyond this, the reigning monarch could claim the right to name his successor.

Matilda's son Henry was now in England at the head of a large army which had been outgeneralled and outmanoeuvred by Stephen and which, as the young general could not afford to pay his men, was becoming increasingly difficult to control. With his own son dead Stephen now decided to end the war by concluding a pact with the son of his enemies.

This was the age of chivalry and when Henry wrote to Stephen asking him if he would advance the money to pay off his men so that he could return to France, Stephen readily complied. But, more than this, he now named Henry as his successor. Two years later, in 1159, Stephen died and Henry, Count of Anjou, was crowned king as Henry II at Worcester Cathedral.

Later Henry II was to be no stranger to the city for Worcester was to be his headquarters from which he mounted his early campaigns against the Welsh. But Welsh wars were a minor matter in Henry's life for, apart from England, he controlled vast possessions on the Continent and the latter part of his reign was to be heavily concerned with campaigns against his sons who, backed by the King of France, had ambitions to carve up his lands amongst themselves. It was to be well over a century before Worcester became the mainspring of the operations of Edward I against Llewellyn of Powys which resulted in the final conquest of North Wales. Only a few years earlier the city had been the scene of bitter fighting when, in 1263, it had been captured by the barons in their war against Edward's father, Henry III. It remained in their hands for two years until the final eclipse of their cause in de Montfort's defeat at the Battle of Evesham.

The later civil war of York and Lancaster largely by-passed the county, though many local men doubtless fought under the Neville emblem of the Bear and Ragged Staff for, as Earl of Warwick, Richard Neville had succeeded to the large Beauchamp inheritance in the shire. The city, however, was to have a close association with the later stages of the struggle in the person of John Tiptoft, who was created Earl of Worcester by the Yorkist King Edward IV and who was destined to act as a counterpoise to Warwick's influence.

Tiptoft was a lawyer, educated largely in France and Italy, and was one of the first 'Renaissance men' to make an impact on the English political scene. Edward singled him out as the man to oppose Warwick's interests which were increasingly proving to be opposed to those of the king. Warwick, tiring of being Edward's second fiddle, was moving steadily towards an alliance with the French and ultimately with the Lancastrians in return for aid to create a virtually independent kingdom of his own which he hoped to carve out of the Duchy of Burgundy.

In the 1460s Tiptoft advanced steadily in power, commanding Yorkist armies in Scotland and negotiating treaties with the enemies of the French king which finally frustrated Warwick's own plans. By 1469 Warwick was virtually isolated and rushed an army into the field in an attempt to overthrow Edward and Tiptoft. But he was defeated at Stamford and only just managed to escape to the safety of France.

In this hour of victory events were to run strangely against the Earl of Worcester. As Constable of England it fell to John

Tiptoft to exact retribution from those of Warwick's supporters who had been unlucky enough to be captured at Stamford. It was Tiptoft who took the brunt of the nation's reaction to Edward's furious burst of temper when he had the dismembered bodies of some of Warwick's men impaled following a series of executions in London in 1470. Angry Englishmen declared that Tiptoft "governed by the law of Padua" and far from being admired as the king's ally against the overbearing Warwick he now found himself hated for being the tool of such bloody justice.

But Warwick, if down, was certainly not out. At the end of 1470 he invaded England with a combined Lancastrian and French army and Edward was forced to flee to Burgundy while the Lancastrian Henry VI was set upon the throne as a puppet-king.

Tiptoft was in real trouble and realized that he must leave England as soon as possible. But his plans evidently went wrong for one day in September he was discovered hiding in an oak in Huntingdonshire.

With Warwick firmly back in power the Earl of Worcester could expect little mercy and, found guilty of treason, was sent to be beheaded on Tower Hill. The man who had come to earn the title of the 'Butcher of England' asked that the headsman perform his task in three strokes in honour of the Trinity and, on 18th October 1470, the Earl of Worcester made his gory exit from the dangerous pastime of medieval power-politics.

But, in general, the power struggles of medieval times left Worcester relatively uninvolved and the city continued to grow and prosper. In these years trade and industry expanded under the city's guilds, especially that of cloth weaving for Worcester was destined to become a leading cloth-town and, in the fifteenth century, its clothiers were responsible for much of its prosperity. Buildings began to be more substantial and from these years dates much of the Commandery—where Charles II was later to sleep before the Battle of Worcester—for much of the St Wulfstan's original friary was now dismantled and the present building is largely the work of this time. Before the Dissolution it was used mainly as an overnight hostel for travellers being situated just outside the Sidbury Gate to the then walled city; travellers could lodge here when the city gates were shut.

Of Worcester's medieval guilds one, the Guild of St Nicholas grew to be more powerful than its companions and the guilds as a body virtually governed the city. In the sixteenth century the old guilds were abolished and many of their religious and social activities taken over by other bodies. But sixteen guilds were re-established in the city to deal purely with questions of trade and employment and included the guilds of the clothiers, bakers, glovers, mercers and coopers. They met originally in Trinity Hall which was owned by the Clothiers Company, but when in 1769 this was sold, moved to what was then known as the Town Hall and which, because of this later association, came to be known, as it still is, as the Guildhall. They had, by then, ceased to exercise any effective power in the city and, by the middle of the last century, were largely defunct.

In medieval times, when the guilds were extremely powerful in the city, Worcester, although the fifth largest city in England, was still very small by modern standards. From Sidbury Gate on the south to Fore Gate on the north was a distance of no more than three-quarters of a mile. The now vanished wall ran from the river to Fore Gate while is eastern perimeter ran roughly three hundred yards to the east of the present High Street and College Street (both names for different sections of the main thoroughfare) and terminated at Sidbury Gate, which stood close to the castle and just beyond the cathedral precincts. The wall extended to a height of fifty feet and was bordered by a deep ditch. Yet, even in medieval times, building was not confined to the area within the city walls and houses sprang up south of Sidbury and north of Fore Gate, the latter developing in Tudor and Stuart times into what is now Foregate Street.

The Severn was bridged here in early times and in 1313 the wooden bridge, which had been many times renewed, was replaced by the Worcester monks with one of stone which was so soundly built that it stood until the second half of the eighteenth century. This bridge was to form one of the major gateways into Wales and the Marches and also gave rise to the suburb of St John's, which grew up on the rising ground on the west bank centred around the Bull Ring and St John's church.

But Worcester's domestic life was not to be one of uninterrupted prosperity: in fact, in common with much of the rest of England, its medieval growth was to be set back for almost a century when it was hit by the worst visitation of the plague in English history.

The Black Death of 1349, which more than halved the population of England in a matter of twelve months, was a fusion of bubonic and pneumonic plague which, in the crowded and insanitary conditions of medieval England, spread with devastating speed. The plague reached Worcester from Bristol and Gloucester probably being first introduced into the city by the boatmen working on the Severn trowes. The disease was no respecter of rank or position and at Worcester the Bishop, Wulfstan de Braunsford, contracted the disease and died within two days. Earlier, when it had been raging in other parts of his diocese, he had issued instructions that if a priest could not be found to hear a dying person's confession then that confession could be heard by a lay person, man or woman. The clergy seem to have been particularly hard hit, for many parishes lost two and sometimes three successive priests within a year and, hardly surprisingly perhaps, a large number also fled their parishes in an attempt to avoid the disease.

The aftermath was to reveal an alarming state of havoc throughout the county. A report made for Bishop Wulfstan's successor revealed a picture of a countryside where lands could not be let because there were no tenants to be found, mills stood idle and forges were unworked. Pigeon houses were abandoned and in ruins while fishponds were choked with reeds. Rents could not be collected because more than two-thirds of the tenants had died. In the fields the harvest lay ungathered and even if it had been brought to market little could have been sold because there were so few people left to buy the produce. It was estimated that in the county as a whole more than two-thirds of the population died and this proportion was probably even greater in Worcester itself. So many bodies had to be buried that the city churchyards proved inadequate for the task and new burial grounds had to be opened up outside the city walls.

It was as a direct result of the Black Death that Worcestershire was later to become one of the major sheep-rearing counties. Labour shortage meant that not enough men could be found for arable cultivation while those that were available, because of the same shortage, demanded much higher wages than had their predecessors before the Black Death. The economic consequence of the plague was a century of mounting inflation and partly to cut costs many Worcestershire landowners went over to sheep-rearing, a fact which in time helped to establish Worcester as a cloth-weaving centre but which also paved the way for the ending of the medieval system of agriculture, later inviting first the enclosures of the Tudor period and subsequently those of the eighteenth and nineteenth centuries. These later movements were to coincide with the rise of industry in the towns so that ultimately the Worcestershire countryside was to be depopulated in favour of sheep and cattle reared on large-scale holdings while the descendants of former peasant proprietors were to lose their connection with the land in favour of one with the new machinery.

By the end of the Tudor period Worcester had expanded to the point where the proportion of development outside its walls was beginning to rival that of the older buildings within. Most of this new activity was along what is now Foregate Street and The Tything, but building was also taking place along and around Sidbury, outside Frogge Gate to the south of the castle site and in the region of St Martin's Gate. St John's was already growing into a considerable suburb and the only two gateways that had not attracted new building by this time were Friar's Gate, which led into open fields to the east of the town and Water Gate, which had originally backed on to the Severn, but which now stood a little way from the silted bank. Then, as now, it was not a practical proposition to build near to the river because of the ever-present danger from flooding.

It was to this expanding, thriving city that Elizabeth I came in 1574. Some authorities say that she addressed the assembled citizens at the site of the Grass Cross, which stood where that part of Worcester's main street now called The Cross runs. But I prefer to think that she spoke from the gallery of the half-timbered house in the Trinity which, since those days, has been known as Queen Elizabeth's House. Nearby, in New Street, is another house with royal associations for here is King Charles's House, forever famous for its back-door which opened on to the outer side of the city wall and through which Charles II, hotly pursued by Cromwell's Roundheads seeking to crown still further their 'crowning mercy', effected a hasty exit after the Battle of Worcester.

After extricating himself from such a hot spot Charles would no doubt have welcomed a dip and nowadays, leaving out of account the rather grimy Severn, Worcester would be able to accommodate him. Not far from New Street, in Sansome Walk, stands a new building which it would be a serious omission not to mention. This is the new Swimming Pool opened in 1972. It embodies all that is good in modern civic design, a functional building which, in its brick-facing and proportions, is worthy to stand beside many of the older architectural examples from the past. The yearly attendances have been estimated at well over 400,000 and the building contains, besides its main pool, a training pool and a sauna.

In New Street's continuation, Friar Street, are a group of especially pleasing half-timbered buildings, a number of them inns. Here stands 'Greyfriars', once the hostelry of the friary and which has been tastefully restored and is now maintained by the National Trust. It would be a good thing if some of the shop-keepers here could be induced to smarten their premises up a little. The continuation of Friar Street used to be known as Lich Street and was an area of great charm—unfortunately the half-timbered houses have been bulldozed in recent years to be replaced by a shopping precinct and the Giffard Hotel, named after one of the city's most industrious medieval bishops and not, as some may be tempted to think, after one of the county's best-known cricketers. This new concrete and glass conglomeration stands a little too close to the cathedral for the comfort of either and while the Giffard seems a reasonably designed building in terms of those who stay in it rather than those who have to look at it, I can think of no possible compliment that can be accorded the shopping precinct which has been assembled rather than built out of pieces that would look just as out of place next door to any other cathedral.

Worcester's original Grammar School once stood near to The Cross. It was founded by Elizabeth I and in the Civil War its scholars are said to have distinguished themselves by carrying earth and stones to strengthen the battered walls and powder to supply the defending Royalist garrison. The school was later housed adjoining St Swithun's Church in the High Street and moved to its present site in The Tything in 1895.

With the exception of the cathedral and some of the older

churches I have now perambulated most of the Worcester that was in existence at the time of the Civil War. When all is said and done not much remains of the early Stuart city, certainly not as much as remains from those times in the towns of York, Chester or Shrewsbury. But this is not to be entirely regretted for Worcester has not been a town to stand still and the next century was to add many Georgian treasures to its architectural possessions.

Much of the street pattern that the embattled Stuarts knew here still persists, greatly to the chagrin of motorists who, in this case at least, I hope will lose their battle for the through-ways, under-passes, by-passes and flyover that have so disfigured so many of our towns. The solution to Worcester's traffic problems seems to be to keep the motor-car out of the city as much as possible and to make the fullest use of existing and improved public transport, including the re-opening of local railway halts. High Street, The Cross, College Street, Fish Street and Dolday would have been known to the hopeful Charles II though in a far different form and I doubt if he would have appreciated the tortuous one-way traffic system which now operates in the region of the Severn bridge.

The exterior of the cathedral he would certainly recognize, though perhaps its interior would not be all that familiar for it was yet to be desecrated by the Puritans and to be restored at the hands of Sir Gilbert Scott.

Although the most common view of the cathedral is that of its West Front which, when seen on a sunny day from the county cricket ground across the river, still seems to echo to the music of Elgar who loved the place so well, it cannot be said to be its best feature. Indeed, when compared to the West Front of cathedrals such as Wells, it can only be said that, by comparison, the work at Worcester is rather shabby. What redeems it is its position on a height above a bend in the river, its neighbouring trees and behind it its real triumph, the truly majestic tower.

The cathedral is a medley of styles from Norman to Tudor times which has fused over the centuries to make a most har-monious and impressive whole. Some of the Norman work begun under the direction of Bishop Wulfstan survives, notably in the crypt, which is generally acknowledged to be one of the finest examples of Norman building in the country—I should warn anyone intending to go down that it can be a rather chilly place. A charge is made for entering the crypt and another for climbing up the seemingly endless flight of steps to the top of the tower.

The nave was constructed over a period of more than two centuries, yet no one part seems disparate from another. The earliest portions are the two western bays on either side which date from the mid-twelfth century—they were the first to replace a section of the original Norman nave, parts of which stood until some years after the Black Death. The continuity of design was achieved by the uniform vaulting of the nave which was completed in 1377.

In the centre of the choir stands the cathedral's most famous memorial, the tomb of King John. John was not buried here by one of those historical accidents but because he especially chose to be buried in the cathedral of his favourite city. In being buried in England he made a break with the traditions of the country's earlier Angevin rulers and their predecessors all of whom had been buried in their native France. The effigy of John in Purbeck marble was said to have been a very good likeness. He did not, of course, expect to be buried at Worcester quite as soon as he was. But, after eluding the forces of the French dauphin by moving through the marshland in the region of The Wash—in which, as most schoolchildren used to know, he had the misfortune to have to abandon the royal plate in the face of a combination of storm and rising tide—John, sharing the fate of many saddle-weary medieval warrior-kings, fell ill with dysentery. The royal party managed to reach Newark, but John could go no further and here, tended by the monks of Newark Abbey, he died, his body later being brought to Worcester for burial.

John has received rather a bad press, but he acted no worse than many other kings of his time. His problems were the same as those facing all English monarchs in the Middle Ages—how to assert the power of the Crown above that of the barons and the Church. His father, Henry II, had lost the struggle with the Church in the aftermath of the assassination of Thomas à Beckett. But the Church's victory had been more apparent than real and John had been quite willing to come to terms with it and accept the theoretical supremacy of Pope Innocent III while he got on with the more practical problem of dealing with his rebellious baronage. It was a problem that his son, Henry III, was to only partially solve in the defeat of Simon de Montfort at Evesham half a century later.

John was buried between the tombs of St Oswald and St Wulfstan—but both these were destroyed at the Reformation and now only two small figures of the saints alongside the tomb of the king remain as their memorials.

In 1218 the four-year-old Henry III, together with William Marshall, the Constable of England who had been one of John's closest advisers, and a host of nobles, attended the rededication of the choir, the older one having been badly damaged by fire a few years before. In 1224 work was begun in replacing the original Norman choir with the present choir, lady chapel and east transept which produced one of the finest examples of Early English architecture.

The fourteenth-century choir-stalls have a beautiful set of misericords, though these have been much restored. They give a picture gallery of daily life in medieval times, and here the sower and reaper and their associates share for once a common ground with kings and angels. Perhaps it is not out of place here to consider those who usually occupy these choir-stalls, the choral scholars of Kings' School whose voices are such a delight to the ear. At the moment there is an appeal in existence which, it is hoped, will help to augment the school's choral scholarships and so enable the great tradition to continue.

To the south of the sanctuary is the splendid Renaissance tomb of Prince Arthur. Prince Arthur was the eldest son of Henry VII and, in 1502 at the age of 14, died at Ludlow where he was President of the Council for Wales and the Marches. Had Arthur lived there would have been no Henry VIII and possibly no Reformation either, for Arthur had earlier been married to Catherine of Aragon. It had been planned that his younger brother Henry would have become Archbishop of Canterbury, which would have ruled out one let alone six wives. But Arthur contracted pneumonia, was buried at Worcester and Henry was destined to rule in his stead and to create an era of religious strife which still raises more than an echo from across the Irish Sea.

In the lady chapel are the effigies of two bishops—one Walter de Cantilupe who was the friend and supporter of the de Montforts, the other William de Blois, brother of King Stephen and who was said to have interested himself in paganism as well as Christianity.

There are numerous monuments in the cathedral and while it may be possible to mention them all it would be rather pointless to compile an inventory that is easily obtainable from the cathedral's own guide-books. Some, however, deserve mention including the tablet to the composer Sir Edward Elgar, whose music and personality so invigorated the Three Choirs Festival and which so perfectly evoked the pastoral character of the county.

From the eighteenth century is a tablet bearing the single word 'Miserrimus'. This once caught the eye of Wordsworth and led him to write a poem musing on the mis-spent life of whoever had caused such a melancholy inscription to be placed to his memory. But the poet fell wide of the mark for the story behind the inscription was very different to his poetic fable. The tablet has been identified as commemorating Thomas Morris, who was vicar of Claines and deprived of his living for refusing to take the oath of allegiance to William III. Morris was a lifelong Catholic and supporter of the Jacobite cause and after his ejection from Claines seems to have spent much of his life at Upton-on-Severn. But, at the time of the Jacobite Rising of 1745, he was living at a small house near to the cathedral. He placed great hopes that the rising would finally restore the Stuarts to the throne and when the Jacobite forces were crushed at Culloden Moor, Morris, who was then 88, was also a crushed and defeated man. He realized that the Stuarts would never now be restored and that the Catholic cause was lost and now gave instructions for the simple inscription to be placed to his memory.

At the west end of the aisle is a bust of Bishop Gauden, another and closer friend of the Stuarts, holding in his hand a copy of Eikon Basilike. Like Samuel Butler's Hudibras, another literary product of the Civil War, Gauden's book can hardly be said to be in today's best-selling charts. But in its day, it was tremendously popular with Royalist sympathizers and at one time was considered to have been written by Charles I himself. This was hardly surprising for it gave a detailed account of the sufferings of the king before his execution and when Gauden subsequently revealed his authorship there were still many who preferred to believe it was the work of the martyr-king.

14

Two other literary figures are commemorated in the cathedral, though they are now both very much neglected authors. Both belonged to the large clan of Victorian lady novelists, one being Mrs Henry Wood whose best-known work *The Channings* was set in Worcester, much of it within the actual cathedral, and the other being Mrs Martha Sherwood, who wrote *The Fairchild Family*, one of the best-known, if least read, of Victorian moralities for children.

From medieval times survives the tomb of Sir John Beauchamp and his wife Joan which stands near the north door. The tomb dates from the end of the fourteenth century and is resplendent with colour. Also dating from this period is the monument to Alexander Neckham, Abbot of Cirencester. Neckham was an intellectual colossus for his times. His book *De Naturis Rerum* was one of the first scientific textbooks to be written in England and he also wrote about the mariner's compass and chess. Born on the same day as Richard I, Neckham was brought up as his foster-brother. He died at Kempsey in 1217.

But the real wonder of Worcester's cathedral is not the great men who are commemorated within it but the many anonymous men, whose names we do not know, who laboured to build it. Along with the priests, scholars and statesmen we should also honour the masons, sculptors and carpenters without whose labour the cathedral could never have come into being. It is too much to hope that the golden age of the English craftsman will ever be recreated to beautify some of the less exalted building with which we live today.

The chapter house was originally the administrative centre of the cathedral-monastery and here the affairs of its manors were conducted. The original Norman building was circular but later repairs became necessary and the building was largely rebuilt in its present decagonal form. Many a monkish scribe must have spent his day here, laboriously recording the business affairs of the monastic manors with a goose-quill pen. It was very likely that it was upon this site that Florence of Worcester wrote his *Chronicle*.

Most of the old cathedral registers are now housed in the County Record Office at St Helen's Church, where the difficult task of preserving old documents can be carried out rather better than in the cathedral—though, due to a continual shortage of capital, not all that much better. The cathedral, however, still contains in the region of 4,000 volumes, one printed by Caxton and three by his near-contemporary Wynkyn de Worde. The library is situated above the north walk of the cloisters.

Beyond the south side of the cloisters, at the entrance to College Green, is the Edgar Tower. This forms the gateway between College Green and Sidbury and was erected as long ago as the reign of King John when it formed part of the original Worcester castle. At the other end of the Green is the Watergate, once used to land goods for the monastery and still, in flood conditions, able to live up to its name. Nearby are the ruins of the Guesten Hall, which was the main hostelry for travellers to the cathedral, and the fourteenth-century refectory, once used by the monks but now used by the boys of King's School whose choral scholars, as I have already mentioned, provide the altos and trebles of the cathedral choir.

The present King's School was founded by Henry VIII after whom it is named, but there was a school here in pre-Reformation days. The school was once almost exclusively housed in former monastic property, but now largely occupies modern buildings to the south of the Green.

Worcester still remains a country town as well as a county town, but there is also a large amount of industry and there has been considerable housing development in recent years. Factories range from the Metal Box Company to the old-established firm of Heenan and Froude (now Redman-Heenan) and the even older-established Worcester Royal Porcelain Company. The title dates from 1862 but the present firm traces its origins to the Worcester Tonquin Manufacture which was established in 1751.

The leading founder of the Worcester Tonquin Manufacture was Dr John Wall of Powick who has already been met with in connection with those of his activities which were instrumental in turning Malvern into a spa-town.

Malvern Spa grew out of Wall's medical interests while the Worcester Tonquin Manufacture was in part a fusion of his scientific and artistic ones. Then as now Chinese porcelain was highly admired and a number of attempts had been made to reproduce it in England and on the Continent. Wall developed a formula which contained Cornish soapstone and this may have been somewhat derivative from that used at a Bristol manufactory known as Lowdins. This firm, however, closed down in

1773 and left the Worcester company as the only one in the field producing porcelain by this method, for Wall's formula was a closely guarded secret revealed only to his manager and two craftsmen engaged in producing the necessary mix.

Early Worcester-ware was cream-coloured and decorated with motifs in the fashionable Chinese style. Although the cream-coloured ware delights the eye and arouses the enthusiasm of the modern collector in its day it was considered to be a serious defect, for the Worcester men were endeavouring to produce porcelain with a bluish hue which would be closer to its Chinese original and later attempted to rectify their formula by the inclusion of a small amount of cobalt.

Unlike the situation which was to exist by the mid-nineteenth century much of the decoration for this early Worcester-ware was added by independent china-painters working in their own workshops and some of the completed ware was also fired at independent premises.

The 'Doctor Wall era' lasted for roughly two decades and afterwards the standard of craftsmanship steadily declined, until, in Victorian and Edwardian times, good work was only being produced in the form of special orders which, in some ways, rather resembles the 'limited editions' of craftsman-companies of present times. The present company will provide visitors with a conducted tour of the premises if they wish.

The manufacture of porcelain is by no means the oldest industry in the city. Glove-making has been carried on in and around Worcester for many centuries, though it was for long a domestic industry and was not brought into factories until the early nineteenth century when what had been a craft associated with a large area in the neighbourhood of Worcester naturally became concentrated in the city itself. The manufacture of the famous Worcester sauce, however, has been carried on only since the middle of the last century and, on a somewhat related theme, the city manufactured its own beer, and very good beer too, until the closure of Spreckley's brewery in the late 1950s.

Worcester was once one of the most prosperous inland ports in the kingdom and the quayside was once crowded with shipping which had brought goods up-river from Bristol. Amongst the small boys who thronged the quayside to watch the unloading of the cargoes must once have stood the young Thomas Chippendale, the designer of so much celebrated furniture, who was born in Worcester and died in London in 1779. In those days it was something of a gamble to build near the riverside and many of the warehouses were often flooded, as tide-marks in the Rectifying House, —the 'Old Rectifier',—and on the walls of the cathedral's Watergate bear witness. Worcester's prosperity as an inland port was greatly increased by the opening of the Birmingham and Worcester Canal which reached the Severn at Diglis Basin in 1815. New warehouses were built and the commerce of the city doubled almost overnight—though at the expense of nearby Stourport, for the new waterway offered a faster route to Birmingham and the Black Country and toll-charges were also much lower.

Many of the quayside warehouses have long vanished and others are due to fall in the process of redeveloping the riverfrontage. But two buildings here may remain, the tower and spire of St Andrew's Church, the spire being known as the Glover's Needle and added in the late eighteenth century, and the chapel of the Countess of Huntingdon's Connexion, whose interior is a rare delight for those with a taste for Georgian design. Unfortunately the future of this rare building hangs in the balance and I only hope the planners may yet see their way to saving it. At the same time, and in almost the same place, I also forlornly hope they decide to demolish the hideous mustard-coloured Technical College which must rank as an exceptional boob even for Worcester's Planning Department.

A little further upstream, on the opposite bank of the river, stands one of the greatest architectural insults any English county town has had to suffer. I refer to the power-station which stands here as a great Moloch and will certainly win no design prizes, not even from the Central Electricity Generating Board. Nearby are the modern printing works of Berrows Newspapers, who moved from their original headquarters in the Trinity in the early 1960s and still print the *Berrow's Worcester Journal*, founded in 1690 and the oldest continually printed newspaper in the country.

On the opposite bank is Pitchcroft, now largely known as the site of Worcester Race Course but once a tract of common land on which the citizens had grazing rights for their cattle. Here was fought, in 1824, the epic prize-fight between Tom Spring, champion of England and Langan, champion of Ireland. Spring

had won his title by defeating Jack Cribb and was the hero of the
English sporting fraternity which went by the collective name of
'The Fancy'. On the day of the contest an enormous crowd
turned up, estimated by Pierce Egan, the leading sporting
journalist of the day, to be over 50,000. Langan was held up by
the crowds in the city and the spectators became restive when it
was thought that he was not going to make his challenge. But
Langan did appear and the bare-knuckle fight lasted for 84 rounds,
the end of a round only being called when one of the fighters fell.
In the end Spring was declared the victor, though Langan, who
was by now almost insensible, declared that he was willing to
fight on.

In recent years the city has put out tentacles to embrace a
number of neighbouring villages, including Fernhill Heath,
Claines and Hallow. Claines has a good pub to recommend it,
'The Mug House', which stands in the grounds of the parish
church; the village was once the home of Dr Treadaway Nashe,
more usually associated with Droitwich.

Just how much more of the nearby countryside Worcester is
destined to fill no one can say. This process of urban encroach-
ment is going on all over the county and its continuance can only
lead to the eventual obliteration of the whole countryside. Even
in the villages the process goes inexorably forward, though
recently I noticed that at least one small, temporary check
occurred when permission was refused for Church lands at
Bredon to be developed for housing.

It is this problem of population absorption, coupled with that
of catering for the motor-car, that threatens to overwhelm not
only Worcestershire but most English counties. If there is a
solution then I am afraid that I cannot see one for it would
appear to depend on there being a limit to population growth,
something which shows no signs of being reached in the
foreseeable future.

It seems pessimistic in the extreme to forecast that we will
witness over the years a gradual shrinkage of our Green Belts,
Country Parks, areas of Outstanding Natural Beauty and, beyond
this, of the agricultural industry itself. Unfortunately, this
process seems all but inevitable. Within our own county I know
of only a few isolated areas where land has reverted from an urban
past. More usually bricks and mortar are replaced only by more

bricks and mortar and land once urbanized is lost as countryside forever.

If Worcestershire is judged on population alone it is already dominantly urban for most people in the county live and work not in the countryside but in the towns. A very large proportion of those who actually live in the countryside also earn their living in the towns and their presence has rendered whole areas of the county suburban.

Perhaps the urban geography that will emerge in a few decades will not have completely obliterated the county, but it will have extended its present urbanized aspects to the point where the remnants of the pastoral county will have become emparked leisure-ground and where what has not escaped will be, I hope, at least an environment that has not repeated the claustrophobic and characterless patterns of so many of our present communities.

INDEX